FIT FOR
HEAVEN

*The Best Catholic Athletes and Coaches
Talk about Sport, Faith, Leadership,
Family, and Heaven*

Foreword by Mark Teixeira

TRENT BEATTIE

DynamicCatholic.com
Be Bold. Be Catholic.®

FIT FOR HEAVEN

Printed in the United States of America. [2]

ISBN: 978-1-942611-22-6

Design by Jenny Miller

For more information on bulk copies of this title or other books
and CDs available through the Dynamic Catholic Book Program,
please visit www.DynamicCatholic.com or call 859-980-7900.

The Dynamic Catholic Institute
5081 Olympic Blvd • Erlanger • Kentucky • 41018
Phone: 1-859-980-7900
Email: info@DynamicCatholic.com

TABLE OF CONTENTS

///

NATIONAL FOOTBALL LEAGUE (NFL)

Danny Abramowicz **13**

Mark Bruener **17**

Philip Rivers **22**

Kellen Clemens **30**

Eric Sutulovich **36**

Zoltan Mesko **42**

Matt Birk **48**

Justin Tucker **54**

Garrison Sanborn **59**

Greg Zuerlein **64**

Dan Quinn **69**

Bruce Gradkowski **74**

Eric Mahl **78**

Luke Willson **87**

John Harbaugh **91**

Alex Kupper **97**

Vinnie Sunseri **101**

John Simon **106**

Ryan Grigson **111**

Joe Lombardi **117**

///

MAJOR LEAGUE BASEBALL (MLB)

Mike Sweeney **123**

Jeff Suppan **128**

Ryan Lefebvre **131**

Rich Donnelly **137**

Willie Bloomquist **143**

Mark Teixeira **149**
Alex Avila **156**
Jack McKeon **162**
Craig Stammen **168**
Mark Kotsay **174**
Grant Desme **179**
Tyler Flowers **188**
David Phelps **193**
Vin Scully **198**
Justin DeFratus **203**
Joe Wieland **208**
Joe Thatcher **213**
Drew Butera **217**
Richie Bancells **222**

///

MAJOR LEAGUE SOCCER (MLS)

Matt Besler **227**
Eddie Gaven **231**
Danny O'Rourke **237**
Drew Beckie **241**
Brian Carroll **246**

///

TENNIS, BOBSLEDDING, GYMNASTICS, GOLF, COLLEGE SPORTS, GENERAL ATHLETIC INTERVIEWS

Mario Ancic **251**
Santiago Giraldo Salazar **259**
Steve Langton **263**
Matt Hicks **268**
Curt Tomasevicz **273**

Dr. Vince Fortanasce **278**
Father Joseph Freedy **286**
Lou Holtz **293**
Gerry Faust **297**
Ben Domingue **302**
James Hairston **309**
Brother Peter Hannah **315**
Dr. Bill Thierfelder **321**
Lou Judd **327**
Father Richard Pagano **333**
Father James Mallon **338**

/ / /

MULTISOURCE STORIES

Mike Sweeney's Catholic Baseball Camp **344**
Notre Dame Football **349**
Athletic Clergy **355**
Catholic Athletes for Christ **360**

/ / /

APPENDICES

Papal Quotes on Sports **367**
Saints for Sports **371**
Sports Prayers **375**

THANK YOU

I would like to thank all the athletes, coaches, broadcasters and executives I've interviewed. Your stories show that having the right priorities in life—most importantly, putting God first—is not incompatible with excellence in one's work.

A special thank you goes to Ray McKenna of Catholic Athletes for Christ, everyone at the *National Catholic Register*—especially Tom Wehner and Amy Smith, everyone at Catholic Digest—especially Danielle Bean and Robyn Lee, and everyone at Dynamic Catholic—especially Matthew Kelly and Shawna Navaro. Your efforts have made this book possible.

FOREWORD

Some people look at professional athletes as warriors who aren't afraid of anything and are always on top of the world. Athletes don't need God, right? This couldn't be further from the truth. In fact, God is THE reason that I am a professional athlete and have had a long baseball career. First of all, I understand that without my God-given ability, I wouldn't be playing first base for the New York Yankees. That's not exactly a job that you sign up for at a career fair! Second, the ups and downs I have experienced as an athlete are much more manageable because of my relationship with Jesus Christ. In baseball and in life, there are many more disappointments than triumphs, but because God sent his only Son to die for our sins, we have already won the most important competition! The only thing left for us is to accept that victory every day by the way we live and pray.

My hope for readers of this book is that they will understand that the challenges athletes face are the same challenges everybody else faces. We are on the same playing field, and what unites us on the same team is following Jesus Christ through our Catholic faith on a daily basis. Some people only ask for God's help when times are tough, but it's important to give all of the glory to God in those championship seasons! These interviews are a great way for us to glorify God and thank Him for all of the many blessings He has bestowed upon us. I know you will enjoy reading the interviews as much as I have.

God Bless You,

MARK TEIXEIRA

5-time Gold Glove Award winner
3-time Silver Slugger Award winner
2-time All-Star
1-time World Series Champion

INTRODUCTION

Most people are presented with only one side of athletes and coaches: that which appears during sporting events. Incredible touchdown passes, mammoth homeruns, and searing service aces are among the actions which entertain viewers of top-level sports. Because there is so much excitement about the physical feats performed, many people give little thought to what athletes think or pray about.

However, I've been interested in what occupies an athlete's mind and soul for many years. The reason for this is quite simple: if you know a man's thoughts and prayers, you know that man. It's been my privilege over the past five years to let readers of the *National Catholic Register and Catholic Digest* see not only the man on the field, but what motivates him, what he expects not only in this life, but in the one to come. Yes, even Super Bowl champions, Major League All-Stars, and Olympic gold medalists have souls to save, so reading about their journeys to salvation will help you on your own.

One of the easiest concepts to carry from sports to the spiritual life is the value of discipline. Everyone understands that discipline is necessary for an athlete to reach his peak. If a tennis player wants to win Wimbledon, he cannot practice only when he feels like it, indulge in junk food, and spend his nights partying. The same general concept is true in the spiritual life: if a man wants to "win" Heaven, he has to deny his lower desires for the sake of the higher good. Eternity with the Trinity is so immense a good that any sacrifice should be seen as insignificant in comparison. Indeed, sacrifices themselves become pleasant when we know of the joy that awaits us; every opportunity of self-denial is taken as a means to become closer to Jesus Christ.

If we suffer with Christ, we shall rise with Christ (cf. 2 Timothy 2:11-12). That is the goal of every "athlete of God": to be one with Our Redeemer, letting Him lead the battle and claim the victory. To be sure, if we follow in the path of the Son of God, we will become fit for Heaven.

TRENT BEATTIE

May 1, 2015, Feast of St. Joseph the Worker

Note: Most of the interviews in this book originally appeared in the National Catholic Register. *The two exceptions are those with Greg Zuerlein and Steve Langton, which originally appeared in* Catholic Digest.

REACHING FOR A HIGHER GOAL

Former NFL Star and Coach Challenges
Men to Put Jesus Christ First

January 7, 2011

Does football season mean that Sunday Mass gets a back seat to the local NFL team?

Danny Abramowicz doesn't think so.

The former All-Pro wide receiver challenges men to become more consistent in the practice of their faith. This is a transition he knows about personally: He used to be far more consistent with football than with Catholicism.

After graduation from Xavier University in Ohio in 1969, Abramowicz was drafted in the 17th round in the annual NFL draft. He proceeded to have a successful eight-year career, the most notable years of which were with the New Orleans Saints, who began their quest for back-to-back Super Bowl championships Jan. 8 by taking on the Seattle Seahawks.

When he retired from the NFL in 1975, he held the league's record for consecutive games with a reception (105). He later became a special teams coach with the Chicago Bears from 1992-1997 and an offensive coordinator for the Saints from 1997-2000.

"Take that same dedication I had and other guys have for sports, and direct it to what really matters, what will last through eternity," he said. "Sports are great, but they need to be put in proper perspective."

Abramowicz does have the right perspective today, and he helps other men to have it as well. His chief apostolate is Crossing the Goal, an outreach to Catholic men which includes a show on EWTN by the same name, along with local conferences, "prayer/share" groups and retreats.

Abramowicz authored *Spiritual Workout of a Former Saint*, released in 2004. He and Claudia, his wife of 44 years, have three children and four grandchildren.

Shortly after taping new episodes for the "Crossing the Goal" show, Abramowicz spoke with *Register* correspondent Trent Beattie.

How did you get started playing football?

I started playing football in the sixth grade at St. Peter's Elementary School in Steubenville, Ohio. We played with leather helmets; I mean they were literally leather. Can you believe that? It was a tough, coal-mining and steel-mining area we grew up in, and sports were a community-building thing there.

What are some of the biggest changes you've seen in football since you started playing?

The equipment has changed tremendously. The nutrition and training have also changed so much. When I played, our biggest guys were 265 or 275 pounds. My last year in coaching (2000), the smallest guy on our offensive line was 300 pounds.

The rules have also changed in favor of the offense. They used to let the defense "clothesline" you, do all kinds of nasty things, so the scores were lower. Now they score more points because of the stricter rules on the defense, but I still think the key is the team that plays the best defense and special teams.

Do you think we as a country pay too much attention to sports?

Sports are great. Most other TV is trash, except EWTN, of course. But with sports, the programs themselves are decent TV. It's just that we have to ask ourselves, "How much time are we spending on the spiritual life?"

On a recent flight I was sitting next to two guys, and for four hours they went on and on about fantasy football. If I closed my eyes, I probably would have thought they were 12-year-old boys by the way they were talking, taking it so seriously. Now you've talked about sports for four hours, but are you going to give the Lord even one hour at Mass? That's when all the whining and excuse-making comes up.

What would you tell someone who skips Mass on Sunday in order to watch a football game?

Well, with most of the games, you don't even have to be there until the fourth quarter to know the result anyway, so it's not like you have to take a huge amount of time out of your day. There's still plenty of time for Mass, for putting things in the right order.

For someone who skips Sunday Mass for a game: You're telling me that God comes after football? The Lord Jesus Christ came to earth, suffered, shed his blood, died, was buried and rose from the dead just so that you could go to Mass if you feel like it?

You'll have to answer to the Good Lord on Judgment Day. You make the choice; you have free will. People don't like to think about judgment, about how we'll all end up either in heaven or hell.

It's up to the free will of man to decide which place you end up.

Do you think that, while the country as a whole is too devoted to sports, more individual Catholic athletes and coaches are willing to share their beliefs today than in years past?

They are, but Protestants are still better than Catholics at evangelizing. Catholics don't know how to evangelize, and that's why we started Crossing the Goal. It's not about just talking the talk, but how you live your life. Your own actions evangelize your family and those around you. If you're a God-fearing coach or athlete, that's an example of a real man.

One of the aspects of Catholicism that has helped you most is Eucharistic adoration. What would you tell someone who is unsure of the efficacy of this practice?

We should receive Our Lord daily at Mass if possible, and then my wife and I go to adoration at least one hour out of the week. You just focus on the Lord. You don't have to worry about anything but the Lord, and he'll touch your heart. The idea for my book *Spiritual Workout of a Former Saint* came to me in adoration, and that's where Crossing the Goal came from as well.

You learn to walk in the Lord's ways, deepening your prayer life. In adoration, it's you before the body, blood, soul and divinity of Jesus Christ in the monstrance, so it's a time of peace, of fulfillment. You're filled with his Presence.

What are some of the things that Catholic men most need to hear and do today?

I've been speaking to men's groups for 25 years, and men need to be challenged to live their faith. Men tend to think religion is for women and wimps. That's not true. When I used to stumble out of bars years ago, now that's a wimp. A real man is someone who takes the initiative and leads his family in the faith. The man is the spiritual head of the family, and women want to be led, not by tyrants, but by loving men who look out for them.

A lot of guys like to be macho and put on a tough-guy show. On the outside, everything looks great, but they're horrified at the prospect of looking inside themselves. They're afraid of what they'll find inside, but what's inside is what really matters. That's what we take with us and what lasts for eternity, so that's where the substance of a real man is found, where virtue originates.

If you go to our website — CrossingtheGoal.com — you can see our resources. We have shows on spiritual warfare, the Our Father and other important topics. We have shows on DVD, playbooks, and you can ask us questions through the site. We give men the tools they need to lead their families.

Aside from your own book, are there other books that Catholic men specifically would do well to read?

Yes, Father Larry Richards has a book called *Be a Man!*, and Tim Gray and Curtis Martin have one called *Boys to Men*.

Do you have a patron saint?

Our patron at Crossing the Goal is St. John the Baptist, and Pope John Paul II is someone we admire as well. Our patroness is Our Lady of Guadalupe, so we've got a lot of spiritual power as far as advancing a culture of life.

///

NFL PLAYER-TURNED-SCOUT FINDS STRENGTH IN CHRIST

Former Steelers tight end uses faith to balance family and football.

January 9, 2012

While college football fans have been cheering for their respective teams at bowl games around the country, **Mark Bruener** has been on the lookout for the right players. And he certainly knows what to watch for.

Bruener has done nearly everything that can be done in the game of football. He was part of a National Championship team at the University of Washington in 1991 and was later a first-round draft pick for the Pittsburgh Steelers. In a league where the average playing career lasts three-and-a-half years, Bruener's spanned 14, and included four AFC Central Division titles and a trip to the Super Bowl.

While Bruener maintains an enthusiasm for football today as a scout for the Steelers, he has long known the importance of faith and family as well. The intrepid yet mild-mannered Aberdeen, Wash., native is happily married with five children, ages thirteen years to four months. Attending Mass and eating dinner together as a family are not considered nice extras, but treasured necessities in the Bruener household.

Mark Bruener took time out of his busy schedule to talk with *Register* correspondent Trent Beattie in early December about his faith, family, and football.

What are your top football memories?

I have many fond football memories, starting with flag football as a youngster, then progressing to contact football in the seventh grade. Football continued to be an integral part of my life through high school.

My first year in college at the University of Washington we went 12-0 and won a National Championship. Coming in and being a part of that as a 19-year-old was awesome. It was great to be under the direction of one of the best coaches ever in Don James. I respect him a great deal, and, in fact, we're still in contact with each other today.

I also remember my first game with the Pittsburgh Steelers in 1995 against the Detroit Lions. That whole rookie season in the pros was memorable, and at the end of it, we played in the Super Bowl. We didn't win, but it was still quite an experience to get there.

Probably what stands out most from the different teams, though, was the camaraderie in the locker rooms and the friendships formed there. Similar to Coach James, there are a good number of teammates I'm still in contact with years after having played with them.

In your current work as a scout, what do you look for in players?

There are the standard items of height, weight and speed. However, there are intangibles you just can't measure, such as the heart of the player. As a scout you're not looking so much for what the player is doing now, but you try to predict how he'll play in the future. Simply because someone plays well in his senior year in college doesn't mean that will transfer into the pros. Then there are examples of players who were fairly good in college but definitely not rated among the best who turn out to be outstanding in the pros.

Scouting is a challenge, but it's a rewarding challenge. The busiest part of the year for me is in the fall, with the regular season games, and then later, in December, we start all the bowl games. It's great to still be actively involved in football.

What do you say to those who think a violent sport like football is incompatible with Catholicism?

Football is definitely a tough, violent sport, but faith helps to keep the player balanced as far as the rest of his life. If there's just football without faith, that physical aggression can carry over into other areas of life, or even on the field in ways that aren't within the rules. With faith, however, you receive the focus and discipline necessary to keep the aggression on the field in the right way and to treat people more delicately off the field.

When off the field in Pittsburgh, you went to area high schools with Father David Bonnar. What was the purpose of those visits?

Father Dave was actually a former high-school classmate of one of my teammates at the time, Jim Sweeney. Father Dave would offer Mass for the team every Saturday night before games, which was a great help to us. When he asked me to go with him to high schools, I was more than willing to lend my assistance.

I would speak to the students about my faith and how it guided me in all that I do, and then I would ask the boys to consider the priesthood as a real option in life. Priests don't come from factories, but from real families, and what they have to offer the Church is irreplaceable. It's easy to take what priests do for granted, but their work is really the continuation of the life of Jesus Christ, the central purpose of which is our own sanctification. That's definitely something worth promoting, so I was very happy to do that at quite a few schools in the Pittsburgh area.

Catholic family life is something that's near to your heart as well.

Yes, stable family life is essential to the wellbeing of the Church and society as a whole. My parents have been married for 45 years, and they have provided me and my siblings with an example of how a family should function.

I can remember as a child going to church at St. Mary in Aberdeen as a family and eating dinner as a family as well. Those are two things my wife and I insist on with our children today. You don't realize as a child the importance of all the things your parents do for you, but as you get older, you do realize that more and more, especially when you have children of your own. There's a saying that the older you get, the more intelligent your parents become.

That was true when I was away from home for the first time in college, and then even more so in the pros. I already knew some people upon arriving at the UW in Seattle in 1991, and it wasn't as far away from my hometown as Pittsburgh. Both of those times, however, I had the opportunity to personally implement the faith that had been passed on to me and to see that it really does carry over quite effectively in the "real world."

Today, I thank my parents for giving me a strong grounding in the Catholic faith and the resulting stability of family life. I aspire to give those same things to my children. I want to be a good example for my boys as to how a husband should treat his wife and to my girls as to what kind of husband a woman should look for. That's a tall order, but the Lord gives us the grace to do it if we ask him.

Do you have a favorite Bible verse that expresses that belief?

Philippians 4:13 is a verse that has been instrumental in my life. Throughout my career I would repeat it to myself before, during and after games, "I can do all things through Christ who strengthens me." That verse served as a "halo" to protect me from serious injury in a long NFL career.

It also protected my family when I was away from home. I wanted them to be secure in my absence, which was made possible by the grace coming from Christ, which is sufficient for all things. Philippians 4:13 expresses an inspiring, powerful reality that all Christians should remember and put to use.

It's easy to get distracted by the vain attempt to measure up to other people's opinions. This can be particularly true with pro sports, where you work in a fishbowl: Everything you do is analyzed and commented upon. However, if you remember who your Savior is, what is required of you by him, and the grace He gives you to do those things, then everything is certain to turn out fine. That's what Philippians 4:3 is all about.

Do you have a favorite devotion?

The Rosary is something that has been instrumental to our family. Growing up, I knew my grandmother prayed the Rosary regularly, but it didn't really hit me how dedicated she was until her death around the third year of my pro career. It was then that I saw how her rosary beads had actually been flattened out from so much usage.

I also hadn't known until then that she would pray the Rosary during my high school, college and pro games. That's probably another reason why I had such a long career that was free of serious injury. Asking anyone to pray for you is a beneficial thing, but asking the Mother of Christ to do so, as we do in the Rosary, is the ultimate in intercessory prayer. She has a maternal concern for us that we can only begin to imagine now, but will only understand completely in heaven.

We buried my grandmother with her worn-out rosary, but today I have my own, which I intend to wear out as well.

///

CATHOLIC QUARTERBACK PHILIP RIVERS PASSES ON THE FAITH

San Diego Chargers' star talks faith, family and football:
'Once I've received the Eucharist,
then I'm prepared to go out and play.'

January 20, 2012

Coming off a disappointing 2011 NFL campaign, San Diego Chargers quarterback **Philip Rivers** is wasting no time to prepare for next season.

The Chargers won four of their first five games last season, but finished with an 8-8 record. The team missed the playoffs, and Tim Tebow's Denver Broncos went instead.

Less dedicated players would take time off, but not Rivers. Dedication is something his father Steve, a high-school coach, passed along to him, and it has been a driving force in his football career.

At North Carolina State University, Rivers broke every school passing record, finishing his collegiate career with 13,484 passing yards, the second-highest total ever for a Division 1-A quarterback up to that point.

His production in the NFL has also been impressive. His 95.2 passer-rating currently ranks fifth all-time among quarterbacks with at least 1,500 yards passing.

Perhaps even more impressive than Rivers' football accomplishments, however, is his dedication to passing on his Catholic faith. The 30-year-old Decatur, Ala., native cherishes opportunities to hand on to his own children the faith that his parents gave to him.

Rivers discussed this and many other things in early January.

What do you think of this past season, and what are you doing now during the playoffs?

This past season was certainly a disappointment. We didn't make the playoffs, and I didn't have my best season, personally. However, I'm thankful for the adversity we experienced because if we take it in the right way, it can help us next season.

We had a fairly strong close to the season, so I remember the saying that "You never lose; you just run out of time." We ran out of time this season, but there's next season, which I'm preparing for already. I watch the teams in the playoffs to see what we can do better the next time we play them.

I really am thankful for this season's adversity, not just from a football perspective, but from an overall life perspective as well. It's made me not just a better player, but a better husband and father.

How do you find time for your commitment to the faith when most of your games are played on the Lord's Day?

It's funny, because it's always been a dream of mine to play in the NFL, but I was concerned about the games being played on Sundays. I love to play football but wanted to be able to attend Mass as well. Now, I do that by going to a vigil Mass or an early Sunday morning one. Once I've received the Eucharist, then I'm prepared to go out and play.

Something that might seem odd on the surface is this: If I put football above my faith and family, I think I'd be worse off as a player, not better. It's a matter of putting things in the right order, which helps you to do each of those things as they ought to be done. Avoiding idolatry helps you to have the right perspective on life, which in turn helps you to live more effectively. Faith comes first, then family, then football.

What do you think of Tim Tebow's statements about faith?

I know Tim a little bit because we have the same agent. I've enjoyed speaking with him from time to time and know that he has strong beliefs. I've been public about my beliefs, as well, but not in as vocal or persistent a manner. Everyone has a different way of expressing themselves, and Tim has his own way, too.

As a quarterback I very much appreciate what a great competitor he is and how he wills his team to win. I always look forward to competing against competitors like him.

What does football mean to you, not just as a way to make a living, but as a game you've been playing your whole life and one in which your father has influenced you?

Football is one of the most popular sports in the country, and there are many reasons for this. You can take so much from football and apply it to life in general. Just some of those things are goal-setting, preparation, teamwork, perseverance and discipline.

Discipline is one of the biggest things that stands out for me in relation to my father. He would always tell me that if you're going to do something, do it all the way. Nothing should be done halfheartedly. That was true not only with football, but with something as simple as cleaning your room or cutting the grass. I would wonder why making a bed was important at all when you were going to use it again later that day. The discipline to do those simple things can help you so much with greater things. Luke 16:10 comes to mind, in that regard.

My father was my coach in high school, and I still talk with him very frequently about football today. I'll call him after practice, and we'll talk about how things went. In fact, Dad still has other players of his who call him up and talk with him as well. That's something very special to me — how he has helped to guide me and others in being a man.

What has your father passed along to you regarding the Catholic faith specifically?

My father converted from being Southern Baptist when I was very young. He was determined that we get to Mass every Sunday, which served as the foundation for everything else. You simply do not miss Mass. Period. When the father of the family says we go, then we go.

When I went away to school at North Carolina State, I was on my own for the first time and really out of my element, but when I went to Mass that first Sunday, everything fell back into place. Even though I was physically a good distance from my family, I knew I was home in the truest sense.

That's one of the gifts of the Church I appreciate most: the oneness or universality of it all. It's the same essential Mass regardless of which city or state or country you're in at the time. I've been to some beautiful churches in Denver, St. Louis and Chicago, but what's even more beautiful than the churches is Jesus (being) always present in the Eucharist.

This is true in any Catholic church you go to.

Because you grew up in the South, you must have encountered opposition to Catholicism.

There were only about 15 of us in my confirmation class, not just for our parish, but for the entire county in Alabama that I lived in. That tells you how small the Catholic population was. However, I wouldn't call it opposition that I encountered, but more of a questioning as to why we did certain things. That can be a good thing, in the sense that you learn so much about the faith because of the questions. That's something my mother helped me with in even more detail than my father. She was especially instrumental in revealing the truth of the Church to my wife, Tiffany, during her conversion.

Most of my buddies from school I didn't see at Mass on Sunday because they weren't Catholic. We got along fine outside of church, but the religious camaraderie wasn't there.

I've known my wife since we were in junior high school, but she wasn't Catholic at that time. However, like my father, she converted, and that has strengthened both of us.

Our bond in the faith is the foundation of our marriage. San Diego has a very solid Catholic community, which has been great for my wife and kids to make friends and be supported in the faith.

This is very encouraging, especially when it comes to living out teachings of the Church that are not as popular as others. The most noticeable of these is being open to life, or what is commonly known as natural family planning (NFP). When you see others making the same commitment to the faith as you are, it can only strengthen you.

Because of the commitment that's required, a lot of people are particularly afraid of the baby stages of raising children. It's easy to talk yourself into thinking you just can't handle all the work that it takes. What I tell people, though, is that the children do grow up; they aren't going to be in need of constant supervision and assistance forever.

Plus, when the time comes to look back on your child-raising years, you may actually want more children. There can be a fear of having too many going in, but a regret of not enough when looking back. There are people who would desperately want to have more but can't.

My mom comes from a family of nine children, and she would have loved more than anything to have had a large family of her own. However, that was not God's plan, and I ended up being the only child for the first 11 years of my life. Then we were fortunate to welcome my brother Stephen into the world, and later my sister Anna.

With the birth of our second son in October, we have six kids now. It's funny because sometimes when I'm out with just three of them, people ask if they're all mine, as if three is an enormous family.

What do you enjoy most about fatherhood?

Every day there's something new to witness. It's fun to watch them grow. Tiffany and I comment to each other on which one is more like mom or more like dad when they do certain things. Each one is different, but I really enjoy watching them play together and love each other. That's very special to see as a dad.

When you have a family of your own, you realize just how much you owe to your own parents, and you find that you do things just like they did. You may not have appreciated those things at the time, but it's funny to see them come back. One little example of this is when I was younger; we would finish a meal, and 15 minutes later I'd ask my dad for a snack. He'd tell me, "We just ate. You're not hungry; you're just bored. Now go play." Today, my own kids do the same thing to me, and I give them the same response my dad gave me.

I love my kids so much and not only enjoy them now, but sometimes I think of what it will be like when they're grown up. When they have families of their own and come back home for Thanksgiving or Christmas, it will be so much fun to see them and all the grandkids.

Strengthening families is a major reason you started your foundation, Rivers of Hope, correct?

Yes, it is. On our way home from a trip to Disneyland a few years ago, Tiffany and I were talking about doing something pro-life, and a great way to do that is by helping foster kids find "forever families." We're so blessed ourselves to have a strong family, but we knew that so many people don't have that same blessing.

In coming up with a name, we all decided on Rivers of Hope, because "hope" is my mom's favorite word, and it really expresses the purpose of the foundation. Our primary purpose is to help find permanent homes for foster children, which is a hope unfulfilled for too many.

I've talked with many foster children, and it is very common for them to bounce from home to home. Two little sisters in particular stand out in my mind. They explained that whenever a social worker would come to the home they were in at the time, one sister would yell to the other, "Pack your bags!" To these kids, seeing a social worker meant moving again. We wanted to help them see the day when that cycle would stop and they'd find a permanent home.

There are hundreds of kids here in San Diego County ready to be adopted, so we want to raise awareness of that. We're not reinventing the wheel, just trying to help the process go more smoothly with the organizations that already exist.

We do other things as well. If someone doesn't have the money to buy a pair of cleats or a musical instrument, or whatever it might be, then we pay for those things. We also do referrals to crisis-pregnancy centers for mothers who need that support. Protecting the most vulnerable is essential to being pro-life.

Another part of being pro-life that you've spoken about is purity. Why is this an important topic to you?

One of the people we've gotten to know here in San Diego is Jason Evert of Catholic Answers. He presents the truth about sexuality, a topic which is so misrepresented in the media. Young people don't realize what a gift it is within the context of marriage, so it's great to be able to use the platform I have to spread the truth. People are able to put a face to a cause.

Speaking of purity, what do you say about some of the commercials played during football games?

It's a shame, because it used to be fun to watch commercials during the Super Bowl, for instance. Now, it's kind of hit or miss, and you have to be thankful for the pause button on the DVR. You know what you're going to see in advance, so you prevent your kids especially from seeing those things. You want to protect their innocence, and that's a preventative way of doing it. But in today's world, praying for our kids is essential for their protection and continued growth in the faith.

I can't put into words how much I enjoy praying with my kids. Most of them are a bit too young to have the attention span for a Rosary, so our favorite devotion is the Chaplet of Divine Mercy, which is shorter. We pray that every day of Lent, and we actually sing it most of the time. If the end of the day is coming, and we haven't prayed the chaplet, one of the kids will enthusiastically insist that we do so.

Do you have a patron saint?

St. Sebastian is the patron of athletes, so I wear a medal of him, along with a miraculous medal and a crucifix. There are many stories I could tell about his patronage, but here's just one. In a 2008 playoff game I tore my ACL [anterior cruciate ligament]. The week following that game was a very spiritual one for me. My mom asked me on the phone, "Do you know that St. Sebastian's feast day [Jan. 20] is the day of the next playoff game?" Amazingly, maybe even miraculously, I was able to play that game.

I also admire St. Francis Xavier, a missionary priest who had quite an adventurous life. Reading stories like his helps to get the right perspective on things. What I have to suffer doesn't really compare with what he and other saints went through for the Lord. Even more to the point, when you think of what Jesus suffered in his passion for us all, it can only help you love him all the more.

///

ST. LOUIS RAMS' QUARTERBACK IS 'CATHOLIC BY BLOOD'

Kellen Clemens looks beyond football for his deepest identity.

August 29, 2012

Kellen Clemens has been playing football as far back as he can remember. After learning the game from his father on their cattle ranch, he went on to set high-school records for the state of Oregon in passing yards and touchdowns. At the University of Oregon, he set single-season passing records and ended his collegiate career as the school's No. 3 man in both passing yards and touchdowns.

After being chosen in the second round of the 2006 NFL draft, Clemens has served as a backup quarterback for the New York Jets, Washington Redskins and Houston Texans. He is heading into the 2012 preseason in that same position with the St. Louis Rams.

Despite his long connection with football, Clemens explained to Register correspondent Trent Beattie that the sport is something he does, while being Catholic is who he is.

How did you start playing football?

My dad played in high school as a quarterback, and then as a defensive back at Portland State. I learned all about football from him on our cattle ranch in southeastern Oregon. However, we didn't have a Pop Warner League where I'm from, so instead of playing on organized teams, I'd play at recess with my friends on the playground. Then, in seventh grade, we jumped right into playing with pads — playing for real, you could say. I've been playing "real" football ever since seventh grade.

What are some of your top football memories?

Playing football in high school was a lot of fun because I was at a small school. That made it possible to play with the same group of guys for four consecutive years. Each year a class would graduate, and a new one would come in; but as far as my own class, we got to play together the whole way through. That's far less likely to occur at a larger school, where a class can be divided up among different-level teams, and then one year someone might get cut. At a small school such as the one I attended, it's more like a family of brothers. We would practice, play games and even do off-season workouts together. We just enjoyed being around each other.

That's something that matters more than the actual game itself: the camaraderie formed among the guys. If you talk with retired players about what they miss from their playing days, they'll tell you they miss the teams they were on and the relationships they formed, rather than win-loss records or awards. The satisfaction of awards doesn't last. Trophies end up collecting dust, but the satisfaction of the relationships does last.

What is most difficult about playing professional football?

The fact that it's a business. It's not the same as playing in high school, where you have a family type of atmosphere and cohesion that endures for a long period of time. While it still is possible to form lasting relationships, it's more of a challenge. You can get cut or traded very quickly, so there's less time to bond.

You have to mentally separate the game from the business aspect. On the one hand, you enjoy the game, but on the other hand, you realize there's the constant pressure to perform with perfection. So many eyes are on you, and everything you do is analyzed. There are certain expectations of you, and this is due in part to the fact that a lot of money changes hands between the fans and the owners, and then between the owners and the players.

Did you grow up in a devout family?

I'm a cradle Catholic, with four sisters, and the faith was always an integral part of our lives. I went to confession, received holy Communion and was confirmed. We were taught the difference between right and wrong and enjoyed the stability that brings. We also benefited from being so close to nature on our family's cattle ranch. That encourages you to be humble and also to respect and work with God's creation.

Then I left my small southeastern Oregon town of Burns to attend the University of Oregon in Eugene, which is the second-largest city in the state. That was a big transition period, where I left almost everything I had previously known. There was a void that needed to be filled, and it became very clear that I had a decision to make: I could either drop the faith and pursue other things, or I could lay claim to it and become the man God wants me to be.

It would have been easy to decide in favor of the first choice, because you don't have your parents telling you when to go to Mass. You're on your own and have to make your own decisions about what you'll pursue. That can be a challenge because there are things in college which seem like fun on the surface but aren't in harmony with the dignity of the human person and don't provide lasting happiness.

I knew that my relationship with Jesus Christ was more important than anything else in college. I made a conscious effort to deepen that relationship, in part by attending daily Mass. I really started to take the faith as my own, rather than simply relying on others to keep it going. That was a key time in my life, and I look back with gratitude for the grace God gave me to make the right decision. Everything else flows from that decision of how you respond to God's call.

I knew being Catholic was important, but what I've come to realize more deeply since college is that being Catholic means everything to me. It's what I am in my very essence. Football is something I do, but being Catholic is who I am. I'm Catholic in my bones, in my blood — however you want to say it.

That is a great way to describe it — Catholic by blood — since Jesus gives us his body and blood in every Mass we attend. One of my favorite passages in the Bible is from John 6: "Truly, truly, I say to you, unless you eat the flesh of the Son of man and drink his blood, you have no life in you. He who eats my flesh and drinks my blood has eternal life, and I will raise him up at the last day." Jesus wants us to be completely united to him forever, and this unity begins here on earth, primarily through the holy Eucharist.

I like to expand my knowledge of the Mass, so one of the most recent books I've read is *7 Secrets of the Eucharist* by Vinny Flynn. The first chapter is about how the Eucharist is alive. In other words, the Eucharist is not just a symbol, but the very Person of Jesus Christ. When you get to know that better, it really changes how you see Mass and how you receive Jesus in holy Communion.

Other than your collegiate years, are there specific times that come to mind when reflecting on your Catholic faith?

There are so many good things to think about, but the first one that comes to mind is from April of 2008. My wife, my daughter (who was only six weeks old at the time) and I had the honor of being at Pope Benedict's Mass in Washington, D.C. We even got to sit right next to the aisle where he would be processing. On his way out after the Mass, Pope Benedict stopped and kissed our daughter, and he traced the sign of the cross on her forehead. That was a very special moment we'll always remember.

What do you enjoy most about family life?

I really enjoy being married. It's exactly what I thought of the sacrament as being when I was younger. Sometimes you can look ahead in life and then the reality can be a lot different from what you expected, but with marriage, it is exactly as good as I thought it would be.

The Holy Family is our model, as far as how to live our lives. That's really raising the bar, because Jesus, Mary and Joseph are the ultimate in how a family should function. The Holy Family is an image of the Trinity, with Joseph in the role of God the Father, Mary in the role of the Holy Spirit, and Jesus actually being the Son. This is a beautiful thing to think about and attempt to pattern your own family after. It's striving for that perfect interaction of the Trinity.

There's a lot of pressure in the business of football, so when you come home to your family, it's quite a relief. My kids (we now have a son and a baby on the way) accept me unconditionally. They don't care how well or badly I played that day, or if I played at all. They just want a hug and to be told they're loved. Family life puts the business of football in the proper perspective, in large part because of the simplicity of kids.

We gave our son Michael as a middle name, after St. Michael the Archangel. I've always been appreciative of St. Michael's protective role in driving out Satan. That protection is something I wanted to pass on to my firstborn son, so that if anything happens to me, he can be the guardian of the home.

I also appreciate St. Sebastian's patronage for athletes and Our Lady of Mount Carmel's patronage of the whole Church. I wear a brown scapular in order to connect to that patronage.

This is an election year, so how are you voting?

You have to vote for the candidate who is most pro-life. That's the fundamental issue that underlies everything else. Without life, there are no other issues to discuss. Some people say that other issues are just as important as being pro-life. Being for the poor is mentioned as one of them. Well, who is more poor than a baby? Who has less power to care for himself? Obviously, being pro-life is being for the poor.

Beyond that, if you take an adult poor person, the best way to help him is not through a remote bureaucratic system, but through local and personal assistance. Individuals, churches and private charities help the poor much better than the government can. They're more effective, efficient and enduring. Not to mention, more compassionate.

Being for lower taxes and less regulations is compassionate as well, because then you allow private citizens to follow their dreams and carve out their own paths. The less government interference there is, the more job growth you get. It's really quite simple. You allow businesses to grow by getting out of their way, and then everyone benefits, especially the poor.

We don't need so-called "investment" from the government, which is only taking more of our tax money and pumping it into programs that don't work. We need real investment, which means less taxation and regulations on private citizens, so they can start or expand their businesses, which in turn means more jobs. This is the truly compassionate thing to do, because then each individual can develop his God-given talents and contribute to the common good.

Mitt Romney is the presidential candidate who gets my vote — and in every other race, it will also be the person who is most pro-life, who respects the dignity of the human person and wants to see each of us have the opportunity to succeed.

///

ATLANTA FALCONS' COACH HAS A SPECIAL TEAM AT HOME

Special-teams coach Eric Sutulovich speaks of his journey of faith.

November 29, 2012

When he went away to college nearly 20 years ago, **Eric Sutulovich** thought he had found a good crowd to hang out with. The name of the group made it sound like he would fit right in, since it included three important aspects of his life: Christianity, athletics and camaraderie. However, there was one large problem with the

Fellowship of Christian Athletes: Those in the group weren't shy about telling him that, as a Catholic, he was going to hell.

Sutulovich knew they were wrong, but couldn't explain why in detail. It wasn't until a few years later that he would be able to do that, in large part because of *Catholic Answers Live*, the popular radio program. This was the springboard for his delving into the world of Catholic apologetics, an adventure that would eventually result in his family being united in faith.

Sutulovich, the special-teams coach for the Atlanta Falcons, told his story to *Register* correspondent Trent Beattie. At press time, the Falcons (10-1) were tied for the best record in the NFL.

What do you think of the season so far?

Everyone sees the record and is impressed, but every game is a battle, and we've been fortunate to have things go our way in a tough league. We've learned things with each game and have built more confidence. It's been a good experience — better than being on the other side, with no wins and many losses, which I have been — but the bottom line is: They don't hand out trophies for [having the best record]; they hand them out for winning the Super Bowl. There's plenty of season left to be played, so that's what we'll do, one day at a time.

How did you get into coaching?

Sports were something I enjoyed while growing up. I learned to play various sports from my father and then went on to play football and basketball at Bishop Ward High School in Kansas City, Kan. The coaches of both of those teams really had an effect on me. They really pushed me to do the best I could, and it did pay off.

I was able to get a football scholarship at Louisiana Tech University, and it was there that I first got into coaching. I was working in the weight room while finishing my undergraduate degree, and one of the coaches asked if I wanted to stay on as a graduate assistant. I enjoyed working with the guys a lot, so I accepted the offer. While earning my MBA [Master of Business Administration] at Louisiana Tech, I helped out with the football team's offense.

What happened after grad school?

With my MBA, I went out to make my mark in the business world, but the business world ended up making its mark on me. I went into financial advising — which really wasn't my specialty — because of the possibility of making good money.

That was a bad move on my part. I learned that you shouldn't work in a particular field just for the possible financial rewards; you should look into something you enjoy doing. That way, you're rewarded every day just by the fact that you are where you should be.

How did you return to coaching?

I realized how much I missed football, so I started volunteering as a high-school coach. After that, I coached at a community college, the University of Kansas and two other NFL teams before coming to Atlanta as a special-teams assistant in 2009.

Special teams is something I played, and it's my specialty, so to speak. I really enjoy the specific times of the game where kicking is involved, in part because they can determine the outcome.

Do you find when you speak to children that being in the NFL helps?

Definitely. It's not that I'm actually anybody important, but when you put on that shirt with an NFL shield, kids pay attention. That means something to them, and they really want to listen to what you have to say. It's something that you can use to their benefit.

I value opportunities to talk with kids, especially through Catholic Athletes for Christ.

It's a great group that promotes the teachings of the Church through sports. Ray McKenna, who leads the group, is always busy doing something to promote the faith — whether it's talks, camps (such as Mike Sweeney's) or retreats.

What do you talk to kids about?

It depends on the setting, but for the older ones, I usually tell my own story. The short version of it is this: I was raised Catholic and had good role models for how to live the faith. The two coaches mentioned from high school were regular Mass attendees, so they are examples of that, as was my grandfather — my mother's father. We would go fishing together, and he had a lot of influence on me that way. I was impressed with the personal witness of all these men who made the effort to live out their religion.

I was also influenced by my parents. My dad led by example. He worked all day as a truck driver and then did air conditioning/heating and plumbing jobs in the evening as well, so that his kids would have the opportunity to attend Catholic schools. I remember seeing him come home late at night and having leftovers at 8 or 9, but he would always give Mom a kiss first. He was tired and hungry, but not to the point of forgetting who made the dinner in the first place.

My mom was the real backbone of the faith at home, getting us all up to go to church every Sunday and making sure we were active in the faith during the week. She encouraged me to be an altar boy and to be involved in other ways. She was always going the extra mile at home while my dad was going the extra mile at work. I'm very thankful for the upbringing they provided me with.

After leaving for college, I came across a group called Fellowship of Christian Athletes. It sounded like a good bunch of people to be with, so I went to one of their meetings. Once they found out I was not a Protestant, but a Catholic, they really went after me. I cannot tell you how many times I was told that I was going to hell. Their assumption was: If you're Catholic, you're not saved.

I was initially startled, but knew there were answers to their questions, even though I didn't have all of them at the time. Somehow I understood the Catholic Church was the right place to be, but I couldn't explain in detail just why.

I did my best to answer all the questions I was peppered with, but the real "apologetic awakening" didn't come until a few years later. I was driving home one day from work with the Houston Texans, and the most amazing thing happened. I turned on the radio, and this show called *Catholic Answers Live* was on.

I had prayed for the answers to my questions, and now I was getting them on a very aptly named program. It was just what I had been searching for.

From the radio show, I discovered they also had a website. It included everything I needed to know about why the Church teaches what it does on things like the sacraments, papal infallibility and purgatory. I had always known the answers were out there, but with Catholic Answers I got them all in one place and in sufficient detail. They have a treasury of information that I recommend to anyone, Catholic or not, who wants to get sound explanations of Church teachings.

From Catholic Answers I came across John Martignoni and other hosts on EWTN Radio. I was becoming more and more aware of Catholic radio in general, which is extraordinarily helpful in learning the truth about the Church.

What you learned from Catholic radio enabled your wife to come into full communion with the Church, right?

Catholic radio has played a large role in my life and also in that of my wife, Melissa. She wasn't Catholic when we met, so that made things tough initially. Not that she was hostile, like some of the other people I had met, but she did have questions. I prayed about them and explained things as well as I could at the time.

After I started to listen to Catholic radio, my wife eventually did so as well. Over the years she has also grown in her appreciation of the Church. She was open enough to go regularly to Mass with me and the kids on Sundays, but didn't receive holy Communion. Then, last year, she indicated that she was ready to become Catholic.

We were both very joyful about that and went to church to see what the RCIA [Rite of Christian Initiation of Adults] schedule was like. The meetings were scheduled on a weeknight, which wasn't welcome news. Weeknights are very important to us as a family, in part because during the season they are a large chunk of the time we spend together. My wife didn't want to give that up, but the parish didn't want to give up its schedule either.

In fact, someone there said that maybe it wasn't the right time for her to come into the Church. That was heartbreaking. I had hoped and prayed for so long that we would become completely united in faith, and just when it was about to happen, we were almost discouraged from doing it. We were on the one-yard line and then the ref unexpectedly called a penalty, which shoved us back 10 yards.

While I was disappointed, I didn't give up. That may be due to the Irish or Croatian in me. I had been hoping for this for so long, and I wasn't about to let go that easily. One of the qualities I prize most is perseverance. I even have a sign in my office about it. It's easy to give up, but that's not how things get accomplished.

We eventually found another parish that allowed me to be my wife's sponsor. That way, we would be able to attend meetings, though not regularly scheduled, that would prepare her for being in full communion with the Church. This past summer my wife became Catholic, and now we are a family truly united in faith. My wife and kids are my "special team," you could say.

What do you enjoy most about family life?

Passing along the faith to my kids and seeing them grow. You're blessed to first pass along physical life to them and even more blessed to pass along spiritual life to them in baptism. It doesn't end there, though. You have to keep them grounded in the basics of Christianity, which are provided by the Church.

THE AMAZING ADVENTURES OF A ROMANIAN-BORN NEW ENGLAND PATRIOT

NFL punter Zoltan Mesko's Catholic faith has been refined by his improbable and inspiring journey through life.

January 28, 2013

Even though his favored New England Patriots lost to the Baltimore Ravens in the recent AFC Championship Game, **Zoltan Mesko** is not letting that get him down. The three-year pro has faced much tougher situations, starting in his home country of Romania.

Economic hardships were a way of life under communist rule, despite the fact that both of Mesko's parents were engineers with good jobs. The family had money, but it couldn't buy them much in an economy with oppressive regulations. Then there were days when the family narrowly escaped a violent death. During the 1989 revolution, the toddler Mesko and his parents evaded gunfire that careened through their apartment.

Eight years later, the Meskos were fortunate enough to win the immigration lottery, despite unfavorable odds. The Meskos were among the 55,000 people from around the world who were granted a visa for entry into the United States -- out of the 22 million who requested one.

Mesko, 26, earned a master's degree from the University of Michigan and was a record-setting punter on the school's football team. It was also during his time in Ann Arbor that he started visiting sick children in the hospital, a practice that he enthusiastically continues today through the Zoltan Mesko Foundation.

Amid all his amazing adventures, Mesko's faith in God and his Church has increased, as he explained to *Register* correspondent Trent Beattie after the Patriots' playoff exit.

What are your thoughts on the recently concluded Patriots' season?

We had a good regular season (12-4), but our postseason ended abruptly with a loss to the Ravens. Our team is so talented and dedicated that our goal each year is to win the Super Bowl. We're capable of doing it, so when it doesn't happen, it's a disappointment.

The Ravens have played well, and so have the 49ers. They are evenly matched, so I don't have a clue which team is going to win when they play in the Super Bowl. It's an interesting matchup between two teams that are led by head coaches who are brothers (49ers' coach Jim Harbaugh and Ravens' coach John Harbaugh).

American football is not too popular in Romania, so how did you get started playing the game?

I came to the United States with my family when I was 11 years old. In gym class, we were playing kickball, which I found to be similar to soccer, a sport I was familiar with. During the game, I kicked the ball so hard that it broke a ceiling light in the gym. The teacher was upset about that, so he took me by the collar and said, "You're either paying for that light or you're playing on the football team for us next season." I wasn't getting too much money from my allowance, so playing on the football team seemed like a much more reasonable option than paying for the light.

Did you have a tough time adjusting from Romanian to American culture?

Not really. Romania was a very harsh place to live while the communists were in power. They portray it as equality for all, but the equality you get is everyone being equally miserable. Government control of everything results in less prosperity for everyone.

One time in Romania, my mother wanted to make me a cake. She had to have eggs to do that, so she went to the egg store. (There was no supermarket, just a bunch of different stores that each had only one item for sale.) She spent three hours waiting in line at the egg store. She finally got the eggs, but then, on her way home, she accidentally dropped them. She then spent three hours crying about the experience.

Those kinds of things happen frequently when the government steps in and tries to do things that people should be allowed to do for themselves. When the principle of subsidiarity is rejected, society is unbalanced and unproductive. As Pope Pius XI wrote in *Quadragesimo Anno* (In the 40th Year), it is an unchangeable aspect of social philosophy that government should not usurp the rights of individuals to do what they are capable of doing through their own actions.

My mother and father are both engineers, so we had quite a bit of money. However, because of hyperinflation, the money couldn't buy much. We lived paycheck to paycheck in Romania, so the transition to American culture wasn't too tough. I found things to be so much easier here. Learning English came quickly, since youngsters tend to be like sponges. I just took in everything and was very aware of how blessed I was to be here.

Did your parents encourage you to take advantage of the new opportunities you had here?

Yes, my mother was especially concerned that I do as well as I could. She always wanted me to succeed in school. Sometimes I didn't understand this, but, looking back now, it makes a lot of sense. Doing well academically is like laying the groundwork for a successful life. I actually had a master's degree before I started playing in the NFL.

There's more to that story, though, which shows the possibilities behind adversity. In high school, I was one of the most-recruited kickers in the country. I got all kinds of attention and awards before I ever arrived at the University of Michigan. Once I was on campus, I fully expected to be the starting punter for the Wolverines. This wasn't what happened, though.

I was actually beaten out by a walk-on player. To go from being thought of as the best to not even being able to start on your own team was very humbling for me. It was actually the most depressing time of my entire life, even more so than all the hardships we went through in Romania.

The reason why it was so tough was because of high expectations that were not met. In the United States, there are many more opportunities than in other countries, so your expectations increase, but so can your disappointments. I had put so much into what others were saying about me that I thought I was entitled to things, and when those things didn't come through, I was very sad.

A lot of good ended up coming from the situation, though. I learned to trust in God, despite how dismal things might appear. I also learned to care more about my character than my reputation. As the saying goes: "Your character is who you really are, while your reputation is merely what others think you are." Sometimes the two coincide, but sometimes they don't. That's when firm decisions to do the right thing are so important.

I ended up staying five years at Michigan and earning my master's degree. It was also during this time in college that I started visiting children in the hospital, which helped to improve my outlook on life.

Hospital visits are still a regular part of your life.

Yes, but I didn't plan on them being so. It all started merely as a way to get something good on my résumé for business school. Yet it only took me one visit to realize that this wasn't the right reason to be at the hospital.

Being around children in general is fun because they have a greater capacity for imagination and awe than adults do. They experience wonder at things we as adults don't think twice about. What's even more rewarding is being around sick children because they endure so much. They have an innocence and humility about them that is very endearing.

The most difficult but most rewarding thing is to visit the oncology wards. There you see 4-year-olds going through chemotherapy. Chemo is tough enough for adults, but it's heartbreaking to see children go through it. I just try to be there for them and make them laugh. Laughter really is the best medicine.

Visiting children in hospitals is something I encourage my teammates and anyone else to do. It helps the children, but it also helps those who visit them. The things we get concerned about are put in their proper perspective, and eternity regains prominence. In serious illness, we can quickly see and act on what is most important.

What do you appreciate most about the Catholic Church?

I really like how the Church is for everybody. It cuts across times and places, and it shows itself to be the place where Jesus wants everyone to be. The Church adapts itself well to different situations, without losing its primary purpose of conveying all the means of salvation to humanity. Jesus suffered and died for all, so his Church is for all as well.

Sometimes this is lost on us because we don't take the time to stop and consider it. We're so busy with other things that God's love for us is forgotten. I try to meditate on this and pray every evening and during the day as well. In the car, I often make the decision to turn off the radio and ask for wisdom on certain matters. Driving can be a great time for silence and prayer.

Do you have a patron saint?

My patron is St. Anthony of Padua. I wear a medal with his image, and I also have a picture of him on the wall. He's holding the Christ Child, so his prayers are sought for things regarding small children. In fact, he's someone my mother prayed to before I was born and then after I was born as well.

This reminds me of how in Romania everything was so expensive that people tended to have very few children. You just couldn't afford to do otherwise. I'm an only child, but when I start a family of my own, I want to have many children. They are God's greatest gift in the natural order, so it would be ridiculous to refuse such gifts when they can be accepted so easily.

I have so much to be grateful for, and I've beaten the odds in so many ways: surviving the bullets going through our apartment on Christmas Eve in 1989, winning the immigration lottery, getting a college football scholarship, making it to the Super Bowl (last year), physical health, spiritual health.

Some of these things I've worked for, but others have been free gifts given by God. When you consider the probability of me getting to where I am, it really is staggering. There's no doubt in my mind that God exists and that he does have specific plans for me.

There's so much more for me to learn about life, but I'm already aware of many great things God has given me. This makes me want to share my blessings with others.

///

BALTIMORE RAVENS' MATT BIRK STAYS CENTERED ON CHRIST

As he prepares for Sunday's Super Bowl in New Orleans, the 2012 Walter Payton NFL Man of the Year upholds life, marriage and children.

February 3, 2013

Before the Baltimore Ravens take to the field against the San Francisco 49ers in Super Bowl XLVII, veteran center **Matt Birk** will continue to encourage his team to stay focused on the game. Many distractions will be present, so concentration will be a must in order to play well.

Earlier in his career, Birk let distractions get the best of him, not in a professional sense, but in a spiritual one. The 36-year-old St. Paul, Minn., native was dedicated to football, but it was to the exclusion of what matters most in life: his relationship with Jesus Christ.

Birk's future wife, Adrianna, set a loving example that helped to bring about a change in his heart. Now, the father of six is focused

TRENT BEATTIE /// 49

on Christ before all else. Public defense of the right to life and the institution of marriage radiate from Birk's renewed relationship with his Savior.

In the days leading up to the Super Bowl, Birk, a six-time Pro Bowl selection, spoke to *Register* correspondent Trent Beattie.

The Ravens were not favored against the Denver Broncos or the New England Patriots, but defeated them both in the playoffs. Are you surprised at making the Super Bowl?

I'm actually not surprised. Every team in the league would like to play in the Super Bowl, and that includes us. It's a lofty goal, and it's a tough journey to get here, but we've worked hard to achieve just that. I can't say we were certain we'd be here, but we certainly wanted to be here, so it didn't take me by surprise.

Now, we have to stay focused on the game and not let all the distractions get to us. My motto is: "Be in the moment." In other words, concentrate on the task at hand. Don't waste time thinking about things that are irrelevant to getting the job done. That's a real challenge in a Super Bowl because there are plenty of distractions.

Are people often surprised to learn that someone who plays in the NFL attended Harvard University?

Yes, it catches them off guard. Harvard isn't exactly a school that produces a lot of players for the NFL, so people have to adjust their thinking when they encounter me. They're used to believing that Ivy League schools are incompatible with professional football.

I've always had a lot of interests outside of football. One of my coaches from years ago even called me "The Renaissance Man" because of my varied activities. I've enjoyed other sports like baseball and basketball, along with academics (especially economics, my major), student government, volunteering and even drama. You'll find varied interests with other NFL players, too. We don't fixate on football 24/7.

Did you come from a devout family?

Yes, my parents both took the faith seriously. My father even considered becoming a priest before deciding to marry my mother. Being Catholic meant a lot to them, and they passed that along to their children. In my 18 years at home, I never missed Sunday Mass.

Once I left for Harvard, however, that changed. I got caught up in worldly things. There was a false independence that took hold of me, and I thought of myself as too sophisticated for religion. Because I believed there were more important things for me to do, my participation in the Church declined sharply.

My mindset got even worse when I started playing in the NFL. I bought into all the hype, thinking I was doing the most important thing in the world as a professional athlete. That attitude changed when I met the woman I would later marry. She was a devout Catholic, and she helped me to see what I was missing out on by separating myself from the Church. Thanks to my wife and then others who followed, I now realize the importance of practicing the faith. That's what life is all about.

You've been active in the pro-life movement. What would you say to someone discouraged about the more than 50 million boys and girls killed in abortions during 40 years under Roe v. Wade?

The big picture is really ugly, but instead of letting that dominate your thinking, I would say to keep the faith and concentrate on the one or two things you can do. You may not be able to save thousands of lives on your own, but the one life you can save today does mean a lot.

Whether it's teaching our own children to be pro-life, contacting our elected representatives or working at crisis-pregnancy centers, we can all do something. These examples are in addition to prayer, which everyone can do and which everyone should do. Prayer is the basis of any good action. Each little effort helps to bring about a culture of life, a culture in which children are appreciated rather than disposed of.

I spoke at a pro-life rally in Maryland a couple years ago, and it was a life-changing experience. I heard other speakers, including women who deeply regretted their own abortions. Their work, carried out through the Silent No More Awareness Campaign, was very persuasive. It wasn't just a theoretical discussion; it was real women who had experienced the trauma of losing a child through abortion. They wanted to prevent other women from going through that same thing.

If people were told the truth about abortion, no one would ever seek out the procedure. We hear about "choice" and "reproductive rights," but no one is ever told by an abortionist, "I will kill your baby by ripping off its arms and legs." The women from Silent No More let people know the facts so that better decisions will be made. It's very admirable work.

You're the father of six. With each new child, do you find you appreciate the gift of life more?

No question about it. When I held my first child for the first time, I had such a love and concern for her that I just can't put into words. Parents know what I'm talking about. You just can't express how awesome it is to be entrusted with a tiny child who has been created in the image and likeness of God. It really changes your perspective on life. It makes you think about what really matters.

With each new child, your ability to love grows. It's not a matter of dividing your love among more children, so that each one gets less of it, but you actually have more to give with each new delivery. Children help you to stop thinking of yourself and expand your horizons. This is a joyful challenge. It's more difficult than football or any other job, but also more rewarding.

I also enjoy helping at-risk children through my HIKE Foundation. "HIKE" stands for "Hope, Inspiration, Knowledge and Education." The foundation's purpose is to provide educational opportunities for children who wouldn't otherwise have them. Our two signature programs encourage children to read, especially at home. We want them to know that reading is not just a task for school, but something that can expand their outlook on life and lead to great opportunities for them.

You've also been publicly supporting the institution of marriage. What are some misconceptions that people have regarding marriage?

The major misconception is that marriage is anything you want it to be, rather than the lifelong union of a man and a woman for the purpose of raising children. That's what it has been for all of recorded history and what it continues to be today, regardless of what some people think.

There has been an intense attack on marriage for decades. It has become easier to get divorced, which means the breakup of the closest relationships: those involving spouses and children. This is devastating for the family, especially children, who need a father and a mother. When the marriage is torn apart, each child can feel like he or she is being torn apart.

After all these years of easy divorce, many people have given up on marriage completely. They just live together without any commitment. Needless to say, this isn't the best of situations for them or for the children who might be involved. What's needed is not a flight from responsibility, but a firmer commitment to it.

One of the things I've learned from the Catholic faith that applies to marriage, football and any other aspect of life is to appreciate discipline. On the surface, self-indulgence appears best for us, but that route only weakens us and leaves us unhappy. Self-denial appears to be worst for us, but that route strengthens us and makes us truly content.

Jesus said if anyone would be his follower he or she must deny his or herself, take up his or her cross and follow him. The way of the cross is the only way to be a true Christian, and it's really the only way to get anything worthwhile done. It helps you to become the best version of yourself, to use a term from Catholic author and speaker Matthew Kelly.

In order for us to be the best versions of ourselves, we do not need to reinvent marriage, but to recommit ourselves to it. We need to look at it, not with our own agendas in mind, but with God's plan in mind. He created us, so he knows what is best for us.

Do you have a favorite Catholic book?

One of my favorites is *Made for More* by Curtis Martin, the founder of Focus (Fellowship of Catholic University Students). A friend gave me a copy of the book, and I liked it so much that I bought dozens more copies to give out to others. It's a simple and eloquent work that is especially helpful for convincing young people that happiness is found not in material things, but in God.

I also read *In Conversation With God* by Father Francis Fernandez every day. It's a yearlong series of meditations based on the daily readings at Mass. Great saints are quoted, and wonderful insights are provided.

Do you have a favorite saint?

St. Thomas More was the patron I chose for confirmation over two decades ago. He was a great choice then, but even more so now. We need to be reminded of courageous people like him. They wouldn't allow others to force their immoral beliefs on them. They had their priorities straight and were willing to give up everything for the sake of the truth.

He remained faithful to the truth that marriage is indissoluble. He knew that truth endures, and it takes precedence over political expediency. We need to have the same outlook and act upon it. The world needs that witness now more than ever.

///

BALTIMORE RAVENS' KICKER PURSUES AN UPRIGHT LIFE

Justin Tucker says he gains strength from the Catholic Church to face life's challenges.

August 7, 2013

Last season, rookie placekicker **Justin Tucker** made all 42 of his point-after-touchdown attempts (PATs) and 30 of his 33 field-goal tries. He kicked the game-winning field goal on three occasions, most memorably during the Ravens' double-overtime victory against the Denver Broncos in the playoffs. This feat was followed by victories over the New England Patriots in the AFC Championship Game and the San Francisco 49ers in Super Bowl XLVII.

Curiously enough, however, last season almost never happened for Tucker. Despite an outstanding collegiate career for the University of Texas Longhorns, none of the 32 teams in the NFL selected him in the 2012 Draft. As a result, he had to prove himself during training camp and the preseason in order to make the Ravens' squad.

Challenges are nothing new to Tucker, and neither is the place he obtains strength to overcome them: the Catholic Church.

Tucker, who makes the Sign of the Cross before every kick, spoke with *Register* correspondent Trent Beattie in anticipation of the Ravens' 2013 preseason opener against the Tampa Bay Buccaneers on Aug. 8.

After winning the Super Bowl in your rookie season, is it difficult to find motivation for this season?

Some people might think that, but it's really the opposite with me. After winning the Super Bowl, I woke up the next morning thinking, "It would be a lot of fun to do it again." I don't look back on it and think there's nothing more for me to do; I think of this season as a blank slate and how much I can improve. I have more motivation now than ever.

The team got along very well last season, but how will you manage without the leadership of six-time Pro Bowl selection Matt Birk, also a Catholic, who retired after the Super Bowl victory?

The first two words that come to mind when I think of Matt are "intellectual" and "spiritual." He's someone who thinks through things intently and someone who acts through sincere convictions. Matt was a respected leader on the team, and we will definitely miss his presence on the field and in the locker room.

We still have many of the same guys on the team this year, which is great. We genuinely enjoy being around each other and working together, which is a tremendous blessing. We put in a lot of hours working hard, but we also have a lot of fun doing it. That ability to make work fun can take you a long way.

Do you pray as a team before games?

The Ravens offer a Mass on Sunday mornings. There are quite a few of us who are Catholic and attend Mass together, which is a pretty cool deal. Then, in the locker room, just before the game, we grab hands as an entire team, and someone always offers a prayer that we play to glorify God and to thank him for the opportunities with which we have been blessed.

Just like a family that prays together stays together, our team prays together, and each player knows the man next to him has his back. Our focus is to give all the glory to God, while emerging victorious in the process.

Some people think it must be tough maintaining a Christ-centered life in the NFL, or in any pro sport for that matter, but I've found it to be quite the opposite. I know, without a doubt, how fortunate I am to do what I do, and I am very grateful for my opportunities. All these blessings make me think of the One who gave them to me.

Has the Catholic faith always been a part of your life?

Both of my parents, Paul and Michelle, are Catholic, so I was raised in the Church from birth. The rich traditions of the Church have always been a part of my life. Every time I've faced a tough challenge or had a setback of some kind, I've always gone back to my faith — in the Holy Trinity, the communion of saints, our holy Mother Mary.

The saint I admire most for his firm standing in Christian faith as the "Rock" — or the protector — of the Church is Peter. In Matthew

16:18, Jesus says to Simon, "Thou art Peter, and upon this rock I will build my Church, and the gates of hell shall not prevail against it."

I find Peter's story very inspiring for the Church and all her people across the world. Jesus takes a simple man who he knows has something great inside him and changes his name to Cephas ("rock" in Aramaic). In that moment, Peter is both blessed and challenged with the task of sustaining and protecting the Christian faith for all generations to come. This is still done today through Peter's intercession, but also through other men in the Petrine ministry, or the papacy.

One of the things I truly love about the Church is her rich history, through both good times and bad. Jesus promised us that the Church would never perish, and he directly prompted Peter to carry the Church on his back, just like Jesus carried the cross on his.

Before the Bible was completed, the Christian faith had to be passed down from one generation to the next in some way. This was done verbally, as described in Romans 10:17: "So faith comes from what is heard, and what is heard comes by the preaching of Christ." Knowing today that everything that constitutes Christian teaching was made possible in the first years of the Church, mainly through preaching, which is very closely associated with faith, (is amazing).

The entire Christian world must rely on faith in order to live out its mission. I've been blessed with a public spotlight of sorts, so perhaps it is my mission to be a beacon of faith, a rock.

One of the ways you do this is by making the Sign of the Cross before every kick.

Before and after each kicking attempt, I simply thank God for the opportunity he has given me. I ask that my hard work comes to fruition; I ask for resolve and, most importantly, that his name be glorified.

Aside from prayer, what qualities make a good kicker?

A kicker's mind is his greatest asset. Those with a fearless resolve in crunch time tend to be the ones with the longest careers. The kickers I've studied most on film are Adam Vinatieri (who has four Super Bowl rings to his name), Phil Dawson (former University of Texas placekicker, now with the 49ers), and Matt Stover (former Ravens kicker). All of them have performed in adverse conditions, when their teams needed them most, which requires a sort of resolve and focus that is not easily attained. I particularly admire Matt for his display of faith on the field, pointing heavenward after each attempt.

If you weren't playing in the NFL, what would you be doing?

There are tons of things other than football that I'm interested in, so I'm not really sure exactly which one I'd be doing. Whether it's something music-related or in real-estate development, oil and land, etc., the same attempt to live out the Catholic faith would absolutely be there.

I'm very happy about the opportunity I have to kick in the NFL, and I'll try to do it as long as possible. It's a great adventure, but also a unique platform for sharing what matters most in life: God's love for us. That love is the ultimate motivation for trying to live an upright life.

///

SMALL SACRIFICES BRING GREAT REWARDS FOR BUFFALO BILLS' PLAYER

Garrison Sanborn puts his talents to use, with trust in God.

September 5, 2013

If **Garrison Sanborn** does his job correctly, no one notices he's on the field. As a long snapper, it is Sanborn's job to start the play by tossing the ball to the punter or the placekicker's holder. This unheralded position is something Sanborn has excelled at, all the way back to his freshman year at Jesuit High School in Tampa, Fla.

In 2003, Sanborn took his skills to Florida State University. Despite a Seminole career capped off by being named one of the top long snappers in the country, he was not drafted by an NFL team.

Not one to dwell on the negative, Sanborn redoubled his efforts, and, through systematic and persevering work, he was able to land a job with the Buffalo Bills in 2009.

While Sanborn has achieved his goal of making an NFL team, he and the Bills are now setting their sights on a winning record and a successful playoff appearance. They have an uphill battle, since the team went 6-10 last year, and they begin this season against the perennial powerhouse New England Patriots on Sept. 8.

Sanborn spoke with *Register* correspondent Trent Beattie about how his Catholic faith has provided stability during the ups and downs of his football career.

What are your expectations for this season?

Individually, I want every snap to be quick and accurate, none going haywire. As a team, we want to play well enough to make the playoffs and win once we're there. It is an uphill battle, but we've been working hard.

What are some of the misconceptions people have about professional football?

One is that all NFL players are troublemakers. So much attention is focused on the relative few who cause problems, while most other players are kind of left behind. We might be even more blessed here in Buffalo than the average NFL team when it comes to most players being reliable men. We're a hardworking, blue-collar type of team.

Another misconception is that the "superstar" players have it easy, that they just walk on the field, and everything turns out fine for them. I've been told and have been able to witness just the opposite. Nothing is easy in the NFL. You have to put the work in just to get here, but to be among the best of those who are here, even more work needs to be put in.

A third misconception is that if you have the money, you should spend it. Some players do operate by that mindset, but I'm not one of them. One example of this is that I drive a 2007 Mercury Mountaineer that I bought at the end of 2009.

My father taught me from a young age that you don't need to buy the latest and greatest of everything. It's more reasonable to get something a little less than the ideal, so you don't get bogged down in materialism. You learn that what you've given up really doesn't matter anyway. Small sacrifices bring great rewards.

Have you found small sacrifices have helped you to be a better athlete?

Anytime you want to achieve something, you'll have to give up something else. Sometimes those things are small, but other times they can be sizeable. What makes the sacrifices easier is if you have a clear idea of what you want to achieve in the first place. Then what you give up doesn't seem as important. Even if others look at the things you give up as being important, you see that they really aren't.

Dominick Ciao, the former head football coach at Jesuit High School in Tampa, Fla., saw me snap as a freshman. He told me that I was further along in my first year there than two other Jesuit guys who went on to play at Boston College and Notre Dame. This gave me motivation to work hard in order to play in college.

I ended up being able to play at Florida State University, which has one of the best football programs in the country, thanks in large part to the work of Bobby Bowden over many years. The quality of the program was enough for me to want to go there, but a Jesuit alum named Xavier Beitia, who was playing at Florida State at the time, endorsed the school as well.

Did you keep practicing the faith in college?

In college, it's very easy to abandon the faith, and most students do just that. However, I knew there was something vitally important I would be missing out on if I stopped going to Mass and confession, so I kept up a sacramental life and a life of prayer.

I'm very happy I did that, and I'd recommend doing so to every other student, because the little effort it takes on our part to maintain our faith brings great rewards. By putting God first, we have a solid foundation on which to build. If we forget God, we've got a very shaky foundation, if there's one at all.

I was able to meet my wife, Tara, at Florida State, and we pray together every day. It's such a blessing to be married to someone who takes the faith seriously. If I hadn't kept practicing the faith in college, I would probably have met someone just as unstable as I would have been.

Was there a tough time your faith got you through?

Prior to the 2004 season, in which I would be a redshirt freshman, I was competing for the long snapper starting spot with a junior. I did very well and expected to be the No. 1 guy. However, the job was given to the junior. I was so upset about it that I talked with Coach Bowden. He said that I was a better individual player than the other guy, but because he was a junior, he would be the starter.

I was always under the impression that if you played the best, you'd be rewarded by having a starting position, but this experience ran contrary to that belief. It didn't make sense to me, but, obviously, Coach Bowden knew how to run a football program, because he had 304 wins with the Seminoles. You can't win that many times by accident.

One of the unexpected blessings I got from that experience was having a little more time on my hands. I decided to spend some of that time attending Mass during the week, in addition to Sundays. If I had gotten the starting position early in my career, it may have been easier for me to stop practicing the faith by being overly dedicated to football. Instead, I was more deeply grounded in the life of the Church.

What is one of your favorite aspects of the Church?

I really enjoy the traditions of the Church, which unite us despite our many differences. This summer, my wife and I were in Belgium at Mass, not knowing a word that was spoken. Yet we knew what was going on, because the Mass is essentially the same anywhere. The same concept was played out when we next went to Germany. No knowledge of the language, yet a very deep knowledge of what was happening in the Mass.

Traditions are seen in a negative light by some people, but as long as they're the ones passed down to us by the Church (apostolic traditions), they are very good. St. Paul praised the people in Corinth for preserving the traditions he gave them: "I commend you because you remember me in everything and maintain the traditions even as I have delivered them to you" (1 Corinthians 11:2). Apostolic traditions are also recommended in 2 Thessalonians 2:15 and 2 Timothy 1:13-14.

Have you found a lot of professional athletes to be religious?

I think more professional athletes are religious than the population in general. Pro sports can be very tough; a lot is put on the line, and you're made acutely aware of any weaknesses you have. People are constantly assessing whether you're good enough to keep playing. You realize you need help from a higher power than yourself, so it's easier to seek out a relationship with God.

Also, in pro football, you can't play tentatively. We make a million decisions every play, so if we hesitate, we can't succeed. A great benefit of having a relationship with God is knowing and trusting in his plan and knowing not to doubt the abilities he has given us. Just being able to play with a free spirit and confidently is a huge benefit.

How else has your relationship with God enabled you to play at a high level?

Being closer to God has also enabled me to see that there's more to life than football, which, in a paradoxical way, is a good mindset to have if you want to play well. One reason for this is that you don't let the negatives get a hold of you. There will be negatives in anything you do, but not letting them rule your life is key.

It's easy before a snap with the game on the line to think about all the bad things that might happen. However, my philosophy is to be positive. Instead of thinking of all that could go wrong, I think of all that could go right. It's a simple but powerful thing to think of what should be done rather than what should not be done. When you have a clear idea of what you're expected to do, it's easier to do it.

That clarity helps you persevere when others don't expect much from you or when they have different ideas than your own. I experienced that not only during college, but after college as well.

Despite leaving Florida State as either the No. 1 or No. 2 draft-eligible snapper (depending on the poll), I was not taken in the 2008 NFL Draft. At that point, I could have given up, but I didn't.

I gave myself three years to make an NFL team, and I put every effort into that goal. I worked from 7am to 4pm in an office, then worked out for three hours, ate dinner, made lunch for the next day and fell asleep exhausted. During that time, I used my vacation days to go to tryouts and combines for specialist positions in order to get all the looks I could from NFL teams. After so much work, so many tryouts and making connections with teams, I was finally able to sign with the Buffalo Bills in 2009, and I've been with them ever since.

There have been plenty of guys I've played football with who were more talented than I am, but they stopped playing long before the NFL. I'm still here, and I think it's for two reasons: One, I've always believed in the Parable of the Talents in Matthew 25. God gave me the rare ability to snap, so doing anything other than working my hardest to take this talent as far as I can is as good as burying it in the ground. Two, I've always had a trust in God that things would work out well. With that trust, it's easier to make the necessary sacrifices and persevere.

///

ST. LOUIS RAMS' KICKER GREG ZUERLEIN DOESN'T LET RECORD-SETTING ROOKIE SEASON GO TO HIS HEAD

Catholic Digest, September 2013

In 2012, his first professional season, kicker **Greg Zuerlein** quickly became known for his ability to nail long-distance field goals. Against the Chicago Bears in the third week of the season, the former soccer player made a 56-yard field goal, the longest ever at Soldier Field.

The next week against the Seattle Seahawks, he hit a 58-yarder and a 60-yarder, franchise records for the Rams.

Far from letting this success go to his head, the Lincoln, Nebraska native actually sees playing in the NFL as a humbling situation. Because professional football is a competitive business, Zuerlein has no illusions of a permanent place on the roster being held for him. While he knows that football won't last, he also knows his Catholic faith will.

Zuerlein grew up in a thoroughly Catholic atmosphere, attending daily Mass and going to Confession on a regular basis. The stability this brought to his family is something he wants to continue when he has children of his own.

Did you always want to play for the Rams, one of the closest NFL teams to Lincoln, Nebraska?

As odd as it might sound now, I never thought of playing in the NFL while growing up. When I was very young, soccer was actually my favorite sport to play. I have many fond memories of soccer, such as learning from my dad and my brother (who is ten years older than I am). They helped to lay the solid foundation for what I would do later as a kicker in football.

As I got older and started to play football in Lincoln, my focus was on playing for the University of Nebraska Cornhuskers. That was the dream of every boy in the area. The Cornhuskers have had an amazing record of success, particularly under Tom Osborne, who was head coach from 1973 to 1997. The impressive win-loss records of his teams really get your attention, but beyond them, I really value how dignified, composed, and intelligent Coach Osborne was.

Why didn't you end up playing for the Cornhuskers?

When I was in high school, the Cornhuskers wanted me to be a walk-on. However, I was offered a scholarship for the Mavericks at the University of Nebraska at Omaha, a smaller school.

My parents made it clear at the time that it was up to me to find the funds for college. While I really wanted to play for the Cornhuskers, I thought of all the student loans I would have to pay back after graduation. It was a tough decision, but I ended up playing for the Mavericks in Omaha.

The decision was based heavily on economics, but it ended up being the best thing overall. One reason why is because of the individual kicking instruction I received from specialized coaches. A lot of times this doesn't happen at larger schools because they tend to expect you to pretty much have all the skills down on your own. They just want you to fill a role by going out and playing.

You set a Maverick record for consecutive PATs (points-after-touchdown) at 61, but then had trouble with injuries. Was that a time your faith got you through?

That was the toughest time of my life. I was very dedicated to football, and really enjoyed playing in college. However, I seriously injured my right quadriceps and hip, which took me out of what would have been my senior season (2010). Instead of capping off a memorable career, I was on the sideline with a medical redshirt season.

I prayed more than usual during this time, and one of the key things that happened for me was a desire to live in accord with the will of God. While I certainly wouldn't have chosen to be injured, I realized that God can have different plans than mine, and that He always knows best.

If God wanted me to be injured for a long time and maybe even not play football again, then I was going to do my best to accept that. If He wanted me to recover quickly, then I would certainly work with that, too. His will is our sanctification, so I put my life in His hands in a more profound way than I'd ever done before.

As it turned out, I was able to recover very well and get back into kicking. However, the Mavericks' football program was eliminated in

March of 2011, so I transferred to Missouri Western State University to play for their team in the fall of 2011. I ended up with many more opportunities to kick than I had previously, which was very beneficial for getting a chance to play in the NFL.

Is it difficult to maintain a Christ-centered mindset in the NFL?

Not really. Sometimes people think the high-level of play can go to your head, but I think it can actually be a humbling situation. The phrase that keeps me from getting carried away is: *I will only be tolerated as long as it takes for the team to find my replacement.* This helps me not to take myself seriously and keep things directed toward Heaven rather than earth.

Do you have a patron saint?

My special patrons are St. Sebastian, St. Christopher, and my guardian angel. St. Sebastian is known for his patronage of athletes, so it's easy to see why I'd ask for his help. St. Christopher is known for his patronage of travelers, so I ask for his assistance on the road. I rely on my guardian angel throughout the day, but in a special way on the field.

It's awesome to have friends-in-faith who are in the direct presence of God. Having holy friends here below is helpful, of course, but there's something special about an angel or saint who can't do anything against God's will. Even if your prayer intention is off, they know how to set it right and help to bring about things which are conducive to your salvation.

Did you grow up in a devout family?

I did. At St. Joseph Catholic [Elementary] School I would go to Mass every day during the week, often with my mother and three sisters, and then we would go to Mass on Sundays and other holy days of obligation as a family. We'd also go to Confession regularly, so we were taking in a ton of grace on a regular basis. Our lives were centered on Jesus in the Mass and other Sacraments, so there was a great stability present in the family.

Growing up, I thought everyone lived the same way we did. I even had that mindset at Lincoln [Saint] Pius X High School. I was so surrounded by a Catholic atmosphere that I wasn't aware of anything different. However, that changed when I went to college. Then I saw that not everyone had the benefit of living a sacramental life, which made me appreciate what I'd been given all the more. You just can't replace a loving, structure way of life for a child.

In addition to the sacramental life, what do you appreciate most about the Church?

The consistency of the Catholic faith is one of the things I appreciate most. To have the same teachings over 2,000 years is an incredible thing. A strictly human institution wouldn't have been able to last that long as a cohesive entity. On a human level, divisions are inevitable, so it was necessary that the Church be protected by the Holy Spirit from officially teaching error.

The certainty of faith we have as Catholics is a beautiful thing. We're not left guessing or feeling the need to make things up on our own. We have a reliable Church to count on, so that brings about a real peace of mind. That's what I happily grew up with in Lincoln.

In my opinion, the diocese of Lincoln is the best in the country. We've had great some bishops who have strengthened their flock through faithfulness to the teachings of the Church. They don't make things up as they go along, but order things according to the mind of the Church.

While many dioceses have had a shortage of priests, the diocese of Lincoln has had no such trouble. We pray regularly for vocations, which is what we're instructed to do at the end of Matthew, chapter 9. We also rely on the intercession of Mary, which is described in the context of the Wedding Feast at Cana in John, chapter 2.

Speaking of weddings, you were just married, right?

Yes, I was just married to my longtime girlfriend Megan on April 27. We're very happy and looking forward to starting a family. We want to give our kids the same Catholic atmosphere we were blessed to be given, so the most logical place to do that is right in Lincoln.

///

SEATTLE SEAHAWKS' COACH DRAWS STRENGTH FROM CATHOLIC CHURCH

Defensive coordinator Dan Quinn is guided by the communal aspect of the faith.

November 27, 2013

Community has always been part of **Dan Quinn's** life. Having five older siblings and going to Mass regularly from his youth have prepared him for his present-day coaching duties. As the defensive coordinator for the NFC West-leading Seattle Seahawks, Quinn uses, on a daily basis, what he has learned from his family and faith.

The connectedness Quinn values so highly has also been helpful in his marriage. The 43-year-old Morristown, N.J., native has benefitted from the support of his wife, Stacey. She has been with him over the years as he has moved from coast to coast for coaching changes.

· Dan Quinn spoke with *Register* correspondent Trent Beattie in time for the Seahawks' much-anticipated Monday night game against the NFC South-leading New Orleans Saints on Dec. 2.

With their best start ever to a season (10-1), the Seahawks are often spoken of as having a great chance of winning the Super Bowl. Yet how is the team approaching the season?

We have a really great team and coaching staff. I was privileged to work with Head Coach Pete Carroll in his first season with the Seahawks in 2010, and, after a good two-year stint with the University of Florida Gators, I'm happy to be back with the Seahawks.

As a team, we're not talking about the Super Bowl right now; our primary goal is to own the NFC West. After that, we can move on to bigger things. Whether it's the Super Bowl or anything else, you have to do it one step at a time, so we emphasize staying (in) the moment. That helps to maximize effort and concentration on the task at hand.

It sounds like the philosophy of former University of Nebraska football coach Tom Osborne and former UCLA basketball coach John Wooden: If you prepare as well as you can and execute as well as you can, the results will take care of themselves.

After his tenure with the New England Patriots, Coach Carroll looked into John Wooden's philosophy and was very influenced by it. That's what helped him to build up the football program at USC. He wanted to have a coaching staff that genuinely cared about the players as human beings and wanted them to be in a position to succeed.

When everyone is on the same page and actually enjoys being part of the team, then you can do great things. Of course, talent is important, but the most connected teams are the ones that do well. Really, every good team I've been a part of has had that connectedness. Games really can be won in the locker room before they're won on the field.

You're the youngest of six children. Sometimes the youngest is pampered; other times, pummeled. Which was it in your case?

Four of my five older siblings are brothers, so that should answer the question. Like most boys, we could treat each other pretty roughly, and being the youngest, I certainly didn't escape from my share of bruises.

However, there is a real advantage to being the youngest, in that you can learn from the successes and failures of your older siblings. My brothers had gone through so many athletic experiences by the time I started in football, baseball and hockey. I felt very much at home when my time to play came.

Was the Catholic faith an important part of your upbringing?

Yes, Sunday Mass was a regular part of our week. It was seen in our family as it is seen by the Church: not optional, but necessary. My father insisting that we go to Mass was such a great blessing to me, because it laid the foundation for living life as God wants it to be lived. Giving God one hour of our time is nothing compared to what he gives us back in the Mass.

Regular Sunday Mass attendance helped me to understand coaching better. The importance of structure, discipline and fraternity were clear in church, and they were also made clear to me in athletics. When you have a set routine that you stick to as a family or a team, it is so much easier to get things accomplished.

It's also necessary to take time every day to step back, think and pray. Reflecting on what's happened, what you'd like to happen, how to get there — all in the context of God's will — helps you to see things in their proper perspective. When you take the time to think and pray, then you make the right moves in life, rather than just reacting to things as they come up.

Connecting with God is the way to gain wisdom. In Sirach (6:37), it says: "Reflect on the statutes of the Lord, and meditate at all times on his commandments. It is he who will give insight to your mind, and your desire for wisdom will be granted."

How did you get started coaching?

One year after completing my playing career at Salisbury State College, which is now Salisbury University, I started as a college defensive-line coach. I coached at three schools before going to work for Head Coach Steve Mariucci and the San Francisco 49ers in 2001.

That was a great experience for me, on many levels. At the time they hired me, I was only 30 years old and thought that I knew some things about football. Well, working with Coach Mariucci, not to mention Bill Walsh and Terry Donahue (who were both in administrative roles with the 49ers at the time), was a wonderful experience. I was blessed to learn from some great coaches.

That was so helpful, not only from a football standpoint, but from an overall life standpoint, as well. You're reminded that humility is needed to learn new things and grow beyond your current capacity. John Wooden liked to say that, "It's what you learn after you know it all that counts."

You've had a good number of Catholic colleagues, right?

Being part of a team is great, and going to Mass with others on the team raises it to another level. It seems that ever since I started coaching, there have always been some faithful Catholics around me. I learned early on that being centered on God brings you stability in what can be a very unstable (constantly changing) line of work, and that there are so many lessons you can learn from being Catholic that carry over into the work world.

It reminds me of my father, who actually went to Mass every morning before going to work. He saw Mass as a regular part of his day, and I think it helped him fulfill his duties as a husband and father.

My parents' dedication in over 50 years of marriage has helped in my marriage as well. My wife, Stacey, and I have been married for over 18 years. What has also helped our marriage is Stacey's selflessness and supportiveness. She has been with me through all the moves, from team to team, over the years.

What's the toughest part of your job?

The toughest thing is when 85 guys come into training camp and only 53 will make the active roster. It's great to work with young guys out of college in order to help them realize their potential. You start to develop strong bonds with them, but at the end of the day, they can't all stick around. That's really tough.

I still enjoy my job tremendously, though. Guiding players and helping them to develop, then putting them in a position to succeed — that's great fun, and it's something I've been prepared for by my Catholic upbringing. When you come from a large family and are part of a church community, one major thing is made clear: It's not all about you. That realization is essential to doing well and being happy in life — whether it's on a football team or any other place.

///

PITTSBURGH STEELERS QB THANKFUL FOR CATHOLIC FAMILY LIFE

Backup Bruce Gradkowski enjoys 'how the Church feels like a family.'

December 17, 2013

This season has been a challenging one for the Pittsburgh Steelers. Currently, the team has six wins and eight losses and is a longshot for the playoffs, even if they win their final two games of the regular season. Despite the Steelers' troubles, the team's backup quarterback, **Bruce Gradkowski**, doesn't have a gloomy outlook.

Gradkowski was drafted by the Tampa Bay Buccaneers in the sixth round of the 2006 NFL Draft, after playing college football at the University of Toledo. Following stints with the St. Louis Rams, Cleveland Browns, Oakland Raiders and Cincinnati Bengals, he came to the Steelers in 2013.

The 30-year-old Pittsburgh native is keenly aware of what a blessing it is to be playing football professionally at all, regardless of wins and losses. He is also mindful of the even greater blessing of family life. With a wife and 8-month-old daughter, Gradkowski is happiest when at home or in church with his family.

Bruce Gradkowski recently spoke with *Register* correspondent Trent Beattie about football and family in the light of faith.

This season has been tough for the Steelers. What have you learned from it?

Something that has been reinforced for me is to look at what you can do, not what you can't. People talk about if this or that team wins and all these other things that really aren't under your control. Worrying about those things is counterproductive. You just have to do what you can. What the team has to try to do is take care of our own business and win out. Then whatever happens after that is up to God's providence.

What is the best part of pro football?

The best part is that you're getting paid to play a game. Playing a game is fun on its own, but to be able to say that it's your job to play it — that's quite a blessing. It's something I thank God for every day. At a time when so many people are out of work, I'm very conscious of how fortunate I am.

What is the toughest part of pro football?

The toughest thing is trying to play at a high level on a consistent basis. There's so much talent among so many players in this league, but the key is to be able to use that talent day in and day out. Trying to be the same player every day — a player the others can rely on — that's a great challenge.

There's the joke that NFL stands for "Not For Long" because the average playing career is only about three years. There's a lot of competition, and pro football can be a very strenuous game, physically and mentally. You have to give it your best while you're playing, but also keep in mind that there's so much more to life after your playing days are over.

Since your brother Gino plays for the Baltimore Ravens, you obviously come from a football family, but is it also a Catholic family?

Yes, my younger brother Gino and two sisters were raised Catholic. We were baptized, went to reconciliation and holy Communion and then were confirmed. We attended Catholic schools, and my mom would frequently talk about St. Teresa of Lisieux and call on her intercession. My mom would even take holy water and bless us with the Sign of the Cross on our foreheads before a big game or some other event. Even to this day, she still blesses me when I visit her.

Your first child was born earlier this year. What is the best part of family life?

Aside from the day I was married to my wife, Miranda, the day our daughter, Liliana Rae, was born was the best of my life. It's such a blessing to come home from work and see Liliana smiling at me. That's the cutest thing in the world. I enjoy football, but being with my daughter and wife is the best part of my day.

Looking at my daughter reminds me of how God the Father looks at us: with such indescribable love. He enables us, despite our weaknesses, to live a life of grace as his children. We don't always do it well, but despite our sins, he does forgive us. Sometimes a baby can cry a lot or not go to sleep, but because of the love you have for the baby, those things are easily forgiven.

I love family life and look forward to having a house full of kids. We'll see what happens, but maybe we can give Philip and Tiffany Rivers, who currently have seven children, a run for their money. Regardless, the Church's teachings about the sacredness of marriage and human life are something beautiful to be a part of on a daily basis.

Was there a challenging time in your life that your faith got you through?

There have been many of those times, but one that stands out is when I was at the University of Toledo. A junior college transfer was brought in before my red-shirt sophomore season. I was worried that he would be the starter for the next two years, which would mean I would only be able to play for one season. That would make it less likely that I'd get into the NFL.

My anxiety was relieved in light of a Scripture passage that a teammate told me about: Jeremiah 29:11. It says, "For I know the plans I have for you, says the Lord, plans for your welfare and not for evil, to give you a future and a hope." That helped me to know that, whatever the future might hold, I knew who held the future. Everything is in God's hands.

It might seem like we need to worry about things and frantically try to get our plans to work out, but God is with us every step of the way. He knows what's best for us, and he's the one who provides for us. All we have control over is our own actions, not the results of those actions or how others will respond to them. We can only do so much, and then it's out of our hands.

After realizing this, I just prepared myself as well as I could and tried to be the best player I could be, and it turned out that I became Toledo's starting QB for three years and am now in the NFL. I did put in a lot of work, but all the credit for the results I had goes to God. He's the one who loves us as children and gives us everything we need.

What are some of the other things you appreciate about God and the Catholic Church?

I enjoy how the Church feels like a family. We're not lonely individuals doing our own thing, but a family united with a common purpose. We believe what the Church teaches, we participate in the Church's sacraments, and we operate as members of the body of Christ.

Jesus Christ suffered and died in atonement for our sins, so that we may have everlasting life. I love how this is made crystal clear though the sacraments. We're not just spirit, but matter as well, so it is very good to have sense-perceptible signs showing us the spiritual realities taking place. In the sacrament of reconciliation, when the priest raises his hand in absolution and says we are forgiven, that is Jesus forgiving our sins through the priest. We can hear it with our own ears and not just wonder, "Am I really forgiven for that sin?" Jesus wants us to hear his words and be sanctified by them.

This happens not only in reconciliation but in the Mass as well. My wife and I also make it a point to go to Mass every Sunday of the year, whether it's football season or not. As a pro athlete, there can be timing challenges, but you really have to make the effort to get to Mass. During the season, I either go to a vigil Mass at a parish in the Pittsburgh area or at the Sunday morning Mass provided for the team at the stadium.

The Mass keeps alive the family-like unity of the Church in many ways, because Jesus Christ himself is present there to unite us. He's there through the Bible readings, in those who have been baptized, and in other ways, such as the art of music, stained glass or Stations of the Cross. Yet the most outstanding way Jesus is present is in holy Communion. That's the greatest gift that outshines every other gift, because holy Communion is truly the Word made flesh. Once Jesus has been adored and received, everyone and everything else comes together in the right order.

///

FROM MERCILESS LINEBACKER TO MERCIFUL MESSENGER

Eric Mahl of the Cleveland Browns was transformed by God's forgiving love.

December 24, 2013

Eric Mahl has always loved a challenge. In his youth, it was the prospect of being the best football player ever. This desire drove him to bench press 450 pounds, earn an NCAA Division I football scholarship and later a place on the Cleveland Browns' roster.

The 30-year-old Ohio native's challenge now, however, is sharing the message of Divine Mercy with the world — particularly the poor and most abandoned. This has meant enduring regular rejection and sometimes sub-freezing temperatures on the streets of Cleveland and other cities, in the hope of convincing souls that God's love for them has not expired.

Eric Mahl spoke about his radical transformation with *Register* correspondent Trent Beattie.

Did you grow up in a devout home?

Growing up in the very small town of Monroeville, Ohio, our family never missed Sunday Mass, and I attended Catholic schools. However, it stopped there for me, because I didn't really understand what was beneath the surface of what we did as Catholics. I am thankful, however, for the Catholic upbringing I had, because if I never had it, I probably would have gone even further astray than I did.

When did football enter the picture?

I started playing football in middle school and enjoyed it immensely. From that point through high school, football was where my heart was. Everything I did — whether it was eating, sleeping, working out or making friends — was all centered on football.

Teammates would talk about how it would be wonderful to be as great as certain players from previous high-school teams in the 1970s or '80s, but I wouldn't limit myself by admiring or emulating one player. I wanted to be not only as good as one other player, but the best player ever, and not just on offense or defense, but both.

Frater Matthew Desme, formerly with the Oakland A's organization, said that baseball was his idol. Could the same be said of football, in your case?

Almost. I was so heavily into football, but it wasn't for football's sake; it was for my own. So I'd say my idol was really myself. It wasn't so much the game of football itself that drew me, as it was the challenge of being the best at it. I would work out twice and sometimes even three times a day, just to ensure I would be the strongest player on the team.

That desire to be better than everyone else was present throughout high school, but in my senior year, seeds were planted for attaining a better understanding of what Jesus had to give us through his Church.

I was asked by a woman in our parish to talk to the eighth-grade confirmation class about living out the Catholic faith in daily life. I was surprised she would ask me because I wasn't really living as I should have been. What she saw, however, was my attendance at Mass every Sunday. This was noticeable because so few high-school students would ever attend Mass at the local parish. I was chosen to speak to the eighth-graders by default.

The talk to the eighth-graders went very well — so well, in fact, that I wanted to know about what I had just described. I had the script down, but the possibility of the script becoming real caught my attention. At this same time, devotion to the Blessed Mother, which included praying the Rosary daily, become a part of my life.

How did Mary guide you from there?

At Kent State University, where I had a football scholarship, I was at a Protestant prayer group. The leader wanted everyone to share when they "got saved." This was perplexing to me because "getting saved" was not part of my terminology. I thought that I must have "gotten saved" on the day of my baptism. I realized then that Protestants and Catholics actually do believe different things.

I was driven to look deeper into what the Church teaches on salvation and every other topic. This took place mainly through a little store in Streetsboro, Ohio, called Our Lady's Gifts. When I first walked in, the owner, Madeleine, asked me, "Are you wearing a brown scapular?" I told her that I wore one while playing football in order to prevent injuries, but didn't wear one all the time. Well, that wasn't good enough for her. The scapular should be worn all the time, she explained.

Then Madeleine told me about the Divine Mercy message and devotion. Before I left the store, she had taught me how to pray the Chaplet of Divine Mercy and had given me the novena prayers and the *Diary of St. Faustina*. The promises that Jesus made to St. Faustina about his mercy touched my heart. I wanted to experience that forgiveness and mercy I read about in the Diary.

I continued to visit the store once a week to ask questions, and I was introduced to more great Catholic books. Some of the Carmelite ones were *Story of a Soul* by St. Thérèse of Lisieux, *Interior Castle* by St. Teresa of Avila and *Ascent of Mount Carmel* by St. John of the Cross. Then there was *The Imitation of Christ* by Thomas à Kempis, *Introduction to the Devout Life* by St. Francis de Sales and *The Glories of Mary* by St. Alphonsus Liguori.

As you learned more about the faith, did you become detached from football?

In high school, I was very much into football. I set many weightlifting records and was able to set more in college. However, as I began to learn more about the faith in college, I slowly began to see football in its proper light. I started to realize there were more important things than my own glory. The glory of God was becoming more of a priority for me.

I still had a good collegiate football career and was then able to play for the Cleveland Browns in 2005. Yet I never felt comfortable with the extreme wealth and all the glitz of professional football. I even questioned whether I should play at all on Sundays, but the people I asked were more impressed with the fact I was in the NFL than with my question.

I wanted to continue playing football for myself, but also for the people in my hometown. No one from Monroeville had ever gotten close to the NFL, so I saw myself as an inspiration to the area. Yet, by this time, I was going to Mass and reconciliation frequently, all the while growing in my prayer life. I longed to live a life completely centered on Christ, but didn't have the courage to leave football.

I would even pray, "Lord, please let the team cut me." This hope was uttered a lot, but by the time I was playing for the Jets later in the 2005 season, I prayed it before the Blessed Sacrament and really meant it. Only 10 minutes later, I was called in to see the head coach, who said, "Eric, you're the hardest-working player on the team, but we're going to cut you."

My prayer had been answered, but upon hearing the news, I cried like a baby. I knew it was the right thing, but I wasn't completely detached from football yet. There was still an emotional pull, so it was very tough to leave what I had put so much effort into.

How long did it take for you to be completely freed up emotionally?

Not that long, really. After my initial letdown, I felt a tremendous freedom, like I had been unchained to pursue better things. I started working in medical-equipment sales. I found it fairly easy to make the sales quota, so there was plenty of extra time to spend praying before Jesus in the Blessed Sacrament.

I was so thankful for God giving me so much: a great family, a great job, the ability to embrace my faith more completely. At one point, I prayed, "Lord, what can I give you in return?" I felt him respond, "Give me everything."

What the Rich Young Man in Matthew 19 was instructed to do, I actually did. I sold (or gave away) all that I had — except the clothes I was wearing and one change of clothing — and gave the money to the poor. I then informed my parents I was going to be a hermit, which came as quite a shock.

Many people thought I was depressed, but they didn't know I was in love. I was in love with God, and I wanted to spend the rest of my life in prayer and sacrifice, alone with him. I joined a community of Carmelite Hermits in Texas to pray for the salvation of the world. After three years of praying and meditating on the Gospels, I discovered in a new way that God is love and mercy itself, going to the greatest extremes to love sinful humanity back into communion with him.

This time of prayer and solitude was such a tremendous gift that allowed me to experience a great intimacy with God. I remember when I truly began to understand God's love for all people, but especially for great sinners, it turned my world upside down. I could then see that God was asking me to love him in the poor and rejected.

Near the end of my third year with the Carmelites, I heard in my heart Our Lord saying, "Go to the National Shrine of Divine Mercy [in Stockbridge, Mass.], present yourself to Father Joseph, and tell him of your desires to take Divine Mercy to the poor." I also knew in my heart that I was to go there on a certain date, Feb. 2, the feast of the Presentation of Jesus in the Temple.

I did not fully understand this request of Our Lord, but I knew he was asking for a simple "Yes." I gave that "Yes" joyfully, although I did not know who Father Joseph was or how I was going to get to the National Shrine by Feb. 2. Then the community flew me back to my parents, and my parents helped me the rest of the way.

How was the idea of bringing the Divine Mercy message to the poor received in Stockbridge?

Well, I learned soon after arriving that "Father Joseph" is the honorary title given to the director of the Association of Marian Helpers, and the priest who currently holds the title is Father Michael Gaitley, who has written the bestsellers *Consoling the Heart of Jesus* and *33 Days to Morning Glory*.

It was a joy for me to meet with and open my heart to Father Michael. He listened intently as I let loose with great enthusiasm about bringing the Divine Mercy message to the poor. He explained that, at the time, the Marians in America didn't have a direct outreach to the poor, so he recommended some other religious communities that did. He also gave me some wonderful advice about being Divine Mercy to others. Then he blessed me, and I was on my way.

So how did you get to where you are today, working with Father Gaitley?

After that first meeting, I felt a bit confused. It seemed that the Lord had sent me to see this "Father Joseph," but there wasn't anything for me in Stockbridge. So I visited the communities he recommended, but none of them were a good fit. I was even more confused then, but I decided to stay faithful to the mission by going to the streets of Cleveland and living among the homeless as one of them. I stayed in shelters and ate donated food, all the while listening to those around me and sharing the message of Divine Mercy.

In the United States, there are many places for the poor to get food, clothing and shelter. However, what is far, far more difficult to get is another person's time. People often don't want to take the time to listen to the poor, to interact with them as fellow human beings. By my living as a homeless man, there were no boundaries for me to be their brother. I was able to give them what is so often lacking.

What were some of your biggest challenges in this work?

Many people were drawn closer to God in beautiful ways, but there were certainly challenges. Sometimes I was rejected by the very people I set out to love. That was a real blessing, though, because the rejection helped to draw me into a greater union with Jesus, who was also rejected by those he came to serve.

I was also rejected by some people in the Church — the same people who, years before, had looked very favorably upon me as a member of the Cleveland Browns. There were some people at a certain parish who thought highly of a pro football player in 2005 but judgmentally of a homeless man in 2012. Little did they know that it was the same man. I had been clean-shaven with nice clothes way back when, but last year was wearing a long beard and very plain, even dumpy, clothing.

It might sound depressing, but it was actually the most hope-filled time of my life. Barriers were broken down, and real human interaction took place. Many hearts were touched by the mercy of God. And I was deeply humbled and very grateful to God for allowing me to be an instrument of his merciful love.

How did you get back to Stockbridge?

A year later, on Feb. 2, 2013, I felt the Lord telling me to go back to see "Father Joseph." A friend drove me back to Stockbridge, and I got to talk with Father Michael again. I expected it to just be a quick meeting, but I was surprised at what transpired.

I handed Father an old but attractive image of Divine Mercy, which had been given to me. What I didn't know was that, just 15 minutes before we met, Father had asked the Lord to send someone to help him with a project whose goal was to bring the Divine Mercy image to everyone. When I walked in the door, Father later told me he was praying silently, "If he's the one you're sending, please give me a sign." Well, I gave him the Divine Mercy image, which was his sign.

Now, I pray and work [as a layman] with the Marians at Stockbridge. Father Michael made me his liaison for communities that work with the poor, and we've started our own outreach to those in need called Mercy for the Poor. We've been able, through the generosity of others, to distribute hundreds of thousands of free Divine Mercy images to those in need. We've also been able to distribute more than a million free copies of Father's Marian consecration book, *33 Days to Morning Glory*.

Divine Mercy and Marian consecration are interrelated, because Mary's goal is always to draw souls closer to her Son in order to quench his thirst for love. Mary's role is to be our mother, and every mother wants what's best for her children. When we entrust ourselves to Mary to act fully as our mother, she takes us to the pierced side of Christ and places us in the rays of his Divine Mercy. She really is the "quickest, easiest and surest" way to Jesus!

I look back now and see how merciful God has been in my life. It's beautiful how he took my self-centered desire for greatness and transformed it into a desire to do all things for the greater glory of God and the salvation of all souls.

Jesus' commandment to love our neighbor as he loves us is radical. To love one's enemies is radical, and to be merciful as he is merciful is radical. This doesn't mean we all have to sell everything we have and live with nowhere to lay our heads, but we all must go out of our comfort zones and seek the true good of our neighbor. This is a challenge we face head-on by first experiencing the mercy and love of God as our Father, which will then compel us to share it with others.

///

SEATTLE SEAHAWKS' TIGHT END STAYING LOOSE BEFORE THE SUPER BOWL

Rookie Luke Willson relies on sound philosophy and theology for peace of mind.

January 31, 2014

Many people think of football as a purely physical endeavor. Seattle Seahawks' rookie tight end **Luke Willson** sees it differently. Even before majoring in philosophy at Rice University, Willson had been accustomed to methodically thinking his way through sports and life in general.

This practice is now more important than ever, with all of the distractions leading up to the Super Bowl on Feb. 2, in which Willson's Seahawks will be facing off against the Denver Broncos.

The 24-year-old Windsor, Canada, native continues to rely on a solid philosophical and theological foundation for being the best football player — and man — he can be.

Luke Willson spoke of his Catholic upbringing with *Register* correspondent Trent Beattie in the days leading up to the Super Bowl.

Everyone I've spoken to who has been in the Super Bowl has said the actual game is just like any other, but the increased media hype can be a problem. How have you dealt with all the hype?

There's definitely a lot of media attention, and people like to make it seem as if this is the most important thing ever. I don't put a lot of weight into all the attention, though. All the buildup doesn't really serve to make the quality of the game better. It's more productive to be on an even keel and just take things as they come.

My whole thing is not to over-try. That's a huge temptation for all athletes: to get so psyched up that you actually hurt your chances of doing well. You become tense, and you're not really yourself. That's why you just need to relax, play your game and not try to press things.

We came here to play football, and that's what we'll do. It's not about all the extraneous stuff; it's about playing as a team. That's what we've done all season, and it's great to be a part of such an outstanding team that has gotten this far.

Your family is from eastern Canada, relatively close to this year's Super Bowl site in New Jersey. Will they be at the game?

Yes, my whole immediate family will be there. My mother, father, younger sister and older brothers are all going to be watching the game in person. Football isn't quite as popular in Canada as it is here, but my father played at the University of Windsor, and my older brothers, who are twins, played at the University of Western Ontario, so they'll surely know what's going on. In fact, I learned from them how to play football to begin with.

If you weren't playing football, what would you be doing?

I would probably be playing baseball. I actually got to do just that for a little while last year. After completing my degree at Rice University, I played an extended minor-league spring season for the Toronto Blue Jays. That was my first experience as a professional athlete, and I found it be very helpful for learning how to conduct myself on and off the field.

Outside of sports, though, I might be writing something philosophical. I majored in philosophy, so I'm into thinking things through, with the aim of being a better, more complete person. It's kind of a mind-body wellness that takes into account the whole person. That fits in well with Catholicism, which is a sacramental religion. It's a mix of spirit and matter. The Church sees the human person not just as a soul alone, but a body-and-soul combination.

Have you always been able to connect your Catholic faith with sports?

My faith is a huge part of who I am today, and it always has been huge, ever since I was a child. My siblings and I were raised to believe what the Church teaches and to act in certain ways. Clear demarcation of right and wrong made decision-making pretty easy. That's incredibly helpful for pursuing excellence in life, because you see what's truly valuable and worth sacrificing for and also what you shouldn't even bother to give attention to.

It's an irreplaceable thing to be raised in the Catholic Church, where you have the teachings of Jesus passed down through the centuries. His goal is our eternal salvation, but even if you look only at the earthly benefits you get from being Catholic, they're amazing. The peace of mind that comes from being in God's will is awesome. I'm very grateful for the Catholic upbringing I had. Without it, I wouldn't be anywhere near where I am today. Not even close.

Do you have a favorite Catholic book?

Outside of the Bible and *Catechism of the Catholic Church*, there are many others. One that I have with me now is called *Catholic Christianity: A Complete Catechism of Catholic Beliefs Based on the Catechism of the Catholic Church* by Peter Kreeft, a professor from Boston College. The book is not meant to be a replacement of the *Catechism*, but a summary of sorts.

Dr. Kreeft has a way of organizing and explaining things that makes them very accessible to laymen. He's very precise and insightful, which helps clarify misconceptions you might have. I've read some of his other books, which in turn have led me into reading works of C.S. Lewis, such as *Mere Christianity* and *The Screwtape Letters*.

Do you have a patron saint?

I'm named Luke, so St. Luke the Evangelist is someone who's been a patron from way back. So has St. Paul. Later on, when I was confirmed, I chose St. Sebastian, a patron of athletes, as another heavenly helper. I have a medal with his image on it and also one of St. Michael the Archangel.

As any Catholic should, I also have a devotion to the Blessed Virgin Mary, who is the Queen of Angels and Saints. I pray the Rosary, which is a powerful way to remain in the heart of the Church. Mary's entire existence is centered on Jesus, so when we ask for her intercession, we're allowing ourselves to be sanctified in Christ.

All the sacramentals of the Church have that same goal: greater union with Christ. In addition to the Rosary, other things that are great to use include prayer cards, scapulars and holy water. They're not only expressions of our faith, but means for increasing our faith.

You attend Mass with other members of the Seahawks, such as Dan Quinn. Why is the Mass important to you?

Wherever you go in the world, the Catholic Church is the same. Whether I'm at Mass in Ontario, Houston, Seattle or anywhere else, it's the same Mass. Some of the externals will be a little different, but even if it's in a language you don't know, the core of the Mass — the very heart of what it is — is the same. That's because the Mass is essentially a re-presentation of the life of Jesus, and Jesus is unchangeable.

From the readings of the Old Testament, where Jesus is prefigured, to the readings of the New Testament, where he walks the earth, to the actual sacrifice that happens on the altar, it's all about Jesus. He's the one who sanctifies and unifies us, no matter what differences we might have. This guidance received in Mass is incredibly important, and it's awesome to have it all capped off by receiving the body of Christ.

The whole team doesn't attend Mass, but we do all pray in the locker room before games. That connection is important for playing as well as we can. Camaraderie is all the better when it not only has a social component, but a spiritual one.

After we've prayed in the locker room, I pray alone in the end zone before the game. I thank God for getting me that far and ask for his guidance and protection on that day. I'm incredibly blessed to be where I am, so I can't help but acknowledge that and ask for God's continued assistance to do what I'm supposed to do.

///

SUPER BOWL-WINNING COACH MAKES THE MOST OF EACH MOMENT

The Baltimore Ravens' John Harbaugh discusses his Catholic faith and football, on the eve of the NFL Draft.

May 7, 2014

Following a disappointing 8-8 season in 2013, Super Bowl XLVII champion coach **John Harbaugh** took some time off to recuperate. Then he was back in action.

The 51-year-old Midwest native took a trip in early February to visit the American Armed Forces in Afghanistan. Not long afterward, he was at the annual NFL Combine in Indianapolis, where he and several other Catholic NFL coaches, scouts and administrators participated in a Mass and dinner organized by Catholic Athletes for Christ.

Harbaugh took what he learned at the combine to prepare for the NFL Draft, which takes place Thursday through Saturday. He is also working with the team's general manager on re-signing the right players through free agency. He is keenly aware of the fact that the outcomes of games next season will be determined in part by the decisions he makes in the off-season. This is expressed in a favorite acronym of his, W.I.N., which stands for "What's Important Now."

Harbaugh, whose younger brother Jim coaches the San Francisco 49ers, spoke about his off-season exploits in the context of his Catholic faith with *Register* correspondent Trent Beattie.

In early February, you were in Afghanistan with the troops. Why is it important for you to show your support for them in such an up-close way?

We're blessed with a lot of things in our country, so we need to make the connection between those blessings and how they were and are won for us. They are due to the sacrifices made by our military. Our rights and freedoms are God-given, but we have to be stewards of those blessings for them to be passed on to the next generation. No one knows this better than a soldier, who dedicates his life to winning battles so that freedom will triumph.

I enjoyed the opportunity, which I got through Army Chief of Staff Ray Odierno, to go over and speak with some of the courageous members of our military. I got more out of it than they did, because the whole atmosphere puts what you do as a civilian in perspective. It's humbling to meet people who have given more of themselves than you have, but that also allows you to draw from their courage and dedication.

After you got back from Afghanistan, you went to the NFL Combine in Indianapolis. Is the combine really necessary? Do you get to learn things about players that you didn't already know?

At the combine, the scouts are mostly rounding out their knowledge of players they've already studied a lot. However, coaches are a different story, since we are just beginning the evaluation process on this draft class. Coaches can learn a great deal by seeing the players up close at the combine. We start with that information and build on it up until the draft in May.

You didn't need to look for any kickers, did you?

No, certainly not. Justin Tucker is a tremendous kicker and young man. He exemplifies what we look for in players. There's the obvious necessity of physical strength and skills, but above and beyond those, we look for mental characteristics. Those can make or break a draft pick. Work ethic, decision-making skills and interest in team unity are some of the things that go to make up what we call that "football intelligence." This outweighs physical qualities 3 to 1.

Your father, Jack Harbaugh, was a college football coach, so you moved a lot as a youngster. Did you learn any lessons from moving repeatedly?

Every time my dad got a new coaching job, we saw the moves as exciting. Each move meant a new and better position, so we looked forward to what was ahead. Plus, we were able to spend seven straight years in Ann Arbor, when my dad was the defensive backs coach for the University of Michigan. That let me finish out my high-school days at the same place, so there was consistency there.

My brother Jim and I were always a part of our dad's teams, in one way or another, so we learned plenty of things from that. We knew a lot of the players and coaches wherever we lived, and we would oftentimes have them over for dinner. Our lives were centered on the team, and the team was kind of an extension of our family. We were a close unit.

One of the major things Jim and I learned from our dad was to "attack the day with an enthusiasm unknown to mankind." That's something you can take with you, not only on the field, but in the office as well, even during the off-season. The decisions we make now will affect the outcome of games next season.

That's what the acronym "W.I.N." is all about. It stands for "What's Important Now." In other words, you can't change the past or the future, but you do have the power to change what is happening now. That, in turn, will affect what happens in the future. So, basically, you do the best you can with whatever is in front of you now. That's where the power is.

Who were some of your favorite coaches growing up?

Some of my favorites were the head coaches from my dad's teams. Bo Schembechler from the University of Michigan and Mike Gottfried — who is actually my dad's first cousin — from the University of Pittsburgh are two examples of that.

You can even go all the way back to when I first started playing football as a little kid to find one of my favorites: Tom Minnick, whom I'm still friends with to this day. He reminds me of what it means to be a good coach. Good coaches see the best in their players even when that best isn't fully developed and then they try to bring that out.

Looking back, I don't think I ever had a bad coach. I was blessed to have so many good men who wanted to bring out the best in me. Now, I want to do that same thing for the young men I work with.

Were you always able to relate your faith to football?

As I grew physically, I think my faith did as well. Maybe in grade school the connection between faith and football was a vague, generic thing, but in high school, they started to come together. That's when I went to a Fellowship of Christian Athletes camp that motivated me to make faith more of an explicit thing. Then, in college, I was part of Athletes in Action, and, now, professionally, I've become acquainted with Catholic Athletes for Christ.

We recently had a great event at the combine that was sponsored by Catholic Athletes for Christ. There was a Mass with many coaches, scouts, executives and other staff in attendance. Then we shared a dinner afterward.

Weren't you the one who started having Masses offered for Ravens' players and coaches?

They did have Mass years before I got there, when Ted Marchibroda was the coach. However, it had stopped, so I reinstated the practice when I arrived. There are quite a few players and coaches who attend the Mass. It's a wonderful opportunity to pray and worship with men you already work with.

The Mass makes me recall how every priest today can trace his lineage all the way back to Jesus. There's the unbroken succession of bishops who've ordained priests for centuries, so that each and every Catholic priest is truly connected to Jesus in a sacramental way. That's an amazing, irreplaceable thing the Church offers to us today.

Another thing that I really admire is how thoroughly the Church has thought through so many tough issues over the centuries. Some of the greatest minds the world has ever known can be found in the Catholic Church. St. Augustine, St. Thomas Aquinas and St. Robert Bellarmine are just a few of the Catholics who have contributed so much, not only to the Church, but to the world in general, through their dedication to prayer, learning and teaching.

Whatever questions anyone might have about a moral issue they're wrestling with, the Church has profound answers to propose. Scripture and Tradition are united for a wealth of information on how to live an upright, happy life.

Do you have a favorite Bible verse?

In the Old Testament, the first one that comes to mind is Proverbs 3:5. Trusting in the Lord with all your heart is the key to happiness. We do have to put forth our own effort, but, ultimately, what makes for a good life is letting God be God.

In the New Testament, Romans 8:28 is a favorite. When we trust God, all things do work together for good. The failures and setbacks we might encounter have a meaning that is not obvious on a superficial level, but the meaning does become clear in the light of faith.

My favorite book overall of the Bible is probably the Gospel of St. John. It gets to the heart of who Jesus is in the opening line: "In the beginning was the Word, and the Word was with God, and the Word was God." Jesus is the second Person of the Trinity, equal to the Father and the Holy Spirit, and this was true long before he became man for our salvation.

St. John's Gospel is a great explanation of how love and obedience go hand-in-hand. We can say we love God, but that's not really the case when we disobey his commands. John 14:15 reads: "If you love me, keep my commandments." Love of God is inseparable from obedience. When we walk rightly and search for him, when God's desires become the desires of our own heart, then his great plans for our lives can become real.

Was there a particularly tough time your faith got you through?

I've been blessed to never have been really hit with too much tragedy. However, one of the roadblocks was when my wife, Ingrid, and I were trying to have children. We hadn't expected a challenge in that area of life, so it really took us by surprise. There was a frustration that we couldn't achieve what we were hoping to.

We finally made the decision to let go of the things that were out of our control and surrender them to God. We understood that, even if God didn't want to give us any kids, that would be best for us. He is always working things for our own good, even when it doesn't seem like it.

Well, that realization — and decision to let go of things — brought about peace of mind, and then, paradoxically, it brought about our daughter, who is now 12. When we stopped demanding that things go our way and instead recognized God's superiority and wisdom, things couldn't help but go very well.

///

EXPECTING THE UNEXPECTED IN THE NFL

*Houston Texans' lineman Alex Kupper,
a surprise to make the team in 2013,
now aims to make the 2014 squad.*

July 31, 2014

Alex Kupper thought starting on three state championship teams at Trinity High School in Louisville, Ky., was enough for NCAA Division I schools to offer him a scholarship. He was wrong; but as it turns out, so were the uninterested schools. They passed over a player who, after joining the local University of Louisville program as a walk-on, would earn a scholarship and cap off his Cardinals' career with a Sugar Bowl victory.

Kupper, a 6-3, 299-pound offensive lineman born in Louisville, continued his familiar route of passing under the radar screen and onto the final rosters of teams when he made the final cut of the Houston Texans' 2013 squad. After getting married in the off-season, Kupper is attempting to make the team again this year, beginning at the Texans' training camp, which opened July 26.

A lifelong Catholic, Kupper, 24, spoke with the *Register* about how his upbringing provided a foundation for becoming a successful football player.

Heading into last season, you were not one of the players getting the most attention at the Texans' training camp, but you made the 53-man roster. Do you think the lack of attention helped, because there was less pressure?

Yes, with less noise around, you can just get down to business and play hard. You only have one goal in mind, instead of trying to impress so many different people and worrying about this, that or the other thing. That lack of attention was a good thing, but what was also good was making the final cut and being on the team for a whole season. I can take those experiences with me into this year, which, in another sense, makes it easier now, despite the increased expectations from others.

Did you encounter any surprises in 2013, your first year in the NFL?

I knew the NFL would be different than college football, but I wasn't entirely sure how. One thing that would surprise a lot of people is that playing in the NFL is similar to any other full-time job. You don't just show up for games on Sunday and then collect a paycheck later that week. You work and work during the week, sometimes on things that are tedious but that are still part of the job.

Last year, I was unable to attend a good friend's wedding because of my previous football commitments. It was disappointing, but that's what can often happen when you're dedicated to something, like I am to football.

This next thing isn't the case for every player, but for me, the transition from a winning program in college to a losing one in the pros was probably the toughest thing. Yes, the NFL is a higher level of play, but when you come from Louisville, where we were 11-2 senior year, and then you go 2-14 the next year, it's a sharp transition.

I also have seen how the NFL is a business. It's not just about fan or player loyalty to a team; it's about winning and money-making. Seeing the business side of things is good, but if you get caught up in it, you can easily become a lesser player. The great players are the ones who don't get distracted by all the extra stuff; they're the ones who retain a love for the game and just try to play it as well as they can.

Have you always associated the Catholic faith with sports?

When I started playing football in junior-high school, I had a coach, Paul Passafiume, who had a big impact on me. He's part of SportsLeader, a group that tries to associate sports with virtue. They want athletes to see that sports are not a separate compartment in life, but that your values should shape who you are on the field as well.

We were taught by Paul that God is above everything; family follows, then school, then sports and other things. That's a great hierarchy to have in your mind from the start, because it keeps you from taking lesser things too seriously.

Keeping things in the right order is what helped me to get over not receiving a Division I college scholarship out of high school. I thought I deserved one, but it didn't happen, so I moved on and persevered. After starting as a walk-on at Louisville, I earned a scholarship fairly quickly, and things worked out well from there.

Were you able to persevere in the faith while in college?

A lot of people stop going to church in college, but it was really easy for me to continue going. One of the main reasons is that the University of Louisville is so close to where I grew up — so close that I was even able to attend my home parish, St. Agnes. It is an amazingly beautiful church, with a traditional design, which makes it pleasant to be there. It also has a lot of different groups for all kinds of different needs. It feels like an extended family.

Not going to church was never a real option for me. It's just part of who I am. That's how my parents raised me, my two brothers and two sisters. I can even remember a time in high school when I spent the night at a friend's house on a Saturday. He was one of the few non-Catholic friends I had, so he was surprised when, early on Sunday morning, I was getting ready to leave the house. He asked what I was doing, and I told him I was going to church. He thought I was weird for doing that, but I thought he was weird for not doing it.

There are quite a few football players who have a spiritual life. I've prayed with at least some guys from every team I've been a part of, and that includes the Texans. It's not like we're a religious order, but it's common for most of the team to pray before a game, which often includes an Our Father.

You got married in the off-season. How has married life been so far?

I got married in April to Paige, who is from Louisville. We want to start a family and raise our children in a close-knit community. Marriage is one of the seven sacraments, and it's the way children are meant to come into the world.

Fathers have distinct gifts to offer their children, and mothers have distinct gifts, too. When you combine those gifts, children get the balance they need. Then they can grow and learn in a way that is both challenging and compassionate. There's a definite structure you're called to fit into as a child, but also [that teaches] empathy that respects human weakness. That's the beauty of family life: There's unity in diversity — a variety of gifts that, when combined, make for healthy human beings.

The Church is pro-life, of course, but being a biology major in college might have let me gain an even greater appreciation for the sanctity of life. In one way, it's obvious that life begins at conception, but when you go through the science classes, especially the sections on embryology, this basic fact is confirmed again and again. DNA for a unique human being, made in the image and likeness of God, is there from the very beginning.

We'll be happy with as many kids as the good Lord blesses us, and, while neither of us knows everything we could about the Church, we are learning more, and we plan on making sure our children receive a good Catholic upbringing.

///

FORMER ALABAMA FOOTBALL PLAYER NOW A SAINT

Rookie Vinnie Sunseri is set to make his professional debut for New Orleans.

September 6, 2014

After winning two BCS National Championships in three years at the University of Alabama, defensive back **Vinnie Sunseri** decided to aim even higher. He declared himself eligible for the NFL Draft as a junior earlier this year and was taken in the fifth round by the New Orleans Saints.

While Sunseri has had an abundance of blessings in life, it wasn't until he enrolled at Alabama that he started to appreciate his good fortune. At a time in life that many fall away from the practice of their faith, Sunseri was just beginning to take it more seriously.

Now, as the Saints prepare to open their regular season against the Atlanta Falcons in Atlanta on Sunday, Sunseri sees things in their proper order: Faith comes first, then family and then football. The Pittsburgh native spoke about his changed perspective with *Register* correspondent Trent Beattie.

You're joining a team with an appropriate name for a Catholic player. What were your expectations going into training camp/preseason with the Saints?

On the field, I went in with the mindset of doing whatever the coaches asked me to do. I was ready to contribute whatever I could on defense or special teams. Of course, you want to make the 53-man roster and play the whole season, but you have to take things one day at a time.

When I first went up in practice against Drew Brees, it was quite a thrill. I couldn't believe I was on the same field with players like him. After a while, though, you get settled into a routine. You become more comfortable with the guys and the system, and you can see yourself as a regular part of things and able to make an impact.

Now that the regular season is about to start, the goal hasn't changed, really. I'm happy to be here and just want to contribute to the team in whatever way I can.

Your father was a linebacker coach at Alabama and is currently the defensive-ends coach at Florida State. You must have learned a lot from him about football.

Yes, my father Sal played at the University of Pittsburgh and then with the Pittsburgh Steelers, so it was only natural that he would teach me so much about football. Not everyone can say their father played in the NFL, so I really was blessed from the beginning, as far as knowing how to play the game, having high standards and putting the work in to meet those standards.

In my freshman year at Alabama, I got to play on the national championship team that my dad was an assistant coach for. That was the most amazing football experience of my life, because of the family connection. Anytime you win a national championship, it's a great accomplishment, but when your own dad is on the coaching staff, it takes it to another level. I had been able to watch him coach other guys for years, including the Crimson Tide's 2009 national championship team, but actually being on the same team that beat the LSU Tigers [in January of 2012] for the 2011 national championship was awesome.

You had quite a career at Alabama, especially considering the fact that you only spent three years there.

To be sure, two BCS National Championships in three years is an unbelievable thing. In those three years, our record was 36-4. My dad, though, has been with three BCS National Championship teams, the most recent one being this past year with Florida State, so he gives me grief about how I have "only two" championships to my credit.

The highlight of my sophomore year was the SEC Championship game against Georgia, led by QB Aaron Murray, a friend of mine. We went back and forth, and finally won, 32-28. The highlight of my junior year, which was shortened by a knee injury, was picking off a Johnny Manziel pass when we played Texas A&M.

Alabama has a very top-notch program, and I was excited to be a part of it. There is so much work that goes into all those wins, so you develop deep bonds with teammates and coaches. This is true on the field, but it carries over off the field and even into church with some guys.

Nick Saban, Alabama's head coach, went to Mass at St. Francis of Assisi University Parish, along with me and some other players and coaches. Having other guys around you like that when you're worshipping God is a tremendous blessing. It helps you to remember what's most important in life. Sports are so much fun, but you have to put things in the right order, and that always means God comes first.

Have you always taken the faith seriously or was there a distinct time you started to do so?

There was a time when my dad coached in the NFL, and I would tag along with him. This was when he was with the Carolina Panthers, from 2002-2008, so I would have been 11 to 17 at the time. I was awed by the big guys and high level of play, so I didn't think about going to Sunday Mass.

However, once I got to Alabama, it became so obvious that I should be going to Sunday Mass. I mean, here I am on this unbelievable football team, I have a great family to support me, I'm healthy, and so on, but I'm not even going to church for one hour a week? It just didn't make sense. I knew I had been given so much, and I wanted to give back to God and then to other human beings.

When it became clearer to me that I had countless things to be grateful for, I saw that going to Sunday Mass was the least I could do to give back to God for all he has given me. I became more involved at St. Francis and made Mass a regular part of my life. In addition to Sunday Mass, I happily went to Masses said before games, usually on Saturdays.

Even though I've been Catholic my whole life, I have a greater appreciation for it now. I love everything about the Church, with the Mass at the top of the list. Everything from seeing your friends to singing to hearing God's word and the sermon to receiving Communion and quietly praying afterward — it's all what life should be about.

Was there a tough time your faith got you through?

Last October, I tore my ACL [anterior cruciate ligament], and that was very tough. Even though it was really a low point, I trusted in God, family and friends. I had already established a deeper relationship with God, so the foundation was set for me to lean on him. I also leaned on my dad a lot, because he had gone through a similar injury when he was playing for the Steelers. My mom was supportive as always, and my friends rounded things out. With all that support around me, I was able to recover quickly.

Do you have a favorite devotion?

I pray the Rosary every night. Depending on how long it takes me to get to sleep, I pray anywhere from a couple of the mysteries to the entire collection of the Joyful, Sorrowful, Glorious and Luminous Mysteries. There's no better way to end the day than to ask the Blessed Mother to intercede for you, because then you see Jesus in a very real, flesh-and-blood way. You're reminded that God really did become a man with eyes, ears and hands, just like we have.

The Incarnation was made possible by Mary agreeing to be Jesus' mother, and the Incarnation in turn made our salvation possible, because then Jesus had a body through which to suffer. While Jesus was suffering and dying on the cross, he left us Mary as our spiritual mother, so while she only had one child by blood, she actually has millions of other "children" through the shed blood of her Son.

Mary puts her spiritual children to sleep, so to speak, when they pray the Rosary at night. Our "older brother" Jesus is already enjoying eternal rest, but we see a prefiguring of that when we go to sleep with a good conscience.

If you weren't playing football, what would you be doing?

If I weren't playing football, I might be coaching football, although I would also like to own an Italian restaurant one day. I enjoy cooking (especially Italian food), and I enjoy being around people, so a restaurant seems like a great fit. I also majored in business management at Alabama, so I've learned some things about how to run a small business.

Whatever I end up doing, though, I now have my priorities straight. They are faith, family and football (or restaurants or whatever else) — in that order. God comes before all else.

///

HOUSTON TEXANS' LINEBACKER PERSEVERING IN FAITH

John Simon speaks of scandals, Scriptures, saints and scapulars.

November 28, 2014

Linebacker **John Simon's** first two college seasons with the Ohio State Buckeyes went very well, as the team posted records of 11-2 in 2009 and 13-1 in 2010. However, after the 2010 season, things started to get troublesome for Simon. The 6-foot-1, 252-pound Youngstown, Ohio, native was accused of being part of a group of players who received gifts or services in exchange for Buckeye memorabilia. Despite his innocence, Simon's name was sullied on well-known websites, radio and TV programs.

This disheartening experience helped to deepen Simon's trust in God, as it did for many other Ohio State players. A good number of those who previously showed no interest in matters of faith started asking questions, while some of those who had been casual believers ramped up their interest.

Simon also used the adversity of 2011 as motivation to excel personally. He finished that season with first-team All-Big Ten honors, as he did again in 2012. He was also named 2012's Big-Ten Defensive Player of the Year.

These credentials caught the attention of the Baltimore Ravens, who picked Simon in the fourth round of the 2013 NFL Draft. Simon spent his time with the Super Bowl XLVII champions learning as much as he could from some of the best players in the game. Now, he is attempting to make the playoffs with the Houston Texans, after joining them in October of this year.

John Simon, who attended Youngstown's football-famed Cardinal Mooney High School, recently spoke with *Register* correspondent Trent Beattie.

You joined the Texans in early October. What do you think of your experience with the team so far, and what do you expect from the rest of the season?

It's been a pretty good season so far, but you can't take any game in the NFL for granted; you're always going to have tough opposition, so you have to do the best you can, every play of every game. Two games ago, we beat the Cleveland Browns 23-7, but in our most recent game, we lost to the AFC North-leading Cincinnati Bengals 23-13. We're now 5-6 and still in the playoff hunt, so it will be fun to see what happens during the remainder of the season.

You were drafted out of Ohio State University in 2013 by the Baltimore Ravens, which had won the Super Bowl earlier that year. What was it like, not only to be drafted into the NFL, but by the team that had recently won it all?

Being selected by the Ravens was a great honor for me. There I was, among some of the best players in the game, and it was a fantastic experience. I was able to pick the brains of great players on a day-to-day basis. I not only asked questions about what to do in certain situations, but I got the answers. People were always happy to help out with any game-related questions I had.

I found the Ravens to have a lot of selfless players who taught me, in various ways, two main things: 1) You have to take care of your body, and 2) you have to learn how to see clearly and respond quickly to situations on the field.

The first thing is fairly obvious, since if your body isn't working, you won't be working. You have to eat properly, workout with a purpose and under control, and you have to rest properly. The second thing may not be so obvious, but in order to be successful in the NFL, you need to rise above mere athletic ability. You have to know what to look for during games and then swiftly do the right thing.

Learning to be a better football player is something I truly value about my experience with the Ravens. The team has a lot of good people, and I expect to keep in touch with many of them for years to come.

Have you always taken the faith seriously?

My family would always go to Mass on Sundays, but for most of my young life, I saw that as a hassle. I just didn't understand the importance of what was going on. I had a selfish mindset of *What can I get out of this?* that, thanks be to God, changed at Cardinal Mooney High School. I started to realize that life wasn't about me getting stuff, but accepting what Jesus had done for me on the cross. The emphasis was on him and what he has done, while I was supposed to live out his saving action.

In high school, I had a revelation about how my mindset should be shifted from getting things to accepting God's grace. I started praising and thanking God for the many blessings I already had, instead of looking for material things outside of me. I started enjoying life more because I had a greater sense of God's importance and my own insignificance.

Since we're constantly in need of God's help, we still need prayers of petition, but they should be mostly about getting the strength to do God's will, rather than getting specific material objects or goals. The main thing is just doing what the Lord expects of us, regardless of where we might be or what things we might have.

Was there a difficult time that your faith got you through?

There have been many tough times in my life, but they probably aren't all that tough when compared with what others have gone though. Maybe the toughest thing was heading into my junior year at Ohio State, when there was a scandal over some players getting tattoos and other things by signing autographs or trading team memorabilia. My name appeared on several well-known sports websites, radio and TV programs as one of the players involved. To almost any onlooker, I was in real trouble, but the reality was: I had done nothing wrong.

It's really aggravating to be falsely — and very publicly — accused of wrongdoing, but I leaned on the Lord during that time. Jesus was falsely accused of things as well, so it brought me closer to him. It's one thing to meditate on certain mysteries of his life, but to experience something similar in your own life makes it even more intense.

The whole thing actually served as a means to draw the team closer together and inspire many guys to look into the important questions of faith. Some who had no previous interest started asking questions and going to Bible studies, while others who were already somewhat into their faith became even more interested.

Difficult times make you search for what is truly important, what truly lasts. Our standing with God is what matters most, and flowing from that is how we're connected to others in faith. These are the things that will endure long after any sufferings or trials here below have vanished, like it says in Revelation 21.

Do you have a favorite Bible verse?

Three of my top verses — or passages, really — are Psalm 23, Hebrews 3:5-6 and Ruth 1:16-17. Psalm 23 is a favorite of many people, since it expresses the believer's relationship with the Lord. There's a big emphasis on Providence — how, no matter what might happen, it is all for the good of the believer. Hebrews 3:5-6 is about perseverance in the faith under the Lordship of Christ. Ruth 1:16-17 is similar to the first two passages, because it's about faithful determination despite any trials that might occur.

My fiancée Brittany and I read the Bible and discuss what we think certain passages mean. Of course, anyone can have their own opinion about Scripture, but as St. Peter tells us in his second epistle, Scripture is not a matter of private interpretation. So we make sure to take our cue from the Church, which brought us the Bible to begin with. The written word of God is a gift bestowed on the faithful through the Church, so it should be expected that we can learn more about this gift through the Church.

Do you have a patron saint?

Well, I tend to think that the apostles John and Simon are the best saints around, but my name might make me a little partial. I also owe much to St. Simon Stock, who received the brown scapular from the Blessed Virgin Mary.

I've been wearing the brown scapular for about four years now. My father wears one, and he explained the promise related to it of not perishing in hell. That's something you have to jump at. Who wouldn't want to spend eternity with the Father, Son and Holy Spirit, as well as Mary, Joseph, all the other saints and all the angels? If we persevere in the faith, eternal happiness will be our ultimate destiny.

///

INDIANAPOLIS COLTS' GM SPEAKS OF PLAYOFFS, PARENTING AND PADRE PIO

Ryan Grigson values Catholicism now more than ever.

January 7, 2015

At Purdue University in the early 1990s, **Ryan Grigson** was going down the wrong path. The ways of the world had taken precedence over the ways of the Gospel for the 6-foot-6-inch, 290-pound tight end and offensive tackle.

Yet Grigson received a wake-up call that changed his life. He was almost fatally injured during a game and then spent weeks at the hospital in intensive care. Faced with his own mortality, Grigson became much more open to the fullness of the Gospel.

After being released from the hospital, Grigson eventually took up football again, but with a different mindset. He completed his collegiate career as a captain of the Boilermakers and then played two seasons professionally. Not wanting to leave a game that had been part of his life for many years, he embarked upon an administrative career in professional football.

The Highland, Ind., native worked as a scout with the St. Louis Rams and the Philadelphia Eagles, and in January 2012, he was hired as the general manager of the Indianapolis Colts. The team had posted a 2-14 record in 2011, but under Grigson's management, they have registered three straight 11-5 seasons and have gotten progressively better in the playoffs.

Two years ago, they lost in the opening round; last year, they lost in the second round; and this year, they are hoping to go even further. In order to do this, however, they have to get past the AFC West-champion Denver Broncos in Denver, something no team has been able to do this season.

As the Colts prepared to take on the Broncos on Jan. 11, Grigson, a 42-year-old father of six, fielded questions from *Register* correspondent Trent Beattie.

You're facing the AFC West-champion Denver Broncos in Denver on Sunday. What are your thoughts on that game?

It's obviously going to be a great challenge. They are talent-laden across the board and have Pro Bowlers and even Hall of Famers at key positions. They can beat you in so many different ways that they're a hard group to account for when game-planning. We will have to play our best football to this point to have a chance in their backyard, and we definitely can't expect to come out of there with a win if we shoot ourselves in the foot with turnovers, penalties, mental errors, etc. So again, it will have to be an all-hands-on-deck mindset and a true team win to get it done out there.

What do you like most about working in the NFL?

The best thing about being in the NFL is competing and working every day for a Super Bowl victory. It's a great challenge, but it gives me a certain drive and energy to push this organization in every way to try to attain it. No matter how difficult it can get, I love coming to work every day, and I try to keep in mind that there are only 32 of these general-manager jobs in the NFL.

Do you come from a devout family?

When I hear the word "devout" I think of my 91-year-old grandmother. She has been a strong example of the old adage that the best Gospel is lived, not preached. As long as I can remember, she has shown me a consistent example of what it means to be a good Catholic: whether it's seeing her pray the Rosary every single night, never missing Mass, sending prayer cards to people and really just obeying the Golden Rule, but expecting nothing at all in return.

My mom was widowed at a young age, due to my father's terminal brain cancer. She was left with two young sons to raise, but she never complained. She always had me and my younger brother, Dru [the director of college scouting for the Arizona Cardinals], at Mass, rain or shine.

Lastly, my godmother is someone else who helped to shape my faith throughout my life, with constant encouragement and reminders to stay the course, no matter what. I was basically raised by three strong women who took turns keeping me in line growing up, and, trust me, I wasn't the easiest kid to raise.

Did you get in trouble at school?

I attended Our Lady of Grace School in Highland, Ind., from first through eighth grade. The priests, nuns and other teachers in that school taught me so much and showed me *a lot* of tough love as I went through some hard times with my family. Everyone responds differently to different types of teaching or coaching, but I definitely needed tough love as a kid, and the clergy and faculty at school gave me plenty of it.

We went to Mass every day, but, as a youngster, you space out and don't pay attention sometimes. Yet, looking back, I think you still take away something subconsciously, even when you're just sitting there. You're hearing the word of God, being in his presence and receiving him in the Eucharist. Those cumulative days at Mass helped to mold my faith at its earliest stages, and I'm extremely grateful for that.

You have your own family now. What do you like most about family life?

It might sound kind of ordinary, but, to be honest, just being around my wife, Cynthia, and our six children — Sophia (12), Noah (10), Luke (9), Levi (7), Ava (6) and Jonah (newborn) — is what I like most. No matter the activity, I enjoy being close to all of them. I'm always showering my kids with affection, and I probably annoy some of them at times, but I want to make the most of the moments I have with them. You've got to do that when your job has a tendency to take up a lot of your time.

I think marriage, especially in a large family, has its challenges, but you learn so many valuable lessons. As a husband and father, I am constantly exposed in my human weakness, and it gets discouraging because you want to be better for them. Yet God is always there to forgive, strengthen and help to further mold you to get over each hurdle. All the lessons make you that much stronger for the next challenge.

It is such a blessing, but also such a tremendous responsibility, to be a husband and father. The difficult experience with my father's death has helped me to deeply appreciate what it means to be a father. It's not something I take for granted.

Was there a particularly tough time in your adult life that your faith got you through?

Without a doubt, I would say the toughest time was at Purdue, in 1992, when I got seriously hurt in a football game. The injury [a hit to his abdomen, which resulted in pancreatitis, kidney failure and then pneumonia] almost cost me my life; and then it put me in the hospital for a long time. For a good while, I was on machines in intensive care, and my body was so beat up, but my spirit was willing, so it was a time I feel God used to truly get my attention.

I had been a young kid away from home and slowly going down a wrong path, but during my time in the hospital and afterward, I really had a thirst for Scripture, and I opened up my heart and mind completely to the Good News. I prayed more than ever before and just had a better sense of what it means to be a Christian man.

You hear the expression that there's faith in foxholes. The hospital stay was kind of the same; because when you're faced with being that sick, I don't care who you are, you want to go to heaven and not the other destination. So being in the hospital was a wake-up call for me, and I was certainly changed forever because of it.

Even when the world and my job get the best of me today, it doesn't take long to remember what I learned in the hospital bed all those weeks: that we are nothing without God, and there is no hope when he is out of the equation. However, no matter the state of your soul or your current state of affairs, if you're still alive and willing to bring him into the equation, he can make everything right.

What are some of your favorite aspects of the Catholic Church?

I love the sacraments, especially the sanctity of the Mass. I have also recently been trying to go to confession more often. I find it healing to speak to someone about faults and missteps. It is humbling, and it isn't easy to do, especially when it's face-to-face, but it is cleansing and therapeutic, making it worth the effort.

I also appreciate the order and the history of our Church. I've always marveled at the unbroken succession of popes since St. Peter the Apostle. Whenever the Church has gone through turbulent things in my lifetime, I've found solace in the fact that incredible history and deep roots are there.

One aspect of Church history is found in sacred architecture. I'm not opposed to new church buildings, but I am traditional at my core, and I personally like being in some of those beautiful, old churches when I pray. When it comes to places of worship, I want to be in one that looks worthy of housing Christ's body and his blood.

I heard that you have a devotion to Padre Pio. How did that come about?

Like many other saints, I was introduced to Padre Pio by my grandmother. She gave me a book about him when I got married in 2001, which was before he was canonized. The book sat on my shelf for about three years, and, finally, one day, I grabbed it when I was headed out on a scouting trip.

Padre Pio has a long history in my family, it turned out. My great-grandmother actually had a picture of him in her house many, many years ago and knew of all the miracles happening with him over in Italy. Her parish priest actually advised her to take the picture down because I guess the Church hadn't investigated all the things going on, so there was still some controversy.

I was especially drawn to Padre Pio because of the stigmata. If someone bears the wounds of Christ, I figure he or she is obviously close to him or he chose that person for a special mission. The phenomenon of stigmata is a fascinating topic, and Padre Pio's whole life is fascinating. He also endeared himself to me for the simple fact that he liked to enjoy cold beers with friends. There was a normalcy and humanness about him, despite his extraordinary life and circumstances.

While I was with the Philadelphia Eagles from 2004 to 2012, our training-camp site was just 20 minutes from the Our Lady of Grace Shrine and Padre Pio Spirituality Centre in Barto, Pa. I would go on pilgrimage there with whoever wanted to come along. This included a great friend and co-worker stricken with brain cancer like my late father. My friend's cancer has been in remission for eight years now, and he has a strong devotion to St. Pio, still going on pilgrimage every year and placing petitions for me and my family. St. Pio has definitely enriched my faith, and I know that, through his intercession, I've had prayers answered.

Ever since I was given a lives-of-the-saints book as a kid, I've been fascinated by those holy men and women. In many cases, they were very ordinary people who became extraordinary because they let God fully reign in their hearts and minds. This complete surrender is inspiring, and, while it is certainly a challenge, it is what we are all called to do.

///

JOE LOMBARDI'S SUPER BOWL AND SUPER FAITH STORIES

The grandson of the legendary Green Bay Packers coach speaks of past, present and future NFL championships in light of the Catholic faith.

January 23, 2015

Not many people can say their last name is on the sterling silver trophy presented each year to the best team in the NFL. However, while **Joe Lombardi** is one of the few who can lay claim to that honor, he is not taken in by it. The Super Bowl trophy is named after his grandfather, Vince Lombardi, who, as head coach of the Green Bay Packers, won five NFL championships.

As quarterbacks coach of the New Orleans Saints in 2010, Joe Lombardi helped his team win the trophy named after his grandfather. Now, as offensive coordinator of the Detroit Lions, he hopes to win the Super Bowl again one day, but he also knows that there are more important things in life. Faith and family come before football in the Lombardi household, which prays the Angelus, the Rosary and the Divine Mercy Chaplet on a daily basis.

Joe Lombardi, a 43-year-old father of six, spoke with *Register* correspondent Trent Beattie about football and Catholic traditions in anticipation of Super Bowl XLIX, set to take place on Feb. 1 between the New England Patriots and the defending-champion Seattle Seahawks.

The Lions played the Patriots in the 2014 regular season, so you got to see them up close. What do they need to do in Super Bowl XLIX to prevent the Seahawks from repeating as Super Bowl champions?

The Patriots have an outstanding offense led by Tom Brady, but they can't rely solely on it against the Seahawks, who have a tremendous defense. Because the Patriots won't be able to run up the score, I think the key for them will be their own defense. They've got to control the running game of the Seahawks and try to force Russell Wilson to beat them with his throwing arm.

You won a Super Bowl as the quarterbacks coach with the Saints in 2010. Was there special importance for you in winning a trophy with your grandfather's name on it?

Winning the Super Bowl was special, but not just for me. I think everyone else on the team liked it as much as I did. People on the outside looking in might see things in a different light, but, from a coach's perspective, you get too focused on all the work involved to notice a family name on a trophy.

I guess you could say I was carrying on a family football tradition, but the specifically Catholic traditions, which were passed on through my family as well, are the ones most important to me. I wasn't able to meet my grandfather, since he died nine months before I was born. However, his Catholicism lives on through me, so that's what really means the most.

Did your grandfather's football lessons get passed on to you through your father?

They did, but I don't recall my dad sitting me and my two older brothers down every week and telling us outright that we were getting a lesson from Grandpa. It was more of something that was always there, kind of like a part of your identity. Your respect for the game is a part of a heritage you carry with you.

Somewhat paradoxically, one of the things passed on was that success is not a matter of genetics. You're not born a winner; you have to make the effort to become one. Anyone can do something well if he has the sincere desire to do that. There has to be a commitment to getting the task done and a dedication to the fundamentals of one's position.

I've been blessed, not only to have a grandfather like Vince Lombardi, but also to have been around so many other talented coaches. My high-school coach at Seattle Prep was Rollie Robbins; at the Air Force Academy, it was Fisher DeBerry; at the University of Dayton (the first place I coached), it was Mike Kelly; and with the New Orleans Saints, it was Sean Payton.

The Lions were 7-9 in 2013, but after a new coaching staff came on the scene, went 11-5 and made the playoffs. What needs to be done to get even better next year?

We want to continue to improve, have a great regular season and go further in the playoffs. We're already going in that direction, because we've gotten better from 2013. We've played smart football by cutting down on turnovers, and our defense did extremely well. Our offense needs to be more explosive, though.

There's a lot of talent spread in the league, so there's a cluster of teams that, if certain things turn out right, can win the whole thing. I think we're one of those teams, so we have a real shot at being the best next year. You start out with an overarching goal like that and then break it down into smaller goals: Right now, the players need a rest from the season; then they start working out on their own; then we have training camp, preseason etc. It's all done one step at a time.

Besides your own work, you need to have certain things outside your control go your way. This happened with the Saints in the 2009 regular season and 2010 postseason. One example was almost losing home-field advantage for the playoffs, but, because of the Bears' overtime victory against the Vikings in late 2009, we were able to play at home, including against the Vikings in the NFC Championship game. They say luck is the residue of design, but we had zero control over a game between two other teams. That's where you have to be thankful to God for gifts that are handed to you.

Have you always been thankful for your Catholic faith?

I have not. Unfortunately, it's all too common for people in my generation to have gotten lost in the catechetical haze of the 1970s and '80s. Parents sent their children to Catholic schools under the assumption that they would receive a Catholic education, but that's not what usually took place. Maybe part of it was my fault, by not being interested in hearing the truth, but there wasn't great faith formation in the classroom.

I first started becoming truly interested in the greatness of the Catholic faith around the time I got married 15 years ago. My wife, Molly, and I were concerned about all the health dangers of contraceptive pills, so we looked into natural family planning [which the Church approves]. A priest we met with wanted us to listen to a talk on CD from Dr. Janet Smith called "Contraception: Why Not"; but we said we were already sold on the topic. He insisted that we listen to it anyway, and we were blown away by what Dr. Smith said. Even though we were on the path it recommended, our beliefs and motives were reinforced or augmented in many ways.

That was the first step toward becoming more fully Catholic?

Yes, we started looking into what the Church teaches, and our search has produced so many great results. Now, we love being immersed in Catholic traditions, including the extraordinary form of the Mass. We attend a parish that has this one Sunday a month, and the other Sundays they have the ordinary form in English, but with the priest facing ad orientem ["toward the east," or in the same direction as the congregation] and with suitable music.

The Eucharist is the source and summit of our faith, so we should do everything we can to make it look and sound like that, rather than downplaying the fact. That's why I find it worth the effort to search for a Mass that's done well. It helps me to get a sharper sense of heavenly things and to pray better.

One thing that has helped me get a better sense of the Mass is a book called *Jesus and the Jewish Roots of the Eucharist*. In it, Dr. Brant Pitre gives a historical context for the sacrifice of the Calvary, which is the same as the sacrifice of the Mass. He shows what the Passover was like at the time of Jesus, why Jesus started the Eucharist during Passover, what the Jews were looking for in the Messiah and the meaning of the manna in the desert. Overall, you're able to see that Jesus is the fulfilment of Old Testament prophecies and practices.

Do you think that if people would look into the history and theology of the Mass they would get more out of it and attend it more frequently?

No question about it. It's mind-boggling to learn what really takes place in each Mass. It's not a random collection of man-made rituals; it's something that originated with Jesus (and, in a sense, came before him, since it has its roots in the Old Testament), and it has been passed down to us. Each of its parts has deep meaning because they are reflections of Jesus.

One of the things I like to do is not only going to Sunday Mass, but making a day of it with the family. Instead of going our separate ways after church, we meet up with another family or two and enjoy a meal together, play with the kids, etc. I get to do this all-day thing now that the season is over, and it's a great blessing.

Are there other Catholic family activities you enjoy?

Our family tries to pray the Rosary and Divine Mercy Chaplet every day. Marian intercession and the mercy of God are so closely related, so we've even started the Angelus at 6am, noon and 6pm. The first one, that early in the morning, is a challenge, but even if we pray the Angelus at 8, it's 6 somewhere, right? Plus, no matter what time of the day it's done, prayer is always a good thing.

It's a privilege to be the father of a Catholic family, where you not only pass along natural life to your sons and daughters, but supernatural life, too. That's what matters most, what's way more important than any Super Bowl victories, however fun those may be. I try to get this across to men's groups I talk to through Catholic Athletes for Christ's Speakers Bureau. The Super Bowl is the attention-grabber, but the more relevant thing is to live your life according to the teachings of Jesus, which are found in their entirety in the Catholic Church.

///

MASS-GOING MARINER SUITS UP

March 22, 2010

A 10th-round draft pick for the Kansas City Royals in 1991, **Mike Sweeney** made his major league debut on Sept. 14, 1995. He spent the next few years playing in both the majors and the minors, not yet a sure thing in the Kansas City lineup. During spring training of 1999, it was rumored that he would be traded, which was not welcome news.

After going to church and turning to Our Lord in prayer, Sweeney realized that he needed to "let go and let God." He resolved to put Our Lord first and let him be the guide in his baseball career, and this brought him peace of mind.

In the end, the Royals did not trade him, and he ended up hitting .322 for the season in 1999, along with 22 home runs and 102 RBIs. He was even more productive the next year, posting a .333 average, 29 home runs and 144 RBIs. While playing for the Royals, Sweeney was named an All-Star five times (2000-2003 and 2005).

This past season he played as a designated hitter for the Seattle Mariners, helping the team to win 24 more games than they did in 2008, to finish with an 85-77 record.

Sweeney recently spoke with *Register* correspondent Trent Beattie.

You're one of eight children from an Irish Catholic family. How important is family to you?

Family is very important to me. On Nov. 9, 2002, I made a covenant with Jesus when I married the love of my life, Shara. My parents, my two brothers and my five sisters mean everything to me, but my priority is now my wife and my three children, Michael, McKara and Donovan.

I still honor my parents and love my siblings with an agape love, but Scripture says that "A man is to leave his mother and father and cleave to his wife." Also, Ephesians 5 gives us men the greatest challenge when St. Paul writes that "Men are to love their wives like Christ loved the Church." It is a challenge but a great compass setting.

You had some medical problems as a baby, but ended up getting through them in a providential, even miraculous way. Could you tell us more about that?

On July 22, 1973, I was born two months premature in Orange, Calif., to a 20-year-old saintly woman and an ex-professional baseball player with the California Angels who to this day is my hero. I didn't know it at the time, but the Lord had a plan for my life — and it wasn't dying in that hospital. I had praying parents, grandparents and other family members that lifted my 4 pound young body up to the Lord and, by God's grace, their prayers were answered.

After weeks in the hospital, I defied the odds and today I stand at 6 feet 2 inches and weigh 220 pounds. I guess it's not how you start but how you finish!

You've shown respect for family in general by promoting pro-life causes. Why are these causes important to you?

My mom is the one who planted the seed in my heart to protect the unborn by plastering her van, aka "The Pro-Life Mobile" with stickers and running the pro-life ministry at our parish, St. Elizabeth Ann Seton in Ontario, Calif. Growing up, we often were honked at or given the "bird" from those poor souls who didn't respect life the way we did, but it was all worth it.

When I married, my wife and I took on similar roles. Shara volunteered at The Rachel House, a crisis-pregnancy center in Kansas City. Through my foundation [MikeSweeney.org], we started the Lunch for Life, where we raised money and awareness for the unborn and agencies that supported life.

The greatest gifts have been blessing those who chose life in truly crisis situations by supplying them with money and necessities to get them on their feet. Also, helping pay for the adoptions of babies for those who have a heart of gold to love these children but have an empty pocket. As you can tell, those stickers on my mom's van brought a love for the unborn to my heart.

There are quite a few other actively pro-life major leaguers, aren't there?

The newspapers are full of negative stories, but the majority of major league baseball players are God-loving, faithful men who love Jesus, the Blessed Mother and the unborn. I just wish stories of these great men would make the front page rather than end up as clips on the editing room floor.

Do you have a favorite devotion (such as the Rosary or Divine Mercy Chaplet)?

My favorite thing to do as a family is pray the Rosary. A friend of mine, Father Willy Raymond, who works with Family Theater in Hollywood, reminds me of words Father Peyton made famous: "A family that prays together stays together." It is such a joy to see your 6-year-old son and 4-year-old daughter ask when it's their turn to say the Hail Mary. We are never closer as a family than when we pray the Rosary.

How does your faith impact how you see the game of baseball and how you see and interact with teammates?

1 Corinthians says, "If you have the faith to move mountains and have not love, you have nothing." The greatest fruit of the Holy Spirit that can flow through us if we are not being selfish is love. One way people will know that we are Christians is through the love we show to them.

Baseball is a great game that I have loved to play since I was a boy. It has been said that I have been a great leader and teammate through my career. My greatest asset is the love that I have for my teammates.

Whether in a workplace, school or locker room, love is the foundation necessary to make an impact on someone's life. Once the teammate, co-worker or student knows you care about them, then and only then are they ready to march with you or become better at their task.

It's better to give your friend a kick in the pants while you are hugging them rather than blasting them from behind when they least expect it.

Do you have any favorite Catholic books you read on the road?

My favorite Catholic book to read on the road is the Bible. I like to joke with my Protestant brothers on the team that we have the "unedited version of the Bible." As you know, our Catholic Bible has 73 books while the Protestant Bible was condensed to 66 when Martin Luther broke away from the Church.

Some people think of Catholicism as only being for old women, but do you think there has been an improvement recently with how men are committed to the faith?

Many would be amazed at the number of godly men that play in the major leagues. It's sad that our pews are filled only with elderly women, and as men, we are not stepping up.

Is it difficult to attend Mass while playing baseball professionally?

It is difficult to attend Mass on the road in the midst of a long, arduous season, but I make the effort because Jesus did so much for me. After leaving the stadium on a Saturday evening at midnight, getting up at 7am to attend 7:30am Mass is not the most exciting thing to do on the way to the stadium — but there is not a better place to be on a Sunday morning than at Mass.

I love speaking with my wife after a Sunday game about that day's Mass as I walk onto our team airplane. Only in the Catholic Church can I go to Mass at St. Patrick's Cathedral in New York and my wife attends Mass in San Diego and have the same Liturgy of the Word. It's fun to discuss the different homilies and churches from the road.

How does it feel to re-sign with the Mariners?

It is joy to put on a big league uniform again as I am living out my childhood dream. I realize this is a gift from God so I want to use it to glorify Him and His Church.

What do you think of last season and what are your expectations for this season?

2009 was the most enjoyable year of my career so I am eager to build on the joy that was experienced last year. My hope is to be a light to the guys in the clubhouse and help the Seattle Mariners win a World Series.

///

MAJOR LEAGUE FAITH

St. Louis Pitcher Marks 15th Anniversary Playing Ball

July 12, 2010

Right-handed pitcher Jeff Suppan was drafted by the Boston Red Sox out of Crespi Carmelite High School in Encino, Calif., in 1993. After a relatively short stint in the minor leagues, he made his major league debut July 17, 1995, at the age of 20.

Suppan has played for six major league teams over the past 15 years. A top highlight of his career was the 2006 postseason, in which he was named the National League Championship Series MVP and won the World Series with the St. Louis Cardinals.

After spending three full seasons and the first two months of this season with the Milwaukee Brewers, he returned to the St. Louis Cardinals in the middle of June.

Since then, his pitching numbers have improved over those he had in Milwaukee.

Suppan has been active in the Alexandria, Va.-based organization Catholic Athletes for Christ, and he had the opportunity to meet Pope Benedict XVI in 2005 during the Vatican's first conference on sports. He is also one of the featured athletes on the "Champions of Faith" DVD, issued in 2007.

He and his wife, Dana, own and operate the restaurant Soup's Sports Grill in the Woodland Hills area of Los Angeles.

How does it feel to be back in St. Louis?

It's great to be here again; it brings back so many fond memories.

What are your expectations for the rest of this season?

As an athlete, my expectations are simply to be prepared. To give my best every time I get the opportunity to be on the mound, I need to be prepared both mentally and physically. These are the things I can control, so I try to maximize that sense of preparation.

As a team we have to take the long view — playing hard until the last game. If we keep it simple and focus on one game at a time, we should be in good shape come the end of the season.

Are your favorite career moments the ones most people would think of, such as winning the World Series, or are there others that are more outstanding to you?

Obviously, winning a world championship is an incredible moment — one that I will cherish my whole life.

However, many of my favorite moments are the smaller things, like making a pitch with runners on to get out of an inning or giving a teammate advice that helps him out in his career.

But there are other incredible moments that are even less obvious and more personal—like being in the stadium in the early morning when no one is in the ballpark. It is such a peaceful time.

You had the opportunity to meet with Pope Benedict XVI in 2005 for the Vatican's first conference on sports. What was that experience like?

I had planned on giving the Pope a St. Louis Cardinals jersey because he had been a cardinal, too, you know. However, the airline lost my luggage, so I couldn't do that, and, in fact, I ended up wearing the same clothes for two days.

Meeting Pope Benedict was overwhelming for me, as I'd never been able to do that before. Being in his presence was a way of experiencing God's love for the Church. By providing us with a visible leader, as explained in Matthew 16, God's fatherly concern for us is expressed in giving us a father/leader in the person of the Pope.

It was also good to see that more people are realizing that sports can be a venue for living out the faith. Sports don't have to be a separate compartment in someone's life, a compartment which isn't touched by the faith.

What advice would you give a young man who aspires to play in the major leagues?

To play in the major leagues takes talent and dedication. You have to accept some personal sacrifices to make it there and in order to stay once you get there.

The best advice I can give is to be well-rounded and take your education seriously, because there is a lot of life after you're done playing. Even if you do make it and have a long career, you can't play forever!

It's also helpful to know your true motivation on why you play the game. You'll have a tough time making it if you're playing because of someone else's passion for the game, not your own.

Is it difficult to attend Mass on Sundays during the season?

There are many challenges for a ballplayer trying to get to Mass on Sunday. One big challenge is that we play on Sundays. Another is that we are in different cities every week. You have to be proactive [and] look on the schedule to see where you're playing each Sunday. I like to go to parishesonline.com and find the closest Catholic church; then I pick the Mass time that works best for my playing schedule.

Do you have a favorite saint and/or devotion?

I don't have a favorite saint, but I am interested in St. Thérèse of Lisieux. I say the Rosary and the Divine Mercy Chaplet, but my discipline in saying them needs some improvement — but I'm working on it!

How has your Catholic faith influenced who you are today?

I found out that when you go out into the world your faith has to be your own. You have to understand why you believe what you believe in. Reading the Bible and the *Catechism of the Catholic Church* is helpful, along with utilizing other resources like Catholic Answers. ... My Catholic faith is an integral part of my life. It has made me into who I am today. I think I owe my faith in large part to my parents. They brought me up in the Church, and my faith has grown ever since.

///

HOPE SPRINGS ETERNAL ON THE DIAMOND

Baseball Announcer Connects Faith and Life

March 18, 2011

Ryan Lefebvre is hopeful that the Major League Baseball season, opening March 31, will be a winning one — but his hopes extend far beyond the diamond.

Lefebvre, the television announcer for the Kansas City Royals, began a broadcasting career during his freshman year at the

University of Minnesota in 1992 when he called football games on the radio for the Golden Gophers. He was hired by the Minnesota Twins in 1994 and has been a television and radio announcer for the Royals since 1999.

At one time, Lefebvre looked to his career success for happiness, but could not find it there. He sought in vain to fill an emptiness that remained within. The 40-year-old Lefebvre recounted his struggles with alcoholism, depression and anxiety in his 2009 release *The Shame of Me: One Man's Journey to Depression and Back*. He has learned a great deal about the role of faith in daily life and has made noteworthy improvements, but still considers himself a work in progress.

Lefebvre spoke with Trent Beattie during spring training in Arizona.

What are you looking forward to with the Royals this season?

This year it has been said by many publications that the Royals have the best minor league system in baseball. Hopefully this will help reverse the trend for the past five seasons, which have all been losing ones. ... Something that's interesting about baseball — whether it's the players or those of us who work in broadcasting — is that it's not just a job, but a lifestyle. For five months in the off-season you're on your own schedule 24/7, but during the seven months of the season, it's totally the opposite. You're on someone else's schedule almost 24/7. You're away from home about four months of the season, with a day off every 10 days or two weeks.

What is one of your best baseball memories as a broadcaster?

One of my all-time favorite games to call was David Wells' perfect game in 1998 at Yankee Stadium. I was with the Minnesota Twins at the time and got to call that one on TV and radio. That was very memorable, along with the final game at Tiger Stadium in Detroit in

1999. Robert Fick hit a monstrous Grand Slam in the bottom of the eighth inning, and it ended up being the last hit in Tiger Stadium.

What was one of the lessons your father, former Major League player and manager Jim Lefebvre, taught you regarding baseball that could be translated into everyday life?

One of the things that really stood out for me from his managerial days was that he was always very poised with the media. I would be in his office with him and some reporters, and even when he was asked a sub-par question, he didn't treat it as such. He treated each question as if it were important, even if it really wasn't. The only exception would be if he knew the reporter was trying to bait him.

My father not only treated the reporters with respect, but so many other people as well, especially those behind the scenes. He knew the parking lot attendant's name, the security guard's name, the bat boy's name. Those people not always considered important were seen as such and treated as such by my father, so that really stays with me.

You've been around professional athletes your entire life. What are some of the major misconceptions that people have about professional athletes?

The biggest one is that because they make a lot of money and are famous that makes them happy. The fact is: It's really just the opposite. People tend to think that professional athletes are extraordinary people, but I've often remarked that professional athletes are ordinary people in an extraordinary situation. Most of them love what they do — that is, their specific sport. That's good so far, but then comes the added aspect of, Wouldn't it be great to play my sport in front of a crowd of thousands, to be on the cover of a magazine, to sign a multimillion-dollar contract ...

Those external goals can be traps that make you think happiness is found in things outside of yourself. The more you strive for them and the further you advance in getting them, the less content you become; but then you're deceived even further into thinking you need more of them to be happy. There's a saying that you can never get enough of what you don't really need, and the odd thing is: The more things you have, the less happy you tend to be.

I can definitely relate to this trap because I fell into it myself. When things aren't taken for what they're really worth and managed properly, all kinds of problems can ensue.

How did your experience with depression and anxiety begin, and how did it continue?

It began when my parents divorced; I was very young, about 5 years old. I didn't really notice the problem, though, until I was in high school. I was out of my comfort zone at an upscale all-boys Catholic school in Los Angeles, and that's when the alcohol abuse began. Even though I was in what would be called the "in crowd," I still felt out of place. Instead of dealing head-on with the issues I was facing, I decided to self-medicate with alcohol.

Then, oddly enough, the problem took a new turn, when I gave up drinking in January of 1998. People were congratulating me on being sober, but the reality was that I had to face unresolved issues without my usual medication. Obviously, becoming sober was a great step in the right direction, but there should be proper support there when that happens. Otherwise, you're confronting issues alone, and that's when the depression can set in.

Depression and alcoholism are really the same thing, which is the inability to cope with life's problems. By August of 2005 I was overwhelmed with problems and was so desolate. Picture a 34-year-old man on the floor in the fetal position crying his eyes out. That was me. I couldn't take it anymore and decided to get help. I called my mother, went to counseling and to a life coach. Instead of hiding my problems, I accepted them and shared them with other people who could help.

Was there a correlation between the lack of practicing the faith and depression?

My priorities were out of whack. I thought that attaining certain outward goals would make me happy, so I was very much into accomplishing them. They weren't bad in themselves, but when you treat them as being more important than they really are, then you're in trouble. It can become an idolatry of sorts, and then other things which are inherently sinful can intrude as well.

I learned the hard way that nothing material can make us happy. We can get little highs here and there, but if we really want lasting happiness, then we have to humble ourselves and let God into our lives. Once the focus is off self and material things, we can begin to heal, become happy, and then help others do the same.

One of the great ways to do this is through the sacrament of reconciliation. Instead of just thinking of it as confessing sins, there really is a reconciling that goes on. It's about asking for forgiveness from God and from those we've hurt, mending broken or bruised relationships. The confessing part is a means to an end, and the ultimate end is everlasting happiness with Our Father in heaven.

This ultimate end is realized even further by receiving the body and blood of Jesus in holy Communion, which is a pledge of future glory given to us, as the Church teaches.

Were there other aspects of Catholicism that you found particularly helpful in getting better?

My Catholic faith was the most important thing overall. In college I would always turn to the Church, including participation at daily

Mass. That's a necessary start, but it's not the whole story. You can't just go to Mass every day and then expect everything to turn out fine without any other means to help. It's not just the sacraments alone that help us; God wants us to work through our problems. A father gives his son a lot more in the long run when he expects him to make an effort, rather than just doing everything for him and giving him everything in one shot. God the Father is the same way with his children.

Do you have a patron saint, favorite devotion or favorite book?

I picked up a St. Daniel medal from a Catholic store years ago in New Mexico and wear it around my neck. He's pictured with a lion and is known as a patron of wisdom and understanding. I pray for wisdom and understanding, but they don't usually come easily. We seem to learn best through trials. It's not like God taps us on the head with a wand and then everything is perfect. There are struggles to get through — but they do make us better people if we take them in the right way.

As for reading, I've started lectio divina [prayerful reading of Scripture], which I learned from the Benedictine monks at a nearby abbey. My wife and I go there for retreats, and they tell us that most retreatants are actually non-Catholics. There seems to be a desire on the part of everyone to just step back and get in touch with the sacred, to simplify things and be at peace.

Simplifying things is so important, and spiritual reading is no exception. In *The Seven Storey Mountain*, Thomas Merton makes the distinction between spiritual reading and reading spiritually. We can read things which are good in themselves, but do we actually implement them in our lives, or do we just use them as academic points to back up our own opinions? Ultimately, it all boils down to charity: love of God and love of neighbor for the sake of God. That's what Jesus tells us in the Gospels.

///

OTHERWORLDLY SERIES

Baseball Coach Rich Donnelly Shows
You Can Go Home Again

October 10, 2011

Rich Donnelly has a World Series story that is out of this world.

Donnelly's daughter Amy had passed away four years before his trip to the World Series in 1997 with the Florida Marlins, but her presence was felt keenly at the end of the seventh game. The coach has recounted the story to thousands of people around the country every year.

His story has a special impact on other parents whose children are struggling with terminal illnesses or have already died. Because only they can know what it's like to lose a child, Donnelly says he has a soft spot in his heart for such families.

In fact, family was what brought Donnelly back from his own wayward path earlier in his career. The loving example of his wife and the early death of his daughter persuaded him to become more committed to his Catholic faith.

The 65-year-old Ohio native is still active in baseball, serving this past season as manager of the minor league Brooklyn Cyclones of the New York Mets organization. He took time out after a game in the middle of August to talk with *Register* correspondent Trent Beattie about his career, family and faith.

What are some of your career highlights that stand out?

Anytime you get to put on a uniform and hit the field is a highlight, but signing my first professional contract in 1968 with the Minnesota Twins was a specific one for me. Then, in four years of minor-league ball, we won four league championships. I retired myself at the ripe old age of 25 to become a coach, and I've been doing that ever since.

I've been able to coach in the major leagues for 25 years. I served as third-base coach for manager Jim Leyland on three different teams: the Pittsburgh Pirates, the Florida Marlins and the Colorado Rockies.

In our years at Pittsburgh, we won three pennants, and then at Florida we won the World Series in 1997. That was great. I remember as a boy watching the Brooklyn Dodgers and New York Yankees playing in the World Series, and then going out in the back yard, thinking that maybe one day I would do that.

What do you remember about the 1997 World Series against the Cleveland Indians?

What's interesting is that the games themselves I didn't see differently than any other series of games. You just go out and play as you normally would. It was only after we won that I really noticed the big difference with all the hoopla that surrounds it.

But, of course, the main thing I remember about the 1997 World Series is the story regarding my daughter Amy. She had seen me at a game in the early 1990s talking to players when they were on third base. I would cover my mouth so the opposing team couldn't read my lips. After the game, Amy asked me, "Dad, what do you say to the players when they're on third base? 'The chicken runs at midnight' or something like that?"

It was just a stilly thing, but it became a catchphrase for our family after Amy was diagnosed with brain cancer. In many tough months of treatment, it was something we said to each other as a family in order to lighten things up a bit. Amy ended up passing away in 1993 at the age of 17, but the story didn't end there.

In 1997, Craig Counsell was on our Florida Marlins team that won the World Series. My sons Tim and Mike had nicknamed him "Chicken Wing" because of his unusual batting stance, in which one of his arms would flop around. Well, I was at my post at third base during Game 7 of the World Series. It was a long game, going into extra innings. In the 11th inning, Edgar Renteria hit a single, and I waved Counsell ("Chicken Wing") into home.

My sons had been batboys for the game, and, after we won, they ran up to me to celebrate. Tim pointed to the clock, which read "12:00." It was exactly midnight, and Tim said, "Look, Dad, the chicken runs at midnight."

I think it was Amy talking to us from heaven. It was the highlight of my professional career, but, more importantly, it was a faith-and-family highlight, reminding me of eternity. The things of this world, no matter how flashy, will all pass away. What matters is where we spend eternity.

That's something it took you a while to learn, right?

When I was younger, I actually did have that type of focus, but lost it later in life. The happiest time of my life was when I was a kid. I was a daily communicant, and my faith was my whole life. In high school, I was probably one of the last people to actually build a May altar in my bedroom.

Then, after I left home and my career progressed, the values of the world gradually got a hold of me. I'm ashamed to say it now, but in my 30s, I became embarrassed to be known as a Catholic. I wanted to be seen as a tough guy, a winner, a great baseball man. I was full of myself, very egotistical, and that kind of attitude only leads to misery.

From the outside looking in, I had it all together. I was a professional baseball coach making lots of money, surrounded by other people making lots of money.

I've known many millionaires in my life, even some billionaires, and they're always looking for something else. There's no contentment — just that restlessness St. Augustine refers to in his well-known prayer: "Our hearts are restless, O Lord, until they rest in thee."

Let me tell you: Nothing in the world can make you happy like Jesus Christ can. Nothing. It took me a while to relearn that.

I would lie in bed at night wondering why I was so miserable and finally asked the Lord what was wrong with my situation. What came back to me was the thought of the happiest time of my life — my youth. I would serve at the altar, on the doorstep of heaven, and was just filled with the Lord. I wasn't rich or famous, but I was content. That realization, along with the loving example of my wife, Roberta, helped to bring me back to participating more fully in the Church.

Then what really capped it off was Amy's death. Nothing will get you to turn your life around like the death of a loved one. It really makes you think of your own weakness and need for God's grace and mercy. We're all going to die one day, but we don't like to think of that. We'd better think of it, though, if we truly want what's good for us. At the point of death, what a consolation it will be for devout Christians to have lived according to the teachings of Jesus Christ.

How does your family play in your overall view of life?

I have eight kids and seven grandkids so far, and we're very religious. We do things together as a family, and I enjoy being around them a lot. My wife is a great example of someone who really lives the faith. Of course, it's necessary to pray and go to Mass and confession, but we also have to take the grace we obtain and use it in our interactions with others.

That's what we learn in the parable of the talents: You've got to invest what you've been given. My wife does just this, treating people respectfully, giving of herself, and putting herself last. Then, after death, the last shall be first, right?

Mother Teresa would sometimes give speeches, and what made them so powerful was her own life. She didn't just go up there and tell people what to do in words; she had already given her own example in deeds. That's why something she said would get a greater response than the same thing coming from someone else. That's the power the saints have, which comes from their inner conversion and living the faith from the inside out.

Do you have a favorite saint?

As a kid I looked up to my older brother Romey, who played in the Cincinnati Reds organization. I admired him a lot; he was my mentor and tutor, and I wanted to be just like him. Unfortunately, he was diagnosed with Hodgkin's disease, so I prayed a novena to St. Jude, the patron of hopeless cases, for his cure. I was 14 at the time, and my brother was 28, the age at which he died. Even though my request wasn't granted, I still continue to have a devotion to St. Jude.

You know, I was an impossible case with my bad attitude mentioned earlier, and I did get out of that situation.

How does your faith affect your coaching?

Coaching is like being a father. There's a time to kid around, a time to discipline, and a time to realize that you and your player (or your child) just don't see things the same way.

What's most important is to be honest and fair. The worst thing in the world is for your players or your children to lose trust in you, so you have to be upfront with them.

What you see with children or players or anyone else is that the good ones are always disciplined. They know their limits, are respectful of others, and they contribute to the family, team or group they're in. Those are some things to look for and encourage.

I love to study people, so one of the things I've done in coaching is to study other coaches. I remember years ago reading about Miami Dolphins coach Don Shula, whom my father admired, not for his football accomplishments, but because he would go to Mass every day.

I also encountered Catholic coaches in my own career, like Jack McKeon of the Florida Marlins, and looked into what they do that works, and then take that into my own coaching.

There are also people like [former NFL player and coach] Danny Abramowicz, whom I've known since childhood back in Ohio. We've had similar stories, in that we grew up very devout and happy, then went wayward following our success in sports, but we finally got back on course.

Baseball is so similar to life in general. There's a base-running analogy that matches up quite well. You start out at home, get a little older (first base), then in early adulthood (second base), you're the furthest away from home you'll ever be. (Second base is 120 feet and six inches from home plate.) You get a little older and wiser (third base), and you see home plate. Then you realize that where you want to be is where you already were.

In my case, when I rounded second base, I fell off the base path altogether and went off into left field, but did eventually get back on the right path. Contrary to what some people think, you can go home again.

///

IMPORTANCE OF CATHOLICISM HITS HOME FOR ARIZONA DIAMONDBACKS PLAYER

Major League Baseball veteran Willie Bloomquist appreciates his blessings now more than ever.

April 24, 2012

The way **Willie Bloomquist** sees it, he's living an impossible dream. Of all the players who try to make it to the major leagues, only a relative few actually get there.

Bloomquist is one of those few, but he doesn't attribute this to his own skills.

The 34-year-old Port Orchard, Wash., native says he's not as talented as some other players who never made it to the majors. Why, then, is he there?

In part because of the intercession of St. Rita of Cascia, he says. After hitting a low point in the minor leagues, he began to ask for her prayers, and he made it through the often slow grind.

After playing nine full seasons in the majors, Bloomquist has a renewed appreciation for his Catholicism, family and opportunities to help others. He spoke with *Register* correspondent Trent Beattie prior to the beginning of the Arizona Diamondbacks' regular season opener in early April.

What are some of your top baseball memories?

There are many memories from college and before that, but, as far as professionally, a handful come to mind. The day I was called up to the big leagues in 2002, my first big-league hit and first big-league home run — those are all very memorable.

Then, last year, I was able to make it to the postseason for the first time with the Diamondbacks.

On more of a day-to-day basis, what is most fun is when you can come through for the team in a clutch situation. Getting a big hit to cap off a rally or coming through in another way is the ultimate emotional high in baseball.

What are your expectations going into this season?

I'm blessed to be with a great group of guys, so as long as we play like we're capable of playing, we'll do just fine. You always want to do the best you can and play at a high level, so you're trying to put every effort forth in order to play an imperfect game perfectly. Your own expectations can far exceed anyone else's for you.

However, you have to moderate those aspirations, in the sense of simply playing in the present moment and playing for an audience of One. Everyone wants to be appreciated, but after so many years playing the game, you realize that what other people think — even your friends — doesn't matter. What matters is being pleasing to God. You have to know that your talents come from God, and you have to direct them back to him. It's an act of thanksgiving to carry out your work well.

Have you found that other major leaguers share that mindset?

The more you play the game, the more your eyes are opened to that. When I started out playing professionally, I didn't really notice it, but, in recent years, it has become more obvious to me. Mike Sweeney, Mark Teahen and Mark Loretta are some of the Catholics I've encountered in Major League Baseball. With the Diamondbacks, I'm blessed to be around guys like Stephen Drew, Ian Kennedy, Joe Patterson and Micah Owings, who are believers as well.

There's a funny story with J.J. Putz, who is with the Diamondbacks now, from our days together in Seattle. I've always been known as Willie, but J.J. started calling me Bill when we played with the Mariners. He even got the public-address announcer at Safeco Field to call me "Bill Bloomquist," and it kind of stuck with a lot of the guys. Now that J.J. is playing with me in Arizona, he still calls me Bill, but, recently, someone suggested that because I'm known as a utility player I should be called "Utility Bill." Maybe that one will stick as well.

But, more seriously, having your life centered on Jesus Christ is something very important for anyone, but in a particular way with a sport like baseball. When you consider the fact that the elite hitters in the game are the ones who fail 70% of the time, that tells you how much failure everyone has to deal with every day.

Most people think that playing baseball professionally is all fun, and, of course, there are fun times, but there's a lot of work to do as well. It's not something that shows up when you see a game, but just like any other job, there are things you have to do that you don't necessarily feel like doing. Then there's the added aspect of having everything you do analyzed. If you have a bad day, you can't erase it; it's on TV and in the papers for everyone to see. Traveling constantly is also one of the things that's not too much fun.

That can be tough on the family, too.

No question about it. I admire, respect and appreciate my wife, Lisa, more and more as the years go by. Being married to a professional athlete has many challenges, and she meets those on a daily basis. I love my wife so much. She's the rock of our marriage.

Of course, Jesus Christ is *the* rock of our marriage, but, in a way somewhat akin to how Peter was the rock on which Jesus built his Church in Matthew 16, my wife is the human foundation of the marriage. She's the heart of the home, and I'm very fortunate to be married to such a special woman.

Not surprisingly, then, with a wife like her, I have two great daughters as well. They are very special to me, and I appreciate their simplicity and love. It doesn't matter to them whether I go 0-for-4 or 4-for-4; they love me just the same. We tend to complicate things and get overly sophisticated, but kids make things so simple. I'm grateful for that in my daughters, and I think I'm the proudest dad ever.

Your own father got to witness your Major League debut in 2002. Why was that so special for you?

After struggling in the minor leagues, I was called up from the Seattle Mariners' AAA team in September of 2002. I grew up in the state of Washington, so my parents were close by and went to all the home games that month, which actually has been the best month of my career so far.

It was great for my dad to witness that, especially in light of what would happen shortly afterward. He was in a car accident that caused massive brain damage, and the recovery didn't go well. However, he did recover enough to get to one game in the 2003 season. It was the last game before the All-Star [Game] break, and it turned out to be the best single game of my professional career. I got a grand slam off of Rob Bell and drove in six runs.

Today, my dad doesn't remember enough to know that his son plays baseball for a living, but he was the one who started me out in the sport. He taught my brother and me how to play the game, and that was really something he got a kick out of: being with his sons on the field.

You're continuing that father-son relationship in somewhat of an indirect way with the work you do for a Phoenix hospital. How did that come about?

Last year, my wife and I decided we were going to start giving back to the community here in Phoenix. We focused on Phoenix

Children's Hospital, where there are many kids going through very difficult illnesses. We decided to bring at least one kid to every home stand — on us.

We give them a signed jersey, and then they get to watch batting practice and meet the guys on the team. This can be very uplifting for the kids because it gives them a chance to get away from their problems for a while.

Last June, we invited a kid named Abe Speck to a game. When Abe was just a little kid, he had some complications growing, so he spent time at the hospital and continues to do so on occasion. Last year, as an 11-year-old, we brought him to a game against the San Francisco Giants.

One of the questions Abe asked before the game was if I had any rituals after hitting a home run and if I pointed to anyone in particular. I told him I'm not really a home-run hitter, and, even beyond that, I don't usually make a show about it when I do hit one. He pressed me and asked if I got a home run that night if I would point to him. I said I didn't really think I would hit one, but if I did, then I'd point to him. Then he was like, "No, you're going to hit one out tonight, so, when you do, will you point to me?"

Well, in my second at bat I made contact with the ball, but it really wasn't that good of a hit. However, it sailed into the stands. It was a home run. I don't know how to explain it, except to say that some higher powers were at work. As I rounded second base, it kind of hit me, and I started to tear up. Then, as I got to third and was going home, I saw Abe in the crowd with his mom and his friend Max. Of course I pointed to him, and they were all crying as well.

Later in the season, we started the Abe and Max Fund, named after Abe and another kid named Max (not the one who was at the game). One of the things that can be very trying for kids in the hospital is being isolated for long stretches at a time. Depending on the treatment they're going through, they can be kind of quarantined and are prevented from being in touch with their friends. We raise money that goes toward things like Nintendo DS, Kindle Fires and iPads so they can be entertained or communicate with the outside world.

You've had communication with the outside world, so to speak, in regard to St. Rita of Cascia. What is something you've learned from that?

After a great college career, I was in the minors and was really struggling. I just thought maybe I was washed up and finished. It was a very low period in my life, and playing in the majors just didn't seem possible.

However, someone told me about St. Rita being the saint of the impossible, so I looked into it and learned more about her. I prayed to her for help, and shortly thereafter I started playing better.

Then, not long after that, I was called up to the majors and have been blessed to play there for many years. When you look at it from a mathematical point of view, I really am living out an impossible dream. The chances of making it to the majors are very slim, especially when you consider the fact that there are players who are more talented than I am.

So I am thankful for St. Rita's intercession, and I keep a medal of her in my wallet all the time.

What are some other things you appreciate most about the Catholic Church?

I like the tradition of the Church. For an entity to be around for 2,000 years, it has to have something special to it, and the Church is very special to me. Through all the years of criticisms leveled against it, the Church still stands strong. It is the Church Jesus refers to in Matthew 16: The gates of hell will not prevail against it.

I also like the fact that anywhere you go in the world the Mass is the same. It may be in English or in Latin or in another language, but the very core of it remains unchanged. The essential Mass is the same for all Catholic believers throughout the world.

I've always believed in God, but, in recent years, I've become more appreciative of the importance of Catholicism. There have been some life-changing events that really pointed me to what really matters. It's been an awakening to understand better what God has to offer through his Church.

As competitive as I am, Catholicism gives me the opportunity to play as well as I can on the field and then leave the game behind when I go home. Without that, you can get really frustrated and self-destructive. We weren't meant to go it alone and get caught up in our own problems, but to live as the body of Christ and have a heavenward trajectory.

///

YANKEES FIRST BASEMAN MARK TEIXEIRA ON THE IMPORTANCE OF FATHERHOOD

Catholic ball player recalls ideal childhood, strives to provide the same for his own kids.

May 17, 2012

Mark Teixeira is widely known as one of the best all-around players in baseball. After being awarded the 2000 Dick Howser Trophy, college baseball's equivalent of college football's Heisman Trophy, he was taken in the first round of the Major League Baseball Draft in 2001.

His professional career includes a World Series championship, two All-Star Game appearances, three Silver Slugger Awards and four Gold Glove Awards.

Teixeira is also known for his generosity. He has established multiple scholarships, including one named after a friend who was killed in a car accident while in high school. Generosity is something he learned at the side of his father, John, along with a strong work ethic.

John Teixeira played baseball at the U.S. Naval Academy and passed along his own athletic knowledge and discipline to his son through the game.

Encouraged to use his abilities to their fullest, Mark Teixeira encountered his greatest coach and his greatest fan in his own father.

In anticipation of Father's Day, Mark Teixeira spoke with *Register* correspondent Trent Beattie.

You've played for three other major-league teams, but is there something special about playing for the Yankees?

I played for the Texas Rangers, Atlanta Braves and Anaheim Angels before coming to New York. Each of those teams was great to play for, and you're blessed to be able to play on any major-league team, but with the Yankees, it's raised to another level.

It's bigger and better here. So many fans, so much media attention, and such a history of success. Twenty-seven World Championships is quite an accomplishment, which makes the Yankees not only the greatest baseball franchise, but the greatest sports franchise, of all time.

You're a three-time Silver Slugger Award winner, but also a four-time Golden Glove Award winner. Do you work on fielding as much as you do hitting?

Everyone likes to get hits, so batting practice is something enjoyable to participate in and to watch. When you get an award for offensive skills, like the Silver Slugger Award, that's nice. Hitting the ball and scoring runs are fun and necessary parts of the game.

A lot of people really only care about offense, though, because it can be a spectacular show.

What is not usually as impressive, but can be just as important, is the defense. I do put a lot of effort into defense, so getting an award that recognizes that, like the Gold Glove Award, is nice as well.

For every aspect of the game, though, you can't focus on results or awards. If you did that, you'd go crazy. There are so many games and so many plays in the season that lots of failure is inevitable along the way. You just have to put in the right amount of effort and remember to work from the inside out, doing what you are capable of doing, rather than grasping for things beyond your reach. Then let the results happen as they will.

That's something you learned from your father while growing up, right?

My father taught me a lot about sports, and that was a key thing: just working as hard as you can, and then letting the results happen as they will. You'll be rewarded in some way for the effort you put in, even if it's not in the way you originally intended.

Some kids dream of playing a sport professionally, but when I was a kid, the ultimate goal in my mind was to play in college. I just had more of a one-step-at-a-time approach to it. Enjoy the little things along the way, and don't get caught up in the noise around the game. That way, you really get to know the game itself, and enjoy the game for what it's worth, rather than trying to seek approval from outside sources.

You did get approval from your father, though.

My father was my No. 1 coach and my No. 1 fan. Early on, in high school, he said he taught me everything he knew about baseball, so the coaching part is kind of over, but he remains my No. 1 fan. I talk with him almost every night, and we go over what happened in the game that day.

While he did cheer me on for as long as I can remember, he was more concerned about being my father first and my friend second. There was a lot of structure and discipline in the house: You don't talk back to your parents; you don't use foul language; you don't drink or use drugs.

The discipline wasn't just for the sake of discipline, though. There was a productive purpose.

You were expected to show respect to others and to yourself by using and developing your God-given talents. You can only do that through gratitude, purposeful action and self-denial. Cutting corners or being idle doesn't make it happen. If I hadn't been taught that or lived by that, I wouldn't be where I am today.

I'm very fortunate to have the upbringing I did. It was a very balanced family life, and I think the structure made the affection more genuine.

My dad always took the time to be with me, even though he had a very busy schedule. He showed me affection, told me he loved me; and so, I just had a very secure upbringing. It was a childhood everyone would want to have.

Did your father's conversion to the Catholic faith influence your own faith?

Even though my dad came from a nondenominational type of background, he would attend Mass every Sunday with my mom, my sister and me. So when he was confirmed with my sister, it wasn't that much of a change in day-to-day life, really. He was essentially Catholic already, but then he had more of a formal, official entry into full communion with the Church.

He did influence my faith, but it was more of a steady influence, rather than one that changed sharply at a certain point.

My mother's side of the family, which is Italian, also had an influence on my faith. Her older brother, my Uncle Chuck, is a priest, and he was the heart and soul of the family when I was growing up. He brought spiritual realities into everyday life in an energetic way.

Your mother comes from a family of eight kids. Did you learn to appreciate family early on?

Definitely. We had a large extended family, and family has always been important to me. I have three of my own kids now, two boys and a girl, and there's nothing more important than being a parent. You're blessed by God to be able to cooperate in the creation and upbringing of another human being with an immortal soul. There's a tremendous joy, but also responsibility, in that reality.

I appreciate how the Church is so dedicated to that: to being pro-life and pro-family.

I love being a parent and am grateful for what I've learned from my own parents. As Pope Benedict has reminded us in his encyclical *Deus Caritas Est*, God is love.

Parents are called in a special way to share in the providential concern for their children that God has for all of us. When you think of a little child and how much he needs you, it reminds you of how much you need God, even as an adult. Children have a way of making you think of Providence and how the generations are connected.

I'm reminded of the continuity of life when I think of an important story within our family. My paternal grandfather was injured while working on a sugar plantation in British Guiana, a small country on the northern coast of South America. His condition was so serious that they flew him to New York for surgery at Columbia Hospital.

While there, he met a nurse whom he would later marry. My grandparents met through this unusual event almost 80 years ago.

Fast-forward to 2010. My grandfather died, and less than a week later, my second son was born at Columbia Hospital in New York, the very same place my grandparents met. As one soul was leaving this world, another was being born into it.

I know God orders all things well for my son and for his great-grandfather, and this was a unique reminder of that spiritual reality.

The reality of life and death hit home for you in high school when one of your close friends died in a car accident. How did that heighten your awareness of eternity?

When you learn things growing up, they often start on a theoretical level. You only have so much real-life experience, so you don't always understand the importance of what's being passed on. You take it on faith and maybe shelve it mentally until you actually come into contact with something it can be applied to.

When someone who attends the same classes and plays on the same sports teams as you do is suddenly gone, it's very jolting. That's what happened with the death of my friend, Nick Liberatore, the summer before our senior year. One day he's there, and the next he's gone.

With a game like baseball, you have so many chances to start over and come back, and that's true with life in general. However, at some point, we all have to leave this life, so that's when all the second chances are over. That's when the stark reality of how much we owe God comes into play.

It's the ultimate reality check.

It goes back to the way I was raised: I was loved very much, but with that love comes responsibility. There were certain things my parents expected of me, and there are also things God expects of us. When death hits us in the face, it's the perfect time to examine our consciences as to how we stand before God. Then we have the blessing of going to confession and receiving forgiveness, as introduced by Jesus in John 20. He said to the apostles, "Whose sins you forgive, they are forgiven, and whose sins you retain, they are retained."

There's great peace of mind with that sacramental unburdening.

While Nick's death was an extremely sad thing to happen, I do appreciate the fact that the high school we went to (Mount St. Joseph in Baltimore) is named after St. Joseph, the patron of a happy death. The Blessed Virgin Mary and Jesus were likely present at St. Joseph's death, which any Christian would want, right?

Before all of our games in high school, we would say an Our Father and then ask St. Joseph to pray for us, so that's a peaceful thing to consider.

When Nick died, his family started a scholarship in his name at our high school, and I've since then made it a permanent scholarship through an endowment. It's important to share what you've been given.

You've given to or created other scholarships as well, right?

Yes, that's something I take very seriously. After signing my first professional contract in 2001, the first thing I did was to give some of that money to the Georgia Tech baseball program. Then, in 2009, I set up an endowment for a permanent baseball scholarship at the school. I was very blessed to have a great coach at Georgia Tech, Danny Hall, so it's a good thing to give back to the program that gave me so much.

Some people talk of choosing to play certain sports, but I think, in a way, baseball chose me. I enjoyed learning many sports from my father growing up. We would play tennis, golf, basketball and go hunting and fishing. But baseball seemed to be the sport I was particularly blessed to play.

In our family, we were expected to develop our talents and use them properly, so that's something I've tried to do. It's also something I try to pass along to my children. I had the best childhood possible, so if I can be half the father to my children that my father was to me, then I'll be happy with that.

///

CATCHING UP WITH MLB ALL-STAR ALEX AVILA

Young Cuban-American player relates accounts of physical and spiritual revivals in the context of the communion of saints.

July 9, 2012

At only 25, **Alex Avila** is already making his mark in the professional baseball world. The starting catcher for the Detroit Tigers played in the 2011 All-Star Game, and, later in the postseason, his team made it to the American League Championship Series.

This near miss of a World Series Championship came not too many years after Avila had indicated such a possibility to his father, Al, who is vice president and assistant general manager of the Tigers.

Al Avila was telling his son, who was in high school at the time, that he did not care whether he played baseball. He simply wanted him to be happy and would support him in whatever field he chose. His son chose the baseball field, and, today, both of them are content with that decision.

Register correspondent Trent Beattie threw some questions to Alex Avila in anticipation of the 2012 All-Star Game, which takes place July 10 at Kauffman Stadium in Kansas City, Mo.

What was it like to start the 2011 All-Star Game?

It was one of the best experiences of my career so far. You have the best hitters and best pitchers out there going against each other, so it's a special thing. It's already special to be playing among the best players around on a day-to-day basis, but in the All-Star Game, you find the best of the best. It's taken to another level.

It was also somewhat of a break for me and my four Tigers teammates who made it to the game, which took place in Phoenix last year, as well. We had played 37 games in 38 days previous to the All-Star break, so it was somewhat relaxing to play in a different sort of game. Even though we had to travel to get there, it broke up the routine we were used to.

What was even more enjoyable than the game, however, was just being with the other guys in the clubhouse. We would swap stories and interact together, not only to prepare for the game, but for the sake of the camaraderie itself. It was good to be there.

Another place it was good to be at was the American League Championship Series last year. What do you remember from that experience?

That was a lot of fun as well. We got very close to winning it all last year, and it reminded me of a conversation I had with my father when

I was in high school. It was getting around the time when I was really showing some promise and had the possibility of playing professionally. My father didn't want me to think that because he and his father were so involved with pro ball that I had to be as well. He sat me down and explained that he didn't care whether I played baseball or not, that he would support me in whatever I decided to do.

My father never pressured me into playing. In fact, it could be said that I pressured him into playing. Whenever the time came for some kind of break, he would always want to go fishing, which is common in south Florida, where we lived, but I would always want to go to the batting cage or do long toss. This was in addition to the countless other times I would be playing baseball in games and practices. It was just something I always enjoyed doing.

But back to the ALCS. In that high-school conversation, I said to my father that baseball really was what I wanted to do and that, who knows, maybe one day he and I would be with the same team and win a World Series together. That almost happened last year, so if we both stay healthy, it could all come together.

It can be tough to stay healthy as a catcher, which is a demanding position. Do you ever plan on changing to another position?

No, not at all. Getting a little beaten up comes with the territory, but there are too many good things about being a catcher to change to another position. You're actively part of planning and implementing the game plan, and you get to be involved in every play.

Calling a good game brings me more satisfaction than hitting a home run. It's more of a comprehensive, all-encompassing, quality experience than one great hit. It's connecting and working with the team, but especially the pitcher, in a unique way.

I've been blessed to catch some great pitching performances already in my short career. I caught Armando Galarraga's near-perfect game in 2010. Last season, I caught [American League MVP and Cy Young Award winner] Justin Verlander's no-hitter, which was in addition to his other near no-hitters.

People ask me if it's difficult or stressful in situations like that, with the pitcher doing an unbelievable job. They think maybe there's more pressure, but that's not the case at all. When the pitcher is playing well, it's much easier. Everything just works. It just falls together almost effortlessly.

When a game or life in general is not effortless, do you find strength in your Catholic faith?

Absolutely. One of the toughest times in my life was when our family moved from south Florida to Detroit. My father had worked for the Florida Marlins as their vice president and assistant general manager, a position he now holds with the Detroit Tigers. I was a sophomore in high school, and that time of life can be full of adjustments already. Adding a move to another state, another climate and almost another way of life, was difficult.

The underlying theme with our family, however, was the importance of our Catholic faith. Just like Jesus himself, who is the same yesterday, today and forever, as it says in Hebrews 13:8, the Catholic faith he taught us remains the same. He is one with his teaching. No matter where you are in the world, that doesn't change.

Baseball is a great way to connect with people, but sharing the same religious beliefs is an even deeper connection. Not that the two have to be separated, as they really aren't in our family.

Some of your baseball-faith connections involve Tommy Lasorda, right?

My paternal grandfather was vice president of the Los Angeles Dodgers when Tommy Lasorda was still managing the team, and even a little beyond that. This is how our family came to know Tommy, who is actually my godfather, and his name, Thomas, after St. Thomas Aquinas, is my middle name.

There are so many stories that come to mind about Tommy and my grandfather, who are still both working for the Dodgers today, but in more limited capacities. They would go somewhere to eat lunch, and they'd start bantering about baseball. It might begin at 12:30 and sometimes wouldn't end until 9:30 that night. They'd really get into baseball and end up making a day out of it. You get those two in a room — and watch out.

Both of my grandfathers actually fled from Cuba during the Communist Revolution in the 1950s, so it's not surprising that they share in Tommy's conservative political outlook. When your own government won't allow you to participate in the most basic freedoms — freedom of religion, freedom of speech, freedom to own private property — then you want to come to a country where such things are allowed. We take those freedoms for granted, but they aren't automatic anywhere, even here, unless we work to preserve them.

If my grandfathers hadn't escaped from Cuba, they may not have survived, and the same is true with my parents, who were very young at the time. That would obviously leave me out of the picture. You have to praise the Lord for the gift of life.

Even before my paternal grandfather's escape, he had an amazing story of survival or, you could say, revival. According to the doctors, he was supposed to be stillborn. They said he had already died in his mother's womb. His father, my great-grandfather, was beside himself and asked St. Barbara (*Santa* Barbara) to intercede for him on behalf of his wife and son.

His son, my grandfather, was born dead, as the doctors had indicated. However, neither the doctors nor my great-grandfather gave up, and, despite the fact that my grandfather was showing no signs of life for about five minutes outside the womb, he came back to life. They revived him or St. Barbara revived him — however you want to say it.

Ever since that time, even up until today, our family has had a special appreciation and veneration for St. Barbara. Every year on her feast day, Dec. 4, we gather for a family reunion and celebration. We celebrate that day and conclude at night with the singing of prayers to God in thanksgiving for the intercession of St. Barbara, through whom he has worked a miracle. It's something that my wife and I will continue to do.

Aside from the intercession of St. Barbara, what do you appreciate most about the Catholic Church?

One of the best things, maybe the best thing, is the sacrament of reconciliation. We just talked about a physical revival, but in this sacrament, there are spiritual revivals. Sinners are brought back to life. Bringing sinners back into his friendship is the main reason Jesus came to earth, so participating in that beautiful reality is something we are privileged to do as Catholics.

It can be easy to take this sacrament for granted, but we really shouldn't. It's available to everyone, but it's not taken advantage of. As they say, the lines to Communion on Sunday are long, but the lines to confession on Saturday are short.

We come up with all kinds of excuses for not going to reconciliation, but those excuses are basically a cover for the decision we've already made not to go. It's a shame, because there is no sin, however great, that cannot be forgiven through the ministry of the priest. To think otherwise is a strange sort of pride, because then you think that your misdeeds are greater than God's love and mercy.

Confession of sin and reconciliation to God is in the New Testament, especially near the end of St. John's Gospel, but it's also indicated in the Old Testament. Psalm 32 is an example of that. It describes how, before sin is confessed, we become weak and believe that life is very difficult. "Because I kept silent, my bones wasted away." Then it describes how, once sin is confessed, guilt is removed: "Then I declared my sin to you; my guilt I did not hide ... and you took away the guilt of my sin." The Psalm ends on a high note, talking of how mercy surrounds the one who trusts in the Lord and that we should rejoice in the Lord.

This points toward the superabundant grace of the New Testament priesthood, through which we can have any sin forgiven. God and the rest of heaven want this more than we want it here below. St. Barbara, St. Thomas Aquinas and all the other saints rejoice in heaven over our return to God. This is what Jesus referred to when he said that there will be more joy in heaven over one sinner who repents than over 99 righteous men who have no need of repentance. It's not just a matter of a two-part relationship of me and God, but a real communion of saints. We're the living, breathing, mystical body of Christ.

///

OLDEST MANAGER TO WIN WORLD SERIES STILL ENJOYS KID'S GAME

Jack McKeon, 81, credits daily Mass and St. Thérèse with helping his baseball career.

October 1, 2012

Most 80-year-olds would never consider managing a professional baseball team. Then again, most 80-year-olds would never be asked to manage a professional baseball team.

Yet, in June 2011, **Jack McKeon** accepted the then-Florida (now Miami) Marlins' offer to lead the team as interim manager.

McKeon's previous stint with the Marlins included a World Series Championship in 2003. He was a relatively young 72 at the time, but was nonetheless the oldest manager ever to win a World Series. The South Amboy, N.J., native attributes his success not only to perseverance, but also to daily Mass attendance and the intercession of St. Thérèse of the Child Jesus, the doctor of the Church whose feast day the Church celebrates toiday.

McKeon, now 81, spoke with *Register* correspondent Trent Beattie about his long history in and appreciation for what he calls a kid's game.

How did you get started in professional baseball?

When I was in high school — I think we had automobiles by then — I played well enough to attract the attention of several major-league clubs. Back then, there wasn't the draft like we have today, so the scouts would actually come to my house to talk with my father and me.

However, my father was adamant that his boys would go to college, so instead of signing with a team, I ended up going to the College of the Holy Cross in Worcester, Mass. Every day, I would pass by a beautiful picture of the Blessed Virgin on the way to the dining hall. I thought it would be a good idea to ask for her intercession to convince my father to let me play baseball professionally.

When I went home for Christmas break my freshman year, I asked my father again about signing with a major-league club. He said, "You really want to play professionally, don't you?" I told him, "Yes," and he said, "Let's make a deal. I'll let you sign with a major-league club if you get a college degree." I agreed, and, eight years later, I held up on my end of the bargain.

What do you like most about baseball?

I like how it's a kid's game. Grown men play it, but when you really look at it, for what it is, it's a bunch of fun. It's not serious business like most people see it today. It's meant to be fun.

I grew up dreaming of playing in the big leagues, but my minor-league career was less than spectacular. I hit three ways: left, right and seldom. So my goal changed a little bit, but it was still closely related with the big leagues.

I was a good enough salesman to be able to start managing in the minor leagues at the age of 24. At the time, some players were younger and some older than I was, but there was no communication problem. The same was true last year, when I was the interim manager for the Marlins. Some people asked if I had problems relating to the young players. Not at all. Human nature doesn't change, and I enjoyed managing last year, just as I did back when I was 24.

My major-league managing started in 1973 for the Kansas City Royals. George Brett [Royals Hall of Fame third baseman] was on the team, and he's one of the players that stands out when people ask me who my favorite player was.

I don't really have one favorite player, but there are a few that come to mind, as far as baseball skills. Tony Gwynn, Sean Casey and Ivan Rodriguez are some others.

What stands out in your mind about the 2003 season, at the end of which you won a World Series with the Marlins?

In 2000, I actually managed against the Marlins, when I was with the Cincinnati Reds. I remembered thinking at the time that the Marlins were a great team. They had a lot of very talented, very capable players, but they were underachieving. That made me think of how nice it would be to manage that team.

Early on in the 2003 season, the Marlins were 16-22. By then, I was no longer with the Reds, so the Marlins hired me to help turn the team around. When I first met with the players, I told them, "Look, we can do better than this, and not just have a winning record, but win the whole thing — the World Series — if we're willing to pay the price."

Whatever you want to do in life, you have to be willing to make the necessary sacrifices to get it.

When you really give it your all and put every effort into it — not for what the fans or media might think, but for the game itself, your teammates and your own self-respect — then you can leave the ballpark at the end of the day with your head held high. That's true regardless of whether you win or lose; you put every effort into it and then leave it at that.

It might sound contradictory, but while I wanted my players to work very hard, I also encouraged them to relax and enjoy what they did. It's not a matter of clowning around and being irresponsible, but having fun playing a kid's game.

You can try too hard in baseball, in the sense of straining after things which are out of your control. You just have to realize that you can only control your own effort and do the best you can with what's right in front of you.

The 2003 Marlins' team was not only the most talented, but the most unselfish and dedicated team I've ever been with. You can't beat a three-part combo like that, and, as it turned out, no one did stop us from winning the World Series.

Didn't St. Thérèse also have a part in that great season?

Yes, she did. I've had a devotion to St. Thérèse of the Child Jesus for many years, and she helped me to get out of my own way and let God's grace flow through me to do a good job managing. Her intercession helped in a special way to prepare us to win the World Series later in October of that year.

St. Thérèse said before she died that she would do her most important work in heaven, letting a shower of roses fall to the earth. She's a prodigy of miracles and a very endearing person, so you feel very comfortable asking for her help. She's not someone aloof and intimidating, but very open and accepting of your requests.

She's the MVP for the 2003 season — not the "Most Valuable Player," but the "Most Valuable Pray-er."

I would pray to St. Thérèse every day and would go to Mass every morning during the 2003 season. Then, even though I was 72 at the time, I might jog a little and say at least a decade of the Rosary while doing so. That preparation really helps the day go well.

How does daily Mass attendance help the rest of your day?

It puts everything in the right perspective. In professional baseball, there can be a lot of pressure on players and coaches, but when you get grounded in the most fundamental thing of life — which is your relationship to God — then everything else shows itself for what it is.

Instead of taking things so seriously, worrying and fearing failure, you simply do what you can, be generous with those around you, and let God take care of everything else.

It's such a great feeling to have gone to Mass in the morning and start the day in the right way: very invigorating, but relaxing. It's similar to that same paradox of working hard, but doing so peacefully and with a rational plan. It's great — too great to put into words — what the good Lord does for us.

I remember Johnny Coakley, a longtime baseball friend, asking me one morning to go to breakfast. I told him I'd like to, but first I'd go to Mass. Johnny was a Protestant, but he already had a respect for the Catholic Church. He told me the only thing was he didn't know all the signals we used at Mass. I assured him I'd explain everything to him, so he went to Mass with me — and ended up becoming a Catholic.

Johnny thanked me for introducing him to the Catholic faith long ago, and, just recently, he thanked me again, saying that becoming Catholic was the best present anyone could give him. That was three days before he died, which was earlier this year.

Harry Dunlop is another longtime baseball friend who was originally Protestant, but attended Mass with me and became Catholic. Everyone has a free will to make his own decisions, but you can influence people for the better through your own actions. When others see how much the Mass means to you, it means something to them.

Something else that is meaningful to you is your marriage. How has your wife influenced your career?

My wife, Carol, and I have been married for 58 years, and I appreciate every one of them. We have a very solid marriage, and that's due primarily to my wife.

In professional baseball, you're away from home for a good chunk of the year, so that can be tough on the family. My wife took up where I left off, and she raised our kids while I was off managing.

When we won the World Series in 2003, I was so happy, not so much for myself, but for my family. It was the first time they had something big to celebrate at the end of the season.

With me, I could see how rewarding all the work was on a daily basis throughout the season, but they didn't witness that. However, at the end of the 2003 season, they actually had something tangible from baseball to appreciate.

///

WASHINGTON NATIONALS' PITCHER ARMS HIMSELF WITH PRAYER

Craig Stammen sees firsthand benefits putting his concerns in God's hands.

February 19, 2013

Craig Stammen of the Washington Nationals is among the hundreds of players preparing for the opening of spring training later this month.

While the mechanics of baseball are a part of everyone's preparation, Stammen has an added benefit coming into the season: his practice of trusting in God's providence.

The 28-year-old North Star, Ohio, resident learned to entrust everything to God a little over seven years ago at the University of Dayton. After a summer of rookie league baseball in 2005, Stammen returned to campus for the fall semester. It was during this time that he first shared his Catholic faith publicly — a turning point that helped to solidify his core beliefs and aim in life.

In 2012, the right-handed relief pitcher had the best year of his four-year major-league career, going 6-1, with an earned-run average of 2.34 for the National League Eastern Division champions.

When Stammen pitches, he knows that once the ball is out of his hands, everything else is out of his hands as well. More importantly, though, he realizes everything is in the hands of a God in whom he lives and moves and has his being.

How has coming from a small town influenced you?

Coming from such a small place has definitely influenced me in different ways. North Star only has about 250 people in it, so, technically, it's not even a town, but a village. When you live in a community of that size, there's more silence, simplicity and accountability. Much of the noise and extraneous concerns prevalent today are reduced greatly, and you're close to and dependent on your neighbors.

This is a value-based and also a humbling environment to be raised in. You're taught to work hard, but it's not for the sake of one-upping others. Everyone is on a level playing field, in that sense. You're more concerned about carrying out a duty and getting a job well done for self-respect and contribution to the community.

When I bring in friends from out of the area, they say it's like the 1950s, but with technology. We do have computers and all that, but they aren't primary, just tools to be used when necessary. We're more focused on family and friends than the latest gadgets. That perspective keeps you grounded in reality.

The entire village of North Star is Catholic, so even though I went to a public school, it was de facto a Catholic one. When people outside of North Star ask if I went to Catholic school, the answer is, "Well, no, but yes."

What are some of your top baseball memories from growing up?

We would sometimes play baseball as a whole family. I have quite a large extended family, so, with all the open area around us, playing games was easy to do. I also remember playing catch almost every day with my best friend. We would throw the baseball around for hours and talk about playing one day in the major leagues. It seemed like such a faraway, unreal goal back then. It was something to dream about, but I'm blessed to be living that dream out today.

You went on the USO Holiday Tour in December. How did that come about?

I had visited some injured servicemen at Walter Reed Army Medical Center last summer. It was quite an experience: to talk with them at length, learning about the troubles they were going through. Their sacrifices make possible the blessings in civilian life we take for granted. Their service to our country made me want to do something more to thank them for what they've given us.

My teammate Ross Detwiler and I were among the people who visited five countries in five days on the tour. We went to Afghanistan, Bahrain, Kyrgystan, Germany and Ireland. It was quite an adventure to ride in military planes and vehicles to some remote places. I'm used to traveling throughout our own country, but to go so many miles overseas was a totally different experience.

More important than that, though, was being able to interact with the members of our military. We got to see some of what they go through up close, which increased the respect I had for them. Leaving the comforts of home for many months at a time, and going to strange places without many of the simplest things we consider to be necessities, is an experience most of us just can't relate to.

My own daily life is so easy and simple in comparison with what I saw the soldiers go through. I actually get paid to play baseball. How can you ever complain about that?

What are your expectations for spring training this year?

I'm looking forward to spring training, first of all because of what we accomplished as a team last year. We had an improved record (98-64) from 2011 and made the playoffs. This is a great thing to build on for the 2013 season, and spring training is where we do the preparatory work for that. We hope to show this season that we're not a one-year wonder, but a perennial contender.

Have the Catholic faith and baseball always been integrated in your life?

Growing up, Catholicism and baseball were two separate entities in my life. Even though both were important to me, it was made clear that being Catholic came first and playing baseball second. This was and remains true, but I've since learned that the two things can actually be incorporated together.

What I realized at the University of Dayton is that, while you should work very hard to play as well as you can, you need to put everything in God's hands. You do your part, and then let God determine what's best for you. This realization has helped my game a lot. It has made playing in the majors possible, which I had previously thought of as being unattainable.

I used to play for my teammates and school, which was a good thing, but now I play for God, which is an even better thing. It's a much broader-minded way of seeing things, and it takes a lot of the pressure off you. It opens you up to the reality that, while baseball is fun, you can't really enjoy it to the fullest or play it to the best of your abilities without recognizing the God who made it all possible in the first place.

How did you come to this realization?

I was drafted after my junior season at the University of Dayton in 2005. I played in the rookie league that summer and then returned to campus for the fall semester. It was during this time that I went on a retreat.

As one of the retreat leaders, I was supposed to give my own testimony. This was a huge step for me because I hadn't shared my faith in such a public way. I had talked about it with family and friends, but this was the first time I was officially claiming it as my own amidst strangers.

Ever since that retreat, I knew I had to live out what I was stating as true; I had to make a real effort to walk the walk, knowing that certain things were expected of me. Because I belonged to Christ, I had to live no longer for myself, but for him who died for me. It was not just about hearing the truth and agreeing with it, but actually living it.

That sounds like St. Paul in his Letter to the Romans (2:13) and other places.

I've always been interested in St. Paul. He was put in some of the worst situations, but still maintained a positive outlook. From the time of his conversion, he trusted completely in Christ, and that was what drove his missionary work.

Whenever we would have Bible projects as kids, I would choose something regarding St. Paul. He is my favorite saint, someone I look up to and try to pattern my life after, to the limited degree I can. We live in very different times, but the goal of remaining faithful until we get to heaven is the same.

It's funny, because, when people ask me if my faith has gotten me through tough times, I really can't think of anything heavy or burdensome I've been through. Maybe that's just a sign of how blessed I am to have always had faith. Maybe the tough times haven't seemed tough because of my faith. What happens to you isn't nearly as important as how you respond to it.

What do you treasure most about the Catholic Church?

I appreciate how systematically all aspects of the Church's teaching and sacramental life are put together. You don't just make it up as you go along; you receive what is passed down from the apostles. Our Church goes all the way back to them and, of course, to Christ himself.

One of the most obvious ways this is made manifest is in the Mass. I love the order and structure of the Mass — how the priest and people have specific roles, how the word of God is read and then how the Eternal Word himself is made present in the Eucharist. You can't beat that combination. It's something St. Paul wrote of in 1 Corinthians 11, and it's something I've enjoyed since childhood.

Another aspect of my childhood in which St. Paul was involved was "putting on the armor God." I would listen, along with my younger brother and sister, to my mother read from the Bible while we ate breakfast. She would emphasize Ephesians 6, which concerns things like the "shield of faith" and "the helmet of salvation."

We got a kick out of putting on our imaginary gear in order to take on the challenges of the day.

Over the years, we would add more items to our collection of "armor," which increased the time for us to get ready for school. Our weaponry and protection increased, but the length of our football-field-long driveway did not decrease. This made it more likely that we'd be late for the bus, so we ended up throwing our armor on as we ran down the driveway.

I still prepare spiritually in the morning, but I make sure not to be late for any pitching appearances because of it.

///

MLB VETERAN MARK KOTSAY PURSUES PERFECT WORK

*The San Diego Padres' outfielder strives
to implement patience on and off the diamond
and, for Kotsay, it all centers on the Mass.*

March 31, 2013

Thirty-seven year-old **Mark Kotsay** has done nearly everything that can be done in baseball. At Cal State Fullerton his team won the College World Series, and he was named MVP. He then played on the USA's bronze medal-winning squad at the 1996 Olympics in Atlanta.

Kotsay's professional career includes stints with seven teams. In 2011, his Milwaukee Brewers won the National League Central Division title and made it to the National League Championship Series, where they lost to the eventual World Series-champion St. Louis Cardinals.

One thing Kotsay has yet to accomplish is a World Series victory. He hopes that will change this season with the Padres, a team he returned to last season after playing for them 2001-2003. He believes that patience is a primary means through which a World Series victory would occur — and that patience enables us to achieve "a perfect work," according to the First Letter of St. James.

Kotsay spoke with *Register* correspondent Trent Beattie in anticipation of the Padres' first regular-season game of 2013, on April 1, against the New York Mets.

You're entering your 17th season of professional baseball. What are you looking forward to this year?

I've already seen so much in my years of pro ball. I've played on teams with outstanding players, such as Tony Gwynn, Trevor Hoffman and

Jim Thome. I've also been fortunate to have very capable managers, from Jim Leyland at the beginning of my career to Bud Black today. In 2011, I was able to get to the postseason with the Brewers, and that was quite an experience.

One thing that's left, though, is to win a World Series. In order to achieve something like that, you just have to do what you're capable of doing, day in and day out. All the little steps along the journey are how you get there, not by one or two giant steps. After so many years, you learn to enjoy all the little steps along the way to the final goal.

Do you have favorite baseball memories from childhood?

Growing up in between Dodger Stadium and Angel Stadium, I looked up to players like Rod Carew and Kirk Gibson. Gibson's home run off Dennis Eckersley in the 1988 World Series remains a vivid memory.

There are so many memories from my own games, but the thing I appreciate most is having a father who wanted me to do well in life. He was determined to be a great father to me, to be there — not just in body, but in spirit. He wasn't just filling a role; he was giving of his very self.

He wanted me to play baseball as well as I could, so he really pushed me to work at the game. I most likely wouldn't be where I am today had he not raised me like he did. However, there is a fine line when it comes to competitiveness — too much of it can hurt you. My father and I both realized this during my sophomore year of high school. We found that a little distance was needed between the two of us in order for me to relax, play better and become more independent.

You won the Golden Spikes Award and were named the College World Series MVP at Cal State Fullerton. What stands out in your mind from that time in your life?

Those were very memorable years, but they started out being memorable for the wrong reasons. When I entered college, I was only 17, so the normal adjustments everyone makes were even more challenging for me.

When baseball season came around, I barely saw any playing time. I was very disappointed, but didn't give up. I took stock of what was happening and determined what I needed to do to get where I wanted to be. It was a lesson in humility and patience — to accept my own shortcomings — and then do something about them. Everyone wants the playing time, wins and trophies, but few are willing to put in the work to get them.

I learned a great deal from Augie Garrido, who was the head coach at Fullerton during my years there. He wasn't an overly pragmatic, get-the-win type of coach, but a philosopher-coach. He emphasized the fundamentals of the game and hard work. He wanted us to build a solid foundation from which to play well. There are many great college coaches, but I think Augie is the greatest of them all.

By the time I left college, things had changed quite dramatically from my freshman year. I was a starter on great teams, including one that took home a College World Series trophy. I was fortunate to win some personal awards, and then I got to play on the bronze medal-winning team at the Olympic Games in 1996.

Has the Catholic faith always been an important part of your life?

I was baptized a Baptist, but would sometimes attend Mass growing up. I always had a respect for religion in general and Catholicism in particular, but it wasn't until I met my future wife that I became Catholic. I started going to Mass with her regularly in early 2000, and we were married later that year.

The Mass is the thing I appreciate most about being Catholic. No matter where you travel in the world, the Mass is always there. It's the centerpiece of the Catholic faith, the thing that unites us as believers. The unbroken tradition from the time of the apostles is a beautiful thing, something that shows very clearly God's love for us.

There is so much grace for us to get from the Mass, but it's up to us to decide whether we're going to utilize it in our everyday lives. It's not enough just to be there; we need to realize that what's being given is vital to living a virtuous life. If we have eyes to see and ears to hear, our lives will change through the Mass.

How does your faith affect your play?

The easy part of playing sports is being aggressive. That's very straightforward, and everyone — from little kids to adults — knows that aggression is necessary to get the job done. However, something that's much more subtle, but no less helpful, is to be patient.

I've known the value of patience since my college years. Things didn't go my way initially, so I had the choice of getting angry or accepting adversity. Anger seems like the best choice, but that route actually makes achieving your goal less likely. Being angry means being out of control and counterproductive, but being patient means exercising self-control and putting yourself in a position to get things done.

In Proverbs 16:32, it says: "A patient man is better than a warrior, and he who rules his temper [is better] than he who takes a city." That initial aggression is fine, but you have to temper it with the discipline found in patience. It is much more challenging to be patient, but it's also better than being a warrior or conquering a city. With patience, you conquer yourself — and once you've done that, you can do anything else.

It's easier to be patient with the help of the sacraments, sacramentals and the prayers of the Church. Being patient is also easier with the help of a loving wife like mine. She helps me to be patient not only while playing baseball, but, more importantly, while raising our kids. She understands them better and is more compassionate toward them than I am. That's what mothers excel at — helping with all the little quirks of kids that tend to drive fathers crazy.

Have you encountered other Catholics in the major leagues?

It's become more common to have practicing Catholics around the majors. More teams have priests available for Mass. That used to be a rarity, but now it's not unusual.

Probably the most inspiring Catholic baseball player I know is Mike Sweeney. Even though we never played on the same team, we were able to meet up during batting practice and other situations around the games. We share the same core values and have a lot of other things in common.

Mike is a leader in getting the message out that the Catholic Church is the place to be. He knows that other churches have good things in them, but they got all those things from the Catholic Church. The Bible is probably the most obvious example.

Thousands of different denominations talk about how their interpretation of the Bible is the right one, but the fact that we got the Bible from the Catholic Church is overlooked. If we just acknowledged that, we'd know where to go to get the right interpretation.

Mike knows there's so much misinformation about the Church out there, so he's a big advocate of Catholic Answers, based in San Diego. It's also a reason why he conducted his first Catholic baseball camp last summer. Mike is a firm believer that if you want the entire teaching of Christ, then the Catholic Church is the place to get it.

Do you find regular opportunities to share the faith while playing baseball?

There are plenty of ways to share the faith in baseball or in any other endeavor. It doesn't have to be teaching the entire Catechism; it can just be a simple "God bless you" or an invitation to Mass.

Some players point to the sky after hitting a home run or making a great throw, and that's perfectly fine. One thing to consider, though, is whether they'd point to the sky after striking out or throwing the ball past the first baseman.

I like to acknowledge God no matter what happens, so making the Sign of the Cross in the batter's box is part of my hitting routine. That way, I'm stating my faith in God — regardless of what happens in the upcoming at-bat. If it's a hit, great; if not, that's great, too.

An "unsuccessful" at-bat is another opportunity to exercise patience. In James 1:4, it says, "Let patience have its perfect work." You accept things not going your way, and, at the same time, you embrace that cross God has sent you. You're transcending self and affirming God, all in one act of patience.

///

EX-BASEBALL PHENOM DISCUSSES LIFE IN A NORBERTINE ABBEY

The former second-round draft choice of the Oakland A's, Brother Matthew Desme strongly recommends repentance and trust in Divine Mercy.

April 8, 2013

In January of 2010, **Grant Desme** shocked the baseball world by announcing his retirement from the game. Only 23 at the time, Desme had recently been named the 2009 Arizona Fall League MVP and was on the verge of playing in the majors. Despite his athletic success, the former center fielder knew he was called to something greater.

Desme left behind all his worldly goods — including a sizable baseball contract, shiny SUV and state-of-the-art cellphone — to embrace a life of poverty, celibacy and obedience. Now, his confreres at St. Michael's Abbey in Silverado, Calif., know him as *Frater* (Brother) Matthew Desme.

Despite what may appear to many as an overly austere lifestyle, Frater Matthew sees through appearances to the very heart of Jesus, from which he derives his happiness. Now that the former Big West Conference Player of the Year is in touch with Divine love, everything else has fallen into its rightful place.

In a rare interview, Frater Matthew recently discussed his new life inside St. Michael's Abbey.

You entered the seminary in the fall of 2010. How many years do you have left before ordination?

After this school year, I'll have one more year of philosophy, four years of theology and one apostolic year in Rome. It's a long haul, but I'm not looking too far ahead. I'm really immersed in philosophy right now.

How did you get the name Matthew?

We're supposed to submit a list of three possible religious names, and the superior chooses which one we'll use. I ended up having to submit two separate lists of three names each, and Matthew was the sixth possibility overall. Even though it wasn't my first choice, I already see at least one commonality with my own life: St. Matthew was wealthy before deciding to follow Jesus.

Shortly after I entered the abbey, one of my brothers in religion, Frater Alan, suggested that I be called Frater Moses. I didn't like the name at the time, but since studying the Old Testament more in depth, I've come to appreciate the faith and works of Moses. Now I wouldn't mind having that name, but I also like the name Matthew. I think its significance will become clearer to me as time goes on.

Do you miss playing baseball?

When I first left baseball, I didn't miss it one bit. I was very happy to be giving it up for good. However, I have been able to play the game since then, because there are other brothers here who play baseball.

I still don't miss playing professionally, but I've come to enjoy the game of baseball itself more. When I let go of it as my idol, I was enabled to enjoy it for what it's worth. When you're projecting your own designs on something and taking it more seriously than it should be, you don't get what God intended you to get out of it.

When you simply accept things for what they are and don't expect more than what they can give, you experience the satisfaction you're supposed to.

How did you first realize that baseball wouldn't bring you ultimate happiness?

At every stage of my career, I thought happiness was around the corner. No matter how well I played or how far I advanced, I never gained the complete, lasting happiness I was expecting. There were thrills, but none of them lasted. Everything here below is fleeting.

I injured my shoulder while playing for the Vancouver Canadians, a minor-league team for the Oakland A's, in 2007. During rehab, I sat out with another player, who didn't speak much English. I was separated from the team and even from the other player who was injured. It was initially disconcerting, but it was really a period of great grace.

I was removed from the superficial chatter and other noise that I had been accustomed to via electronic media. It was through the silence and solitude that I started to think beyond the baseball field and about life in general. I realized that even if I played 20 years in the major leagues and ended up a Hall of Famer, I would still die one day. No matter what I achieved, I would be just as dead as everyone else in the cemetery.

I then thought of my particular judgment and how I would be held accountable for every decision I made in life. Eternal punishment or reward would follow, based on whether or not I was a faithful disciple of Jesus. It became clear that I had to get into a deeper, more prayerful relationship with the Lord.

Former professional soccer player Chase Hilgenbrinck announced in 2008 that he would be leaving soccer to pursue the priesthood. Did his decision influence yours?

I remember reading about Chase's decision, but it didn't affect my own. At that point, I hadn't seriously considered becoming a priest. I was still on the road back to the Lord in a more general way.

Once I started to consider the priesthood seriously, I almost immediately knew it was for me. There was no gut-wrenching discernment; just a simple knowledge that Jesus was calling me to continue his life and ministry. That was the Lord's loving invitation to me, and I knew living it out would make me truly happy.

I would recommend looking into the priesthood to young men who think they might be called. There's nothing the world needs more than the mercy of Jesus Christ, which is granted through his priests. It's a spiritual fatherhood that is even more profound than physical fatherhood. It's something the saints have written about in almost unbelievable terms. It's mind-boggling to think of what Jesus wants to give us through spiritual fathers.

TRENT BEATTIE /// 183

**What would you say to young men who think they may have a
priestly or religious calling but are afraid of giving up worldly
things to pursue it?**

I was living out every young man's dream. I was playing well enough
to be a Major League Baseball player. I had a big, shiny SUV and
even bigger bank account. That's what most people would think of
as being at the pinnacle of manhood. You've got all these things that
display how strong and capable you are: You become better known,
people want to be around you, and everything looks great.

That's a very superficial form of masculinity, though. It's based on
externals and trying to put yourself before others. I've since learned
an authentic masculinity based on self-sacrificing love. Being a man
is not about stepping on others, but lifting others up. It's about using
the God-given strength you have to protect others and guide them
to eternal life.

Some people have the idea — which I shared at one time — that
Christianity is kind of a soft religion, not worth giving much attention
to. What I've come to know, however, is that if you truly attempt to
live it out, Christianity is anything but soft. A sincere attempt to be
a follower of Jesus requires nothing less than a complete dedication
of your entire being.

This has become clearer to me in the abbey, where we are called
to live out the Gospel more intensely than in the world. Far from
being an idle life, I've found that what's required here calls me to
reach to the very depths of my masculinity to become a more
complete disciple of Jesus. The challenges of baseball are nothing
compared to the challenges of religious life, which is about dying to
self in order to live for Jesus.

Living for Jesus sounds attractive, but dying to self in order to do
that doesn't always seem attractive.

Yet we can't have union with Jesus without first denying ourselves.
Our Lord made this very evident in Matthew 16, saying, "If any man

would come after me, let him deny himself and take up his cross and follow me. For whoever would save his life will lose it, and whoever loses his life for my sake will find it."

We're called to let go of our own selfishness, to "lose our lives" for the sake of finding true life in Jesus. While it may appear unattractive, a life of penance for the love of God is actually the only way to be truly happy. It might seem like you're losing out, but that's just an illusion. Whatever we give to God, he gives back to us a hundredfold, even in this life. This is made clear at the end of Matthew 19, which also indicates that, in eternity, many of the first will be last and the last first.

Repentance is necessary for following any vocation, but trust is even more so. Turning away from sin is great, but it won't last very long without confidence in God's mercy. In order for repentance to endure for our eternal profit, it must be done with trust. Then the initial fear will change into filial devotion. Instead of avoiding sin only because of its consequences, we live out a life of proactive virtue for the love of God.

With trust, we turn our eyes from ourselves to the life of Jesus, which overflows with mercy for us. Our fears are cast aside and replaced with boundless confidence in the unfailing promises of the Lord. St. Faustina spread this message, and it comes to the forefront of the Church's liturgical calendar on Divine Mercy Sunday, one week after Easter Sunday.

Why did you choose to become a religious priest instead of a diocesan one?

I played on baseball teams all my life, so the team atmosphere became second nature to me. I looked for the same type of setting in the spiritual life: a group of men working together for a common goal. Solitary life hasn't ever appealed to me, so I didn't think of diocesan priesthood, which is more of an individual thing in most parishes.

I've played on some great baseball teams, but the team here at St. Michael's is by far the best one I've been a part of. Instead of fighting an athletic battle, we're fighting a spiritual one. We're united in fraternal charity to overcome the world, the flesh and the devil. Every time we offer the sacrifice of the Mass, take part in a Holy Hour before the Blessed Sacrament or pray the Divine Office, we're doing things that have an eternal effect not only on ourselves, but on the whole Church.

Even in the events that aren't part of official public worship — things such as mowing the lawn, forgoing dessert or studying philosophy — you do in community. You're not an isolated man. You're truly part of a team of men that have your eternal welfare at heart. That's an extremely encouraging thing to carry with you through the day.

What is the most difficult part of monastic life?

The most difficult part is dying to self. When you first enter, you make the biggest step of renouncing worldly possessions and pledging to live in community. However, once you're in religious life, there are still situations in which you can be tempted to follow self-will, however petty they might be.

What you find, though, is that the less you follow your own will, the more content you become. In the world, I tried to follow my own will as much as possible, but it only resulted in restlessness. Monastic life is about striving for freedom from self-will and union with God's will, which is our sanctification and happiness.

The Blessed Virgin Mary is, of all creatures, the most free from self-will and the most united with the will of God. It's clear, then, that we can gain so much from her maternal intercession for us. The postulants here make the Marian consecration according to the method of St. Louis de Montfort, which we renew every Saturday.

What is the best part of monastic life?

The best thing is getting to live in God's house, not in a metaphorical sense, but in a true sense. Jesus, who is God incarnate, dwells here in our tabernacle. The same Jesus who preached the Gospel, healed the sick and dispensed other graces on sinners abundantly, lives among us sacramentally. The appearances are different, but the God-man is the same.

Every grace we have flows through the Blessed Sacrament because the Blessed Sacrament is a Person, not a thing. When you realize that, your life changes profoundly. The isolation, discontent and grasping for things give way to an interior freedom that is beyond compare.

Our life here is the continuation of the life of Jesus Christ, who was poor, celibate and obedient. Being God, and therefore lacking nothing, he deliberately chose to live among us without most of the goods of this world. He knew that following his Father's will out of love was the only thing that mattered. That's the only thing that should matter to us, because it's the only way we'll be happy.

Most people aren't called to the priesthood or monastic life, yet everyone can benefit from becoming more "monastic," in the sense of seeing things for what they really are. A right ordering of priorities is essential if you want to get the most out of life. It's ironic that, while in the abbey, even despite all the sacrifices, I'm able to enjoy things more than I did in the world.

Those who think of religious life as odd or even miserable would be surprised at how much joy there is in the abbey. Recreation time is especially indicative of this, because of all the laughter. We do take our vows seriously, but we don't take ourselves seriously.

Do you have any closing words for Christians in general?

Participate in the sacramental life of the Church, which is a life of love. Jesus wants us to experience his healing love infinitely more than we do. If we knew the love he has for us, it would be so overwhelming that we would die, so he hides himself under the appearance of bread and in the ministry of priests.

We're called to nothing less than a participation in the life of the Holy Trinity. Becoming sons of God in the only begotten Son, Jesus Christ, we are heirs to the Kingdom of heaven. This should inspire us to pray every day. Nothing is more necessary than prayer, and nothing could be easier. You don't have to make a pilgrimage across the world — you just acknowledge the God without whom you could not exist for one second.

St. Teresa of Avila said that if you persevere in prayer, you will certainly be saved, but that if you stop praying, you throw yourself into hell. By trying to "go it alone," we lose all the graces God wants to give us; but by admitting our weakness and asking for help, we become capable of doing things which once seemed impossible.

All the saints have become saints through prayer, which is the means of obtaining God's merciful love. My own patrons — St. Matthew, St. Augustine, St. Norbert and St. Faustina — are all messengers of mercy, which they wouldn't have known about had they not prayed. Prayer is the way to touch the heart of Jesus, which is overflowing with grace for sinners. I witness this every day before the Blessed Sacrament.

The only thing that will last after death is our relationship — or lack thereof — with God. This is something that should motivate everyone to see past the superficial things of life that clamor for our attention and instead invest our lives in God, trusting in his mercy.

///

WHITE SOX CATCHER CELEBRATES FAMILY ON ALL-STAR BREAK

Tyler Flowers' daughter is an answer to prayer.

July 15, 2013

As the American League All-Stars take on the National League All-Stars in Flushing, N.Y., tomorrow, Chicago White Sox catcher **Tyler Flowers** will be relaxing with family in his hometown of Woodstock, Ga. Originally drafted by the Atlanta Braves in 2005, Flowers made his major-league debut for the White Sox in 2009.

Neither Flowers (.205 batting average) nor the White Sox (37-55 win-loss record) as a team have had a stellar season thus far, so Flowers sees the All-Star break as a way to get recharged for the second half of the season.

His wife, Nancy, has been a tremendous influence on renewing the faith of his baptism, and their daughter, Mia, is no less than an answer to prayer. Flowers discussed his faith, his family and baseball at the halfway point of the season with *Register* correspondent Trent Beattie.

What's your assessment of the White Sox season so far?

We haven't done all that well, especially when you consider how I planned on the season going. I had high expectations, but they have not been realized, which is a reminder that you can't force your own plans onto a game like baseball, which can be very unpredictable, as far as results go.

I am looking forward to the All-Star break. It's an opportunity to go back home to Georgia for a few days, enjoy some time with my wife and daughter, as well as my parents and the rest of the family.

It will be great to relax and think about things other than baseball. Once that's done, I think the second half of the season will be better because of a rested body and a renewed mindset.

Do you come from a Catholic family?

My mother, Kelly, was raised in a Catholic family as one of seven children. In the past few years, she has been able to convince my father, a non-practicing Lutheran, to attend Mass with her.

My siblings and I were raised Catholic, but it has only been in the last five years that I've really gotten deeper into what the Church has to offer. Even though I went to Catholic schools, it wasn't until late in the game that I learned about things like Eucharistic adoration and the Rosary. I had to rely on my wife, Nancy, to introduce me to those things.

Nancy and I went to Blessed Trinity Catholic High School in Roswell, Ga., and since her maiden name is Fiedler, we would always have lockers next to each other in the hallway. This must have been by Divine design, because she has made my life better in so many ways.

Do you have any children?

We were married in 2008, but didn't conceive any children for a couple of years. I just viewed it as apparently not being God's plan for us yet, and Nancy agreed. Yet, as more time passed without any babies, she became discouraged.

We saw Catholic doctors and found out that nothing was wrong with us physically, so their advice was to pray. We took that to heart and regularly went to Eucharistic adoration. We also went to the sacrament of reconciliation more frequently. Then, once we started praying to St. Thérèse of Lisieux for help, we conceived.

It must have been God's plan to use our lack of children as a way to get us closer to St. Thérèse. She is one of the greatest saints of the Church, so we can gain so much from her. Our biggest gain is our daughter, Mia Therese Flowers, who is almost 11 months old. She is the most wonderful gift of our marriage.

Is it difficult to maintain family cohesion as a professional athlete?

In the off-season, it's not, but during the season, it really can be. The team is on the road a lot, so families don't get to see each other as much as they'd like. That's a major reason why so many players are looking forward to the All-Star break: It's a time to reconnect with family.

I do enjoy playing baseball, but the game's ups and downs can really get to you if you let them. It's easy to become selfish, which leads you down the road to temptations which you wouldn't otherwise notice. I've been fortunate, however, to have selfless Christian teammates to discuss holy topics with. This is an especially helpful blessing when you're away from family.

While we agree on many things, some of my teammates don't understand the role that Mary plays in the lives of Christians. The common misconception is that to be devoted to Mary is to worship her. The reality is: We are honoring her as the mother of our Savior and asking for her help. We ask for the prayers of family and friends here on earth, so why not ask for the prayers of the Queen of Heaven and Earth?

Mary's life was selflessly and faithfully centered on her Son, so we should only expect that she wants all Christians to be united more closely to him. It's not a matter of Mary vs. Jesus, but having an even better relationship with Jesus, through his mother, Mary. Mothers have special relationships with their sons, and it's no different in the Holy Family. It's easy to see, then, why we should definitely want the Mother of our Savior on our side.

What are some ways in which having Mary on your side has helped you?

I love to pray Rosaries, which are very Christ-centered. In fact, Jesus' name is literally at the center of the Hail Mary. It's been said that praying the Rosary is learning about Jesus at the school of Mary.

When you consider what Jesus said about becoming like a little child in order to enter the Kingdom of heaven, it's easy to see the importance of placing ourselves at the feet of our spiritual mother, Mary. Everyone knows it's perfectly normal to see a child with his mother in the natural order, but the same is also true in the spiritual order: Children of God the Father need a mother, and they have one in Mary.

When you become more devoted to Mary, you will inevitably become more devoted to Jesus in the Eucharist. It's easy for me to attend Sunday Mass in Chicago because there's a Mass within the stadium available to players before the game. Ray McKenna, founder of Catholic Athletes for Christ, has made this possible here and in some other cities as well. In those cities where it's not readily available, I look for churches with early Masses. Participation in Mass keeps Christ not only on my mind, but also on my tongue and in my heart.

Another way that Mary has led me closer to her Son is through the sacrament of reconciliation. I appreciate it a great deal because of the relief it can bring to your soul as soon as you finish. The dead weight of sin is lifted off your shoulders, and you experience the great love and refreshment this brings. You're freed to live as a child of God because the grace to do this is imparted to you.

St. Augustine said it is a greater work to make a just man out of a sinner than to create heaven and earth. This is amazingly accomplished by Jesus when you go to reconciliation, and I'd strongly encourage those who haven't experienced this in a while to do so this week. Get back to Jesus and get renewed in his grace.

Do you find your faith has helped you to see not only the things around baseball, but the game of baseball itself in a better light?

That has definitely been the case. I really enjoy playing baseball because of the camaraderie among teammates and the challenges the game brings. It typically takes a combined effort for a team to be victorious, so you have to think in terms of contribution rather than personal reward. This is particularly true in my position as a catcher. You're supposed to make calls that are for the good of the team, and the decisions you make have an effect on everyone else.

On the other hand, I've learned what every player does at some point: Baseball is not always going to be there. The body eventually starts to break down, and you can't do the things you were once able to do. It seems to be just the opposite with God, however. He is always there, but when you're healthy, it's easy to take that for granted. When you're declining physically, it's probably much easier to remember God.

God speaks to us not only through the consolations, but (also) the trials of life. I've experienced that reality this season. I haven't had a year like the one I planned on having, so my plans and God's don't seem to be matching up in that regard. This means I need to quit making plans of my own and go where he leads me. I'm not sure where that will be, but I will keep working hard and keep my heart and ears open to see how I should do his work.

I'm most definitely a work in progress, as far as practicing my faith and being a true follower of Jesus, which is true of most of us. Yet I do know that I've grown in the knowledge and practice of the faith. This is largely due to my wife, Nancy. She has really opened my eyes to a number of things (Eucharistic adoration, Marian intercession and reconciliation, as examples) that bring me closer to Christ. I can't help but be renewed when around her and our daughter, Mia Therese.

///

PERSEVERANCE PAYS OFF FOR NEW YORK YANKEES' PITCHER

*Former Notre Dame star David Phelps'
determination brought him a wife
and a greater understanding of the Catholic faith.*

September 18, 2013

David Phelps knew he was meant to marry a woman in his international relations class at the University of Notre Dame. The only problem was, that special woman was completely unaware of it.

Phelps (no relation to former longtime Notre Dame basketball coach Richard "Digger" Phelps), started off on the wrong foot with the classmate who had caught his eye. However, through prayer and humble perseverance, he eventually gained her respect and her appreciation of the Catholic faith.

Now David and Maria Phelps are happily married, with Jesus as the center of their lives. This holy cohesion provides the foundation for stable living in an oftentimes stressful job.

Pressure is the norm when playing for the New York Yankees, and, this season, injuries have been added to the equation for Phelps, who has spent many days on the team's disabled list.

Phelps spoke with the *Register* in time for his return to the Yankees' active roster on Sept. 14. The Yankees are currently four games out of a playoff position, with 12 games left in the regular season.

What do you think of this season for the Yankees?

It's been an up-and-down season for the team and for me personally. There have been injuries, including my own (an elbow flexor strain), and now we're fighting to get a wild card berth into the playoffs. I'm so happy to be back with the team, because I've spent so much time rehabbing my injury and preparing to contribute in any way I can. I'm so grateful to be back in a position to help out.

I have loved playing for the Yankees, ever since my first action in early 2012. It was April 8 in the last game of a series against the Tampa Rays, in the bottom of the eighth inning. [Manager] Joe Girardi called me in, I threw warm-up pitches, picked up the rosin bag from behind the mound, and tossed it back down. As I came back up, I was surprised to see Derek Jeter in my face. He put his arm around me and said, "It's the same game we've been playing, but with a few more people here."

That greeting from someone who embodies the spirit of the Yankees as well as anyone has meant so much to me. Derek is an amazing baseball player, not just from the standpoint of personal statistics, but also from one of teamwork. A perennial All-Star could easily ignore the new guy, but Derek went out of his way to make me feel welcome.

Have you always wanted to play in the major leagues?

Ever since I can remember, that's been my dream. When I was 6, my older brother and I would play Whiffle ball in the backyard. We would imitate various players from our hometown St. Louis Cardinals, such as 15-time All-Star Ozzie Smith.

That major-league dream was always there, but as more of an ideal, rather than a practical plan. It wasn't until the last two years of high school that I realized it really could happen. I was recruited by a number of college teams and ended up choosing Notre Dame.

There were good things about the other schools, from an academic and athletic standpoint, but Notre Dame was in a class by itself. I visited the South Bend campus on the weekend the football team defeated rival Michigan in 2004. That was a big boost, but everything else about the campus that I would see on a daily basis stuck with me — the buildings, the history, the people. They all came together to form an atmosphere I couldn't find anywhere else.

What are some of your top memories from Notre Dame?

There are so many good memories, and some of the best ones would have to involve my future wife, Maria. We had some great days at Notre Dame, and we have a great relationship now, but it didn't start out that way in the spring of 2007, my sophomore year and her freshman year.

Because our last names were next to each other alphabetically, we were paired up in an international relations class. We were going to be called upon to discuss our reading assignment with the rest of the class. However, I had not done the required reading, so I told her that I hoped she had. She was very put off by that, and understandably so.

Even though things almost couldn't have started off worse, I asked Maria out a few weeks after we first met. She immediately rejected the idea. I deserved the rejection, but didn't give up. I just knew, somehow in my soul, that we were meant to be together.

How long did it take for Maria to see you in a different light?

I asked her out at least 10 more times in the next year, but she said No each time. There was no sugarcoating it either. She didn't want to have anything to do with me. Some of our mutual acquaintances would tell her she should give me a chance, that I was a great baseball player, etc. That year (2007) I was throwing one of the best seasons any pitcher from Notre Dame had ever thrown, but Maria didn't care. Her lack of interest was refreshingly humbling for me.

In 2008, I began to realize that God deserved far more attention than I had been giving him. Instead of going to Mass more regularly, though, I started going to an Assemblies of God church with my roommate. I thought all you needed was to accept Jesus as your Savior, and everything would be fine. Church attendance was seen as nice but not necessary.

Maria would help me grow in my understanding of everything Jesus has to offer us and what we're called to give back to him. After she finally said Yes to me in the spring of 2008, she would ask me what I believed, I would reply, and she would ask more questions. Instead of a one-dimensional, oversimplified, linear way of thinking, Maria had a three-dimensional, vibrant and comprehensive way of thinking.

Maria's influence and that of her family had such an effect on me that, by the fall of 2009, I came to realize what I was missing out on. There are so many great things in the Catholic Church, but the most desirable one is the Eucharist. It had been so long since I had received Jesus sacramentally, and I knew it was time to start doing so again.

I wanted to meet up with a priest in order to discuss my concerns and to be reconciled with the Church. Even though I was drafted in 2008, I would return for the fall semester at Notre Dame three consecutive years in order to finish my degree. This is how I was able to get in touch with Father Paul Doyle, a Holy Cross priest at Notre Dame, in the fall of 2009.

We discussed my concerns, and he heard my confession. All the obstacles that had kept me back from being totally united to Jesus were removed, and I was able to receive him in the Eucharist again. It was a great relief to be back in the Church.

Have Maria and her family continued to influence you?

They have, and I can't tell you how grateful I am for their witness. It is because of them that I now fully participate in the Mass, go to

Eucharistic adoration and pray the Rosary. The Rosary is something Maria suggested I start doing as part of my pre-game preparation. It helps to calm my nerves by drawing down grace and reminding me that there's more to life than baseball.

Another thing I've gained from the Church is an understanding of the theology of the body, a topic I've found to be life-changing. To know not just the biological significance, but the theological significance of what it means to be a man and what it means to be a woman is incredibly helpful. It puts individual actions in the greater context of an all-encompassing divine Providence.

Maria is one of nine children, and her mother is one of 13. Our own marriage has already been blessed with a beautiful child, our daughter Adeline, who was born on March 22, 2012. This was only days before I was first called up to the majors. That call is special for any player, but when it happens so quickly after the birth of your first child, you think of how work is done for the purpose of providing for that child and your wife. Work and family life are supposed to be integrated like that, under the umbrella of faith.

How has your faith affected your work?

I understand the importance of work in providing for my family, but I also know that I won't be playing baseball forever. So whatever work I'm engaged in, it should have God as the primary focus. Our daily actions should be a communication with God, a living prayer.

I'm incredibly blessed to be a member of the Catholic Church, the body of Christ. The Church is amazing, and I love everything about it. When I'm on the road, I search for a parish near our hotel. When I walk inside, I can feel the presence of Jesus in the Blessed Sacrament. Regardless of which city we're in, Jesus remains the same, and his Church does as well.

Since there's so much joy to living a Catholic life here on earth, I sometimes think of how tremendous heaven will be. As long as we persevere in the practice of the faith, we will encounter the reality of the words from 1 Corinthians 2:9: "What eye has not seen, and ear has not heard, and what has not entered the human heart, what God has prepared for those who love him."

///

HUNT FOR A RED OCTOBER

Los Angeles Dodgers' fans hope announcer Vin Scully calls as many postseason games as possible.

October 3, 2013

Legendary announcer **Vin Scully** has called Dodgers' games for an amazing 64 years, the longest-announcing tenure in Major League Baseball history. Dodgers' fans were excited to hear in August that Scully will be returning for his 65th season next year, but they presently hope to extend this season as far as possible.

Blue Dodgers' uniforms aside, such an extension could be called a red October, because of Scully's ruddy hair. The Bronx native has become so closely associated with the Dodgers that no visual of him is necessary. A single word spoken by the 85-year-old immediately brings to mind the face — and the head — that are trademarks of Dodgers baseball.

Scully's illustrious career has included broadcasting some of the most exciting baseball moments of the past six decades, including perfect games from Don Larsen and Sandy Koufax, six Dodgers World Series championships and Hank Aaron's record-breaking 715th homerun.

Scully, whose voice is known as the "Soundtrack to Summer" in Los Angeles, spoke of his reliance on God throughout his career with *Register* correspondent Trent Beattie. This was before the Dodgers knew they would be playing the Atlanta Braves in the first round of the playoffs.

As the Dodgers are heading into their final regular season series this weekend, what do you think of their chances in the postseason?

Looking at pitching, the Dodgers' starting rotation has six All-Star appearances and two Cy Young Awards. A great pitching staff can take you a long way. Aside from that, something interesting about our pitchers is that they actually hit fairly well, which is always a plus.

Four hitters, including two who have been in our regular lineup, are hitting well above .300. We also have five additional players hitting above .270, so they really have great potential to score a lot of runs. However, all the other teams in the playoffs will have great hitting and pitching as well, so whomever we face, it should be entertaining.

What first drew you to a broadcasting career in the late 1940s?

As a youngster in the 1930s, I would crawl under our four-legged radio and listen to the college football games that were broadcast on Saturdays. At that time, the only sports on radio were college football games. I was enthralled by the roar of the crowd — not the games themselves, but the crowd. The enthusiasm expressed by so many fans really drew me in and captured my imagination.

When I was 8 years old in the Bronx, my class wrote compositions for Sister Virginia Maria of the Sisters of Charity about what we wanted to be when we grew up. All the boys wanted to be policemen, firemen, doctors, etc. However, I wrote about being a radio sports announcer. It wasn't what Sister Virginia expected to read about, but it turned out to be something I was actually able to do.

Were you a natural speaker, or did you have to work at it?

I was told when traveling in Ireland as a boy that I had a lovely Irish brogue — a naturally pleasing voice and manner of speaking. I thought of my own speaking ability as somewhat ordinary, but maybe it's a combination of natural talent and diligent preparation for something I enjoyed talking about: sports in general and baseball in particular. I just knew those radio broadcasts were something I wanted to be a part of.

How did you get to be the youngest-ever World Series broadcaster (25 years old) in 1953?

Red Barber was the primary announcer for the Dodgers at the time, but he was at a standstill in negotiations with Gillette, which ran the World Series then. Neither side would budge, so the next person on the list was Connie Desmond, who also had a poor relationship with Gillette.

I was third on the list and was asked by Gillette to announce the World Series that year. I was reluctant to take Red's job because he had already helped me out so much in my short career. I asked him about the situation, and he assured me that it would be okay to take his place. He said that if I didn't do it, someone else would, so I might as well go ahead.

That might be considered the first milestone in a legendary career. What are some of the others you remember fondly?

There are so many opportunities I've been blessed with in my career. In 1955, the Brooklyn Dodgers defeated the Yankees 2-0 in the seventh game of the World Series. I got to announce on the radio that the Dodgers were the champions of the world that year and did so again in '59, '63, '65, '81 and '88.

The victory in '81 was significant because of how we were beaten in previous World Series outings in '77 and '78. Tommy Lasorda, the manager of the team at the time, wanted to beat the Yankees very badly. He asked God that such an opportunity would come about again. His prayer was answered in 1981, and he attributes the Dodgers' World Series victory that year to God.

Tommy liked to say "Because God delays does not mean God denies." In other words, you might not achieve something the first time around, but God, in his providence, might allow opportunities to do so later on.

On an individual player level, some of the most significant pitching performances I got to call were Don Larsen's perfect game in 1956 and Sandy Koufax's in 1965. Some of the most significant hitting performances were Henry Aaron's record-breaking 715th home run in 1974 and Kirk Gibson's amazing homer in the 1988 World Series.

All these performances were great from an athletic perspective, but Aaron's home run was so significant from a cultural one as well. There in the deep South, a black man was given a standing ovation for breaking a white legend's record. It was a marvelous thing to be a part of.

What do you appreciate most about being part of the Catholic Church?

I feel a tremendous degree of comfort in the Catholic Church. It's where I've grown up, where I've had the most important moments of my life. I've benefitted from the dedication of the nuns in grammar school, the reception of the sacraments and a rich tradition of prayer that you can take with you no matter where you are.

When my wife, Joan, died in 1972 at the age of 35, I was devastated, as were our children. We didn't stop praying, though.

The worst thing you can do in times of trial is to stop praying. The tough moments are when you need God the most. He's always there and more than happy to give us his help; we need only ask for it.

There are so many good things about the Church, but that might be the most essential thing I've learned from it: the importance of continual communication with God. That's what all the kneelers, candles, incense, stained-glass windows, holy water and other things are about: directing our minds and hearts to God.

There are many saints named Vincent — Vincent de Paul, Vincent Ferrer and Vincent of Lerins, for example. Do you have a favorite?

I'm not one to alienate any saint who could help me, especially those who share my name, so I'll take the intercession of all the Vincents. In addition to the Vincents, St. Jude's prayers are known for packing a wallop, so I'll take his help as well.

The one saint everyone should have a devotion to is the Blessed Virgin Mary. It has been said, and I believe it to be true, that her prayers are more powerful than those of the rest of heaven combined. No one was closer or more devoted to Christ on earth, so it only makes sense to see the same thing in heaven. Now, the Blessed Virgin seeks to help her spiritual children get home to spend eternity with her Son.

While it's not quite eternity, you've been with the Dodgers for 64 years. Did you ever think you'd be with any team for that long?

The Dodgers brought me in on a temporary basis in early 1950. I worked at their spring training facility in Vero Beach, Fla. It was a trial period, so they could have left me in the Everglades with the alligators. Fortunately, I caught on and have been with the team ever since.

When I was first starting out in the business, I never, ever thought I'd be doing this for 64 years with one team. It never crossed my mind. It was a day-to-day existence back then, and it is so today. You show up and do what today demands, not really looking too far ahead. Eventually, you're able to look back and see all the days added together, which present a beautiful tapestry of life.

///

DISCOVERING BROTHERLY LOVE IN BASEBALL

As preparations get under way for the 2014 season, Philadelphia Phillies pitcher Justin De Fratus is enthused about the Catholic MLB community.

February 25, 2014

Well over a month before their first preseason game on Feb. 26, most of the Philadelphia Phillies were in Clearwater, Fla., preparing for the upcoming season. The team seemed to know collectively, without being told in a meeting, that important preparation needed to be done to make this season different from the last, when they had a record of 73 wins and 89 losses, finishing fourth in the National League Eastern Division.

Pitcher **Justin De Fratus** is thankful to be a part of a team committed to extensive hard work. Having men around him who share the same dedication makes the 26-year-old's days go smoothly. Over and above professional dedication, De Fratus also appreciates those in his line of work who are committed to their Catholic faith.

When De Fratus first entered professional baseball at the age of 19, he didn't find the Catholic community he was looking for. It seemed to him that everyone was Protestant or not religious at all. By the time he was 23, however, the Oxnard, Calif., native was pleased to find that he had not only brothers in baseball, but brothers in the faith.

De Fratus shared his faith journey with *Register* correspondent Trent Beattie before spring training.

You got to Florida a month before spring training began. Did you come to prepare alone or with other teammates?

Basically, the whole team is here, but it's funny how it happened. There wasn't any official shout-out to everyone that we would be here early; everyone just seemed to be thinking the same way. Little by little, we learned about other guys who were venturing down here to Clearwater, Fla., in January.

It's no secret that the past two seasons haven't been fantastic for us, so we're just putting in the effort in the hope of changing that. We want to do everything we can to be a better team this season, and the way to start that is by getting here early. Hopefully all the extra practice will make spring training better, and spring training will make the regular season better.

What are your expectations for this season?

As far as specific numbers, such as an ERA [earned run average] or strikeouts, I don't really have any. Those numbers are outside of your control, so it doesn't help to think about them. What I'm concentrating on is maintaining a consistent mindset that will help me to stay aggressive.

If I prepare well and pitch as well as I can, then the results don't matter. All you can ask is that a pitcher throws the ball well; after that, it's out of his hands, literally. The saying "Let go and let God" is important to anyone, but for baseball players, it might be especially so. God doesn't look upon a player with more love if he throws a shutout. Regardless of the results, God's love is the same.

What are some of the surprises you've encountered in Major League Baseball?

There are two main surprises that really stick with me: The first is understood by first saying that, previous to actually playing in one of the games, my only experience of MLB games was through TV. When you watch on TV, there can be an unreasonable, artificial outlook on the game. You can think of it as part of a movie rather than what real men are actually doing.

Once I got to my first major-league game, however, I was very pleasantly surprised to see that the dirt on the pitcher's mound was the same as the dirt I had seen in baseball games since I was 9. The grass was the same grass, and so forth. That first outing really dispelled a lot of anxiety about just what it would be like to play in the majors.

The second surprise happened after making it to the majors, which had been my professional dream for years. By playing for the Philadelphia Phillies, I had accomplished what I had always wanted to, and that was cool. However, I found that the material success didn't complete my soul. I was shocked, really, at how little I was fulfilled, despite my material success.

That's when you started to take the faith more seriously, right?

I had been raised a Catholic, but the fire for the faith wasn't really ignited until 2007, when I saw the *Champions of Faith* DVD. There were quite a few professional athletes and coaches on the DVD who were serious about being Catholic. That really impressed me, especially when the baseball players would share their testimonies.

What I found in the minor leagues, though, is there didn't seem to be the same commitment to the faith by any teammates. When you're far away from home and sometimes far away from a Catholic church because of the rural locations of stadiums, it's terribly easy to slide away from maintaining a Catholic life.

After making my major-league debut in September of 2011, I had the epiphany of seeing that material success wasn't all there was to life; but it wouldn't be until early in the next season that I would become even more convinced of my need for God.

What happened in 2012?

I was injured and wasn't able to play for most of 2012. That's when everything worldly that could be taken away was taken away. It was like the world had abandoned me, and the only reality left was God. Then I saw more clearly than ever before that if I wanted to be truly fulfilled I needed to become more dedicated to Jesus through his Church.

Nobody likes to be injured, but I look at the 2012 injury as a real blessing from God. He was giving me time to step back and look at life honestly, not just through the lens of worldliness. When you get that quiet time to think and pray, it's really easy to see what matters most in life: loving God and doing his will.

What are some of your favorite aspects of the Catholic Church?

One of the most important things for me is being part of a welcoming community of believers. Some people tend to think of religion as "me and God" but overlook everyone else. You have to remember that when God became man he started a Church for all of his followers to belong to.

I really like that brotherly aspect of being a Christian: that you're on a team — God's team. Not everyone has the same role, but together we can make great things happen. We can support each other and function as Jesus intended us to.

The most important thing, though, is that the Catholic Church was started directly by Jesus Christ. As Catholics, we can trace our spiritual lineage through the bishops over the centuries, all the way back to the first bishops — the apostles — and then, of course, to Jesus himself. This is recorded in Matthew 16:18.

Other Christian groups don't go back to Jesus, but to King Henry VIII or Martin Luther or someone else who broke off from the Catholic Church or, as time went on, from another group that had already broken off from the Catholic Church. Without a central authority found in the papacy, individuals made up their own religions, and the denominations just kept multiplying.

Searching for the truth has been something big for you, hasn't it?

Yes. That search for truth really started in high school. Up to that point, I was kind of on autopilot or cruise control, but in high school, I started looking into the important questions about life. I wondered about why we're here, where we're going, what we should be doing.

I remember a high-school classmate asking me, "If God is so good, then why is there so much suffering in the world?" It was a good question, and as I looked into it with faith and reason, I found an even better answer in the writings of C.S. Lewis.

Without free will, no action we did could really be described as good or bad. If we're forced to do something, then we don't deserve punishment or reward. What we'd do would simply be what we were programmed to do. We would be robots, not human beings.

God freely loved us into being and wants us to freely love him back. In order to do that, we need free will, a consequence of which is that we also have the awful possibility of freely choosing not to love God back. This is called sin, and sin is how suffering entered into the world. So the short answer to my classmate's question is that God didn't cause suffering; human beings caused suffering through original sin and continue to do so through personal sin.

As I looked into the important questions of life, I became more and more convinced that I was in the right place. If I had found the truth somewhere else, I'd be there, but Jesus promised in John 16:13 to send the Holy Spirit to bring us all truth, and that's what I've been able to receive. Not that I have all the truth now, but I've gotten a good answer every time I've searched for one, and I have faith that any other question that will come up has a good answer.

Jesus prayed to the Father in John 17 that we may be one, sanctified in truth, and the Holy Spirit makes this unity in truth possible. The Holy Spirit is the soul of the Church, uniting us as believers. Being brothers in the Spirit is what life is all about.

///

SAN DIEGO PADRES' PITCHER PRACTICES PATIENCE

Joe Wieland looks to recover from arm injury and have a healthy second half of the 2014 season.

March 28, 2014

Heading into spring training in February, San Diego Padres' pitcher **Joe Wieland** was feeling great. He thought his previous arm injuries were behind him, and he was hoping, by this time, to have earned a spot on the team's major-league roster.

Things turned out differently, however. After re-aggravating a tenacious right arm injury, the 24-year-old Reno, Nev., native is now focusing his attention on a successful surgery and recovery. After a March 26 arthroscopic operation, he'll have to spend three months rehabbing his arm before he has the opportunity to return to the big-league roster.

As the Padres looked to open their season against the Los Angeles Dodgers on March 30, Wieland spoke of accepting his recent injury as part of God's plan.

How has spring training gone, and what are you looking forward to now that the regular season is upon us?

I started last season recovering from Tommy John surgery, where a ligament in my elbow was replaced. Throughout the 2013 season, I endured quite a few setbacks as I tried to get my arm back into pitching shape. We never did find out what was wrong with the arm last year. That was no fun, so coming into spring training this year, my big goal was to stay healthy.

Things turned out differently than I had hoped, though. My first three outings were great, but in the fourth outing, the pain started up again. An MRI last week showed that there was a bone spur, cartilage or scar tissue that has been giving me problems. Being injured is never fun, but it's a great relief to finally know what the cause of the pain is.

On Wednesday of this week [March 26], I'll go in for arthroscopic surgery, which is supposed to be quick and easy, as far as surgeries go. Then I'll have three months of rehab, and I should be back in "game shape" by the All-Star break in July.

It will take some patience, but I just have to accept it as part of God's plan and try to make small improvements every day. It's important not to get too caught up in what you'd like to happen in the future, all the while ignoring the good things you already do have. So many people are much worse off than I am. I can walk, talk and do everything else that a healthy person can do; the only thing I can't do right now is play baseball.

When did you start playing baseball?

I played baseball almost from the get-go. My first toys were a ball and a bat, and I'm told my first word was "ball." Baseball seems to have always been a part of my life. I remember my dad coaching me in Little League, even though he hadn't played baseball as a kid himself. Yet he knew what he was doing, and he helped me to become a better player.

I'm a pitcher now, but hitting used to be my favorite thing. I was drawn to any sport that involved hitting, like golf, ping-pong and tennis. I played soccer, basketball and football, as well, but I had always been most into sports that had bats, clubs or rackets.

I fully intended to be a shortstop, until my sophomore year of high school; but that's when I had a great pitching season. The scouts took notice, and that's when the transition to pitching started.

Were you able to connect sports and faith while growing up?

When I was really young, they were separate. I went to Catholic schools, so we would pray before games, but I remember wanting to get that part over with so I could run out onto the field and start playing. Yet, as I got older — say, around 13 or so — sports and faith started to come together.

I made the discovery that any talent I had for sports or anything else did not originate from me, but was ultimately due to God's goodness and generosity. I could then see that sports were not some separate compartment of my life, isolated from God, but were an extension of God's love for me. Without God, I'd have no ability to play sports; and even more to the point, without God, I'd be nothing.

My parents and grandparents were huge, as far as making right and wrong clear to me and my younger brother and sister. They were strict, but it was with a good goal in mind, not just for the sake of being strict. They wanted us to become responsible people who do the right thing.

Something else that really helped to shape me as a young Catholic was the availability of retreats. I was able to go on and even lead some retreats while at Bishop Manogue High School in Reno, Nev., so those experiences helped to solidify my connection with God. When I went to the 2012 Catholic Athletes for Christ retreat, I was able to learn even more than I had previously.

That 2012 retreat was where I met Justin De Fratus, a pitcher with the Philadelphia Phillies. We discovered that we had a lot in common, so we kind of stuck together that weekend.

You were also able to go on that retreat with Jeff Suppan, who played with you for a year while he was with the Padres in 2012, right?

Yes, Jeff is a great man who isn't shy about laying out the faith with anyone at any time. There's a story from the 2012 season, when we were doing pitcher fielding practice. It was after we had been to a Bible study with some other players and were discussing how Catholicism is very biblical.

While the other guys started to become quiet as they did the drills, Jeff kept talking about the Catholic faith. Even as he was going through his pitching motion and scooping up balls in the infield, he was still going on about one aspect or another of Catholicism. I was very impressed with his multitasking abilities, which made it possible to play baseball and evangelize at the same time.

Jeff is an awesome guy who has been a great example to me of how to carry myself as a baseball player and a man. The same is true with Mark Kotsay, whose house I got to stay at last season. Being around Mark and his family was one of the few bright spots from last year, as I was grinding along, recovering from surgery.

What are some of the things you like most about the Church?

You have to go with the Eucharist as No. 1. That's the greatest thing, and you don't get that anywhere else. The Church calls it the source and summit of the Christian life, and that's just what it is. How else can you explain our Savior becoming truly present to us for our consumption? Words can't adequately describe it.

At every Mass, a miracle takes place on the altar. We may not see it with our eyes, but bread and wine become the Body and Blood of Jesus. That's a true miracle, so I count myself privileged to be a part of it. Even now, as I'm talking about it, I'm getting goose bumps. It's a totally amazing gift to have access to the Eucharist.

Another thing I like about the Church is [the sacrament of] reconciliation. We all fall short, so before we can receive the Eucharist, we need to be in a state of grace. That's where reconciliation is so helpful. Many people are anxious before going, even to the point of skipping out on it, but we should pay attention — not to how we feel before going, but how we feel afterwards.

There's no feeling like being told by Jesus, through the mouth of the priest, that your sins are forgiven. It's a very humbling experience, to be honest about how you've messed up, but the grace you get in return is more than worth it. Even if you don't have mortal sins to confess, getting rid of the venial ones that have accumulated is a relief.

Even though I'm one of the people who can get anxious about it beforehand, there's such vitality to the whole thing. You get to see who you really are and who God really is, a reality check that is irreplaceable.

Since you share a name, do you have a devotion to St. Joseph?

Devotions are a relatively new thing for me. I'm learning more about the Rosary, Divine Mercy Chaplet and the intercession of St. Joseph, whose feast day was March 19.

Jesus and Mary, rightfully, get a lot of attention, but St. Joseph can be passed over a lot. If you just take the time to reflect on his role in the Holy Family — that of protector and provider — it's just mind-boggling: how holy he must have been. Here, you have the head of a family whose other members are the Son of God and the Mother of God. St. Joseph was given the amazing task of filling the role of father to Jesus as he grew up on earth.

If a short reflection on St. Joseph doesn't inspire us to look more deeply into his life, I don't know what will. You can't pass over someone like him. He has more to teach me about being a true Christian man than I'll ever understand, but it's very enjoyable to start understanding it at least a little bit better.

///

ARIZONA DIAMONDBACKS PITCHER SHARES FATHER'S DAY REFLECTIONS

Joe Thatcher feels at home with his wife, Katie, and son, Jack.

June 15, 2014

The Arizona Diamondbacks have gotten off to a slow start this season, with a disappointing record of 29-40 as of June 12. However, left-handed pitcher **Joe Thatcher** is not letting those early results get him down. Aside from his knowledge of baseball being a quirky, failure-filled game, the Kokomo, Ind., native finds his greatest joy in being a husband and father.

The 32-year-old shared reflections on his family — and the value of perseverance and prayer — with *Register* correspondent Trent Beattie.

What do you think of this season so far?

The season has not gone as we had hoped. We had high expectations as a team, so the slow start we've gotten off to has been disappointing. But it's not from a lack of work or will. This is just how baseball goes sometimes. You can have bad results one month and great ones the next, all the while not changing a single thing in your own preparation.

Do you have favorite baseball memories with your father?

I have a lot of baseball memories with my father, who went to Indiana State University and played baseball under head coach Bob Warn. I would later attend the same school and play for the same coach, which was a special thing.

Long before college, though, baseball was at the center of most things my father and I did together. From a very early age, it was a bonding activity in which I was encouraged and inspired to be as good of a player as I possibly could. I was very fortunate to have that strong paternal influence behind me.

I remember my father taking me to my first major-league game in Chicago and taking several other family trips there to watch the Cubs or White Sox. When I got older and started traveling for my own games, he was always willing to come along and spend weekends going wherever I went. I will always be grateful for the amount of time and money he spent on baseball so that I could get the most out of my abilities.

Do you plan on having similar memories with your own children?

I have an 11-month-old boy named Jack, my wife Katie's and my first child. I just hope that I can be the father to him that my father was for me. I am sure that baseball will be a part of our relationship in some form. Hopefully, I still have many years left to play and he can be a part of my career and experience some of the big-league life with me, but family has become the most important part of my life now. I will do whatever is necessary to spend time together with my wife and son.

What are your favorite things about marriage and fatherhood?

Being a new father has changed my life completely. Before marriage and family, baseball was what was important to me, but now I feel a great responsibility to be the father and husband that my family counts on me to be. Coming home from a game (whether good or bad) is always a joy. My boy does not care how his daddy pitched; he is just always happy to see me. The love of a child is pure and unaffected by worldly concerns, which can only help us adults have a purer perspective on things.

You weren't drafted out of college, but you made it to the majors and are currently in your eighth season. How important is perseverance to you?

Not getting drafted out of college was a disappointment, but looking back now, it was truly a blessing. It's funny the way that God works, because the outward appearance of things can be very different from the inner truth. No matter what happens to us, God is constantly working everything for our good.

I really enjoyed playing Independent League ball, through which I got to meet a lot of great people. It also gave me a few years to mature as a person and as a player before I got my chance at professional baseball. However, it did take a lot of perseverance to stick with it and keep playing through the tough times. Even in those times, though, I felt that it was what I was supposed to be doing with my life and that God had a plan.

The beauty of baseball is that you can relate it to every aspect of life. The game itself has so many wonderful moments, but at the same time, some moments of incredible frustration. Yet you can learn from all of the ups and downs and then take those lessons into other areas of life.

Is it difficult to maintain a sacramental life and prayer life in pro baseball?

It can be very difficult for professional baseball players to attend Mass at a church on Sunday mornings, but there are ways to step away from the game and fulfill our necessary spiritual commitments. Catholic Athletes for Christ has been very helpful in recent years. More and more stadiums around the league are offering Mass on the weekends. In addition to that, my wife and I try to get to Mass during the week at some point when we are not on the road.

Being in professional baseball and traveling as much as we do, I love knowing that I can walk into any Catholic church in the country and feel at home. I've been to Mass at cathedrals such as St. Patrick's in New York City, and I've been to Mass in many smaller churches in little minor-league towns. Yet in any church, no matter the size or the location, that same pull is there: It's the members of the body of Christ being drawn to worship God together. This connection felt among all Catholics throughout the world is my favorite part of the faith.

Being a member of the body of Christ helps your own prayers to be not only for yourself, but for others as well. You also know that others are praying for you. We won't know in this life exactly how the prayers of others on earth or in heaven have helped us — or even that certain people were praying for us at all — but after death, we'll see how it worked. I do know already, though, that my parents have prayed for me, and, now, I pray for my son.

Do you have a favorite Bible verse?

Philippians 4:13 — "I can do all things in Christ who strengthens me" — is my favorite verse. My mother used to make me and my brother and sister read that passage over and over. Before every game growing up, I would read those words to myself. Looking back, she was ingraining those words into our minds so they would always be available to us. And I believe that there are no truer words in the world. God is great, and anything is possible — including a dramatic turnaround during a baseball season — when you trust in him.

///

L.A. DODGERS' CATCHER GLAD TO CONTRIBUTE TO ALL-STAR TEAMMATES' SUCCESS

Drew Butera is grateful to be able to work with two of the best pitchers in the National League, Clayton Kershaw and Zack Greinke, who will represent the Dodgers tonight in Minneapolis.

July 15, 2014

Some Major League Baseball catchers can look at their team's starting pitchers without seeing any All-Stars. However, Los Angeles Dodgers' catcher **Drew Butera's** men on the mound have 12 All-Star Game appearances among them. The Dodgers' delegation this year for the midsummer classic taking place on July 15 in Minneapolis includes two pitchers, Zack Greinke and Clayton Kershaw, who have helped their team to a National League West-leading record of 54-43.

High-level baseball is nothing new for Butera, 30, who, before being traded to the Dodgers on July 31, 2013, was the backup for six-time All-Star catcher Joe Mauer of the Minnesota Twins. Even before his major-league debut with the Twins in 2010, Butera had gained much baseball know-how from his father Sal, a former Major Leaguer, and also from many other professional players generous enough to share their time with him.

After graduating from Bishop Moore High School in Orlando, Fla., in 2002, Butera played baseball at the University of Central Florida, where he was drafted in the fifth round by the New York Mets in 2005. He played minor-league ball for the Mets until a professional and spiritual turning point resulted in his being traded to the Twins in 2007.

Butera, only the fifth MLB player ever to catch a no-hitter in both the American and National Leagues, spoke with *Register* correspondent Trent Beattie before this year's All-Star Game.

The Dodgers have an abundance of great pitching. Is this intimidating or inspiring?

It's really a blessing to have so many great pitchers on the team. The guys have great talent, but also a great work ethic, which I enjoy being a part of. I prepare before each game with the starter to make sure we have the other team's batting lineup down. We don't leave anything to chance, but do what we can to control everything we do have control over.

The pitchers have good stuff, but more than that, their thorough preparation makes good results possible. They do the same things day in and day out — the work necessary to get things done.

I ask this half seriously, but would you want to travel to and play in the All-Star Game or would you prefer to rest over the All-Star break, as the vast majority of players do?

Well, it's true that if you're not in the All-Star Game, you get some much-needed rest, but I would still love to play in the game one day. Depending on where the game is in a particular year, you might have to fly across the country and back, while most other guys stay at home, but it would be an honor to be there.

Winning the World Series is the team goal, and the team goals are by far the most important. But one of the top individual honors would be playing in an All-Star Game, so that would really be a welcomed privilege, in my mind.

Your father, Sal, played for the Twins, Tigers, Expos, Reds and Blue Jays, so you must have learned a lot about baseball from him.

There are countless baseball-related memories I have with my father. Baseball has always been a part of our lives together. That's been a great blessing: to have the man closest to you growing up with nearly all the answers for the questions you have about your favorite sport.

I've also been blessed to be around other major-league players who were nice enough to play catch with me and give me some pointers. Guys like former Blue Jays right fielder and two-time All-Star Shawn Green (who also went on to play for the Dodgers) would play catch with me in the mid-1990s and tell me how to be better.

Some of the best lessons were about work ethic, no complaining, playing for the good of the team and letting go of results. Wishing for things doesn't make them happen; you have to do what's necessary to get things done. Complaining is easy to do, but if you want peace of mind, gratitude and patience are necessary. Playing selfishly is also easy to do, but playing properly means the team comes first. After all the diligent and selfless teamwork, letting go of results tops everything off. You've done what you can do to achieve a certain result, and then it's just up to God to give you what is best for you, whether you feel it's best or not.

Have you always taken the faith seriously or was there a specific turning point when you started to do so?

I had a good Catholic upbringing: I was raised in a Catholic home, taught the difference between right and wrong, went to Catholic schools, went to Mass and said my prayers. These are all very good things, of course, but it took some adversity for me to get a better grasp of how important being Catholic is. I always thought well of the Church, but when things get tough, you can start to develop a deeper appreciation.

I was playing for the Mets' AA team in Binghamton, N.Y., in 2007, and things were not going well at all. I wasn't playing up to my capabilities, and, considering the goal of playing in the majors, it seemed as if my world was crashing down upon me. I had put so much into the sport, but was not seeing the intended results. That was a really low point in my life.

I remember going to church in downtown Binghamton and sitting in the back. A Mass was being said, but I don't remember anything about it, because I was just praying the whole time for the strength to know and do God's will. When things go well, you can be deceived into thinking that it's all your own doing, but when things go badly, you realize how much you need God's grace. That's what happened to me in 2007, and that particular Mass where I prayed like never before was a turning point in my life.

The very next day, I was traded to the Minnesota Twins, and, while, of course, there were still the normal ups and downs of baseball, things got better overall. I progressed through the Twins' organization and made my major-league debut in 2010. I was so blessed to be the backup for six-time All-Star catcher Joe Mauer.

You can't help but take in good things from Joe, who is one of the most intelligent and productive players in the game.

What are some of the aspects of the Church that you appreciate most?

I'm really into the tradition and history of the Church — not only the obvious things you find in Europe, especially in Italy and Rome, specifically — but also the things you find in the United States. I've been to many beautiful and historic churches in cities like Chicago, St. Louis and Philadelphia.

One of my favorite places to visit is St. Patrick's Cathedral in New York City. It is an impressive building for so many reasons. It's large but detailed, built in neo-Gothic style with beautiful stained-glass windows and statuary. The way everything is organized makes you appreciate the time and effort that went into designing and constructing it. I could spend hours in St. Patrick's among all the beautiful artwork and history there.

One of the fascinating threads of history at St. Patrick's includes Venerable Fulton Sheen, who is now interred there in the crypt under the main altar. Shortly before Sheen's death in 1979, he was embraced by Pope John Paul II at St. Patrick's, the same place that, years before, Sheen would preach Good Friday sermons.

Another venerable American man I recently heard about is Venerable Solanus Casey, a 20th-century Franciscan priest who spent part of his life in New York City. He actually liked to play baseball and was a catcher, so I'm looking forward to learning more about him. I already have two St. Christopher medals, one of which I got from St. Patrick's Cathedral's gift shop, but maybe I'll be getting a Venerable Solanus medal, too.

It's reassuring to think about how the Catholic Church goes all the way back to Jesus, how that same Church was brought to the United States by courageous missionaries and how we're fortunate enough to be a part of it today. We're members of the body of Christ, which continues to live through the ages, with the goal of everyone being saved and united permanently with Jesus in heaven. That's the common theme among all the varied historical situations any given Christian might find himself in. Jesus is always and everywhere pursuing our eternal beatitude.

///

SHARING THE SECRET TO LONGEVITY IN MAJOR LEAGUE BASEBALL

Cal Ripken Jr.'s athletic trainer speaks of three decades with the Baltimore Orioles and his spiritual awakening.

October 14, 2014

Many people know about Cal Ripken Jr.'s record-breaking endurance, but few know about one of the men who helped the modern-day Iron Man break Major League Baseball's consecutive-games-played record.

Athletic trainer **Richie Bancells** was hired by the Orioles on the same day the team drafted Ripken in 1978. While Ripken would make the majors before Bancells, they reunited in 1984 and worked together for the remainder of Ripken's career, which ended in 2001.

Bancells enjoyed his time with baseball's Iron Man, but a couple of years later, he experienced serious anxiety that led to a hospital visit and a re-prioritization of his life. He started to see what could be set aside and what was most important, which led him back into the Catholic Church with a renewed perspective.

Bancells, a Key West, Fla., native and father of three, spoke of his 30 years in the major leagues, including this year's 96-66 Orioles squad, which currently trails the Kansas City Royals in the best-of-seven American League Championship Series, two games to none.

What do you think of your postseason chances this year?

We got to the playoffs in 2012, but this year has been extraordinary. There's a saying that winning solves a lot of problems, and we've won a lot this year, which has solved a lot of our problems. We've had our share of injuries, but we've come from behind and won many games by one run.

It's interesting to see how the team hasn't been firing on all cylinders during the season, yet we've still come together and managed to win. Some of our best players — Manny Machado and Matt Wieters, for instance — are on the disabled list, but here we are in the playoffs. We're a very resilient team, and it will be fun to see how far we can go.

I do know that, while it's great to be in the playoffs, we are aware that the goal is more than just to be here. We want to win the World Series. ... Where we are now is comparable to a fishing analogy I use: We've got a tug on the line, but the fish is not in the boat yet.

This is your 30th year as an athletic trainer in the major leagues. One of the big pluses of that time must have been working with Hall of Famer Cal Ripken Jr.

Working with Cal was definitely a great experience, and it started even before the majors. The exact day I was hired by the Orioles in 1978 was the day he was drafted out of high school. He was a homesick kid, and I was finishing graduate school, when we were both sent to rookie ball with the Bluefield Orioles in the Appalachian League. I got to AAA before Cal, but he got to the majors before I did. I joined him in 1984, and things went well from there.

Cal had an unusual durability about him. He was fit, not only from a physical point of view, but from a mental one as well. He believed he came to the park every day to play ball. It was that simple. Distractions meant nothing; he was a baseball player, period. That mindset came from his father, who had a great work ethic. Cal took that work ethic and used it to break the consecutive-games-played streak in 1995, with 2,131 games, which then ended at 2,632 in 1998.

Before he approached the 2,131 mark, the streak started becoming a topic of discussion. People were talking about him possibly breaking Lou Gehrig's record, but Cal didn't understand what the big deal was. I was taping his ankle one day, and he said to me, "You go to work every day, don't you?" He went to work every day, and that was that.

There are obvious things an athletic trainer does, but what are some of the things people wouldn't know about your job?

Athletic trainers work to prevent, treat and rehabilitate injuries. That's just a normal part of the job, but you end up wearing a lot of different hats in this position, such as counselor and friend.

Players sometimes look to the training room to escape the chaos of the locker room, so they don't even need to have a specific physical concern to see me. The training room becomes a place of peace and quiet — just a casual location to hang out. Sometimes players just want to discuss things, rather then get something fixed. In this lounge-like environment, I've learned when to offer advice and when to listen.

You've also learned to listen to God's word and read it as well, right?

Yes, that's something that has taken many years, but it is finally a regular part of my life. In one way, God's word has always been there, because I grew up Catholic. We always went to Mass on Sundays and First Fridays, I went to Catholic grade school and high school, and my whole life seemed to revolve around the Church.

However, while I knew the rules, I didn't quite get the why of Catholicism. That led me to drift away from the Church in my 20s, because my career seemed so much more important to me.

Looking back, the best way to say it was that my priorities were screwed up. What was supposed to be on the top (my standing with God) was at a much lower level. Work ruled me.

How did you get your priorities straight?

Well, it took a trip to the hospital for that to happen. It was around 2003, and I was experiencing a lot of stress. It seemed like there we so many obligations for me to do, and I just couldn't take them all. There was so much anxiety; my heart would race, and I would have panic attacks.

Over the course of the season, I became exhausted and ended up checking into a hospital while the team was playing the Tigers in Detroit. Staying there for a few days was an opportunity for me to ask myself what was really important in life. I realized that there were things I didn't have to do, that I could say No. This realization brought a lot of relief. I also realized that being a Catholic is not primarily a matter of rules; it's a matter of a relationship.

The Church isn't an end in itself; it's the means through which we meet the real, living, loving Person of Jesus Christ. The Church — in all its various ways — brings Jesus to us. We see that in the sacraments and also in things that call to mind the life of Christ, such as crucifixes, stained-glass windows, statues, Stations of the Cross and sacred music. These are means to an end, and the end is union with Christ.

Today, I feel a very high level of comfort in the Church. It's where I belong, and it's a constant reminder of what is most important in life. Now, I don't see Catholicism as something that is only done from 9 to 10 on Sunday; it's something that is supposed to color everything you do during the entire week.

One of the best ways to describe the mindset is to ask yourself what you'd like people to say about you after you've died. What can honestly be said about the man you were? What sayings or descriptions can be placed, in all truth, on your headstone? It was according to that line of questioning that I started to rearrange my life.

How did the people around you respond to your change?

Some people liked it, and some didn't, but the ones I respected were the only ones whose opinion mattered to me. Now, I surround myself with like-minded people who have a faith-based perspective on life, so there's not much resistance to what I'm doing, and, in fact, there's a lot of encouragement.

Sometimes when people hear I'm getting back from being at Mass, they ask why I'd want to be a Catholic. They bring up sins of individual Catholics, but those don't bother me at all. Those are what specific people have chosen to do, not what we are taught to do by the Church. You don't judge a church based on people who have not followed its teachings.

Plus, where are you going to find a church in which no one sins and everyone is completely perfect? That's only going to be in heaven. I focus on the positives here and find tremendous consolation from being part of the mystical body of Christ. I love the Mass, and I love to go over the readings for every day, even on those days I'm not at Mass. God's word directs my day.

There are so many great Bible passages, but my favorite might be Proverbs 3:5-6, where it says to trust in the Lord with all your heart and do not rely on your own intelligence. Then it says to be always mindful of the Lord, and he will make straight your paths.

///

DEFENDER OF THE FAITH

Major League soccer player keeps his trust in God.

November 19, 2011

Matt Besler and his Sporting Kansas City team almost reached this year's MLS Cup final, which takes place Nov. 20. What makes this an especially noteworthy feat is the team's climb from last place earlier in the season and, on an individual level, the fact that Besler was not even sure he'd be playing professional soccer.

Besler guided his high-school team to a state championship in 2004 and went on to help the University of Notre Dame make four consecutive NCAA tournament appearances. He was named an All-American on the field and the National Soccer Coaches Association of America voted him the Men's Scholar All-America Player of the Year as a senior in 2008.

In the professional ranks, however, the competition was particularly tough, so Besler wasn't sure where he would be playing, or even if he would be playing at all. Nevertheless, he kept his faith in God, stayed focused on the field, and now starts as a defender on one of the best teams in the country.

In between recent playoff games in early November, Besler fielded some questions from *Register* correspondent Trent Beattie.

What are the highlights of the season so far that stand out for you?

I think opening up our new stadium and having such a good home record is a highlight from this season. I also think the fact that we were able to climb back from last place and go all the way to first place to finish as the Eastern Conference champions says a lot about our team. Now we're advancing in the playoffs, when, at the beginning of the season, it looked like maybe we wouldn't even make it to the postseason at all.

Are there quite a few other Catholic pro soccer players (especially from South America)?

I would say that most of the guys that come in from South America are Catholic, but I don't talk to them a whole lot because they speak a different language. Around the league you will find a lot of guys that are Protestant and a good amount of guys that are Catholic as well, regardless of which countries they come from.

How important was faith to your family growing up?

My family was a very Catholic family. My dad was raised very Catholic and went to Catholic schools his whole life. My mom actually grew up Methodist, but she converted to Catholicism when she married my dad. Attending Mass was important for my family, and I think my parents did a good job instilling those values in me and my brothers.

Has your Catholic faith influenced your soccer (and maybe vice versa, such as the discipline necessary for sports helping you to be more disciplined with the faith)?

Having my Catholic faith allows me to always feel confident and comfortable on the soccer field. Competition can be very intense, but knowing there are more important things in life and that God is in control helps to keep things in perspective. Then the confidence is there because you realize that, despite so much work and so many sacrifices, it still is a game.

In the same regard, my soccer career has always kept me on a set schedule and the discipline required to be a professional athlete carries over to attending Mass regularly and praying a lot. If I weren't on as tight a schedule or didn't have as many demands, I may not be as diligent in practicing the faith.

Were there rough periods in your soccer career or life in general that your faith has gotten you through?

Last year I wasn't getting a lot of playing time at all, and it was a tough season for me, but I stayed strong in my faith, and that helped me get through the season. Also, at the beginning of my professional soccer career, I had no idea where I was going to play or even if I was going to play at all. Instead of worrying about it, I put a lot of confidence in the Lord, and it ended up all right.

What are some of your favorite aspects of the Catholic faith?

I really appreciate the eternal aspect of it; Catholicism will always be there. The same can't really be said for soccer. As much as I enjoy playing it, soccer is not always going to be in my life, and everything else is going to come and go as well. However, my faith will always be there as the rock that gives support to everything else.

Former pro soccer player Chase Hilgenbrinck has entered the seminary to become a priest, and former pro baseball player Grant Desme has done the same. Do you have similar plans?

I do not have intentions of joining the seminary at this time, but I do intend on staying strong in the faith throughout my life. Whatever vocation anyone ends up embracing, the basic faith is still the same, with the foundation laid for us at baptism. Married life, religious life and priesthood are all continuations of that initial sacrament that has been likened to a door into the Church.

Do you have a favorite saint or devotion?

I like to pray the Rosary before games; that's one of my rituals. You get into the right mindset by having a routine, and, of course, you get all the grace from the prayers as well. Mary is always willing to help us, if we only ask for it.

My favorite saint is St. Christopher, and I wear a medal with his image on it. I like how he is a strong man and how he used that strength to help someone in need. It shows that power and generosity should go hand-in-hand.

I also heard recently about Blessed Pier Giorgio Frassati, who lived in the early part of the last century. All the saints have something to offer, but he seems particularly interesting because of his youth (he died at age 24), his closeness to our own time, and the fact that he enjoyed playing soccer and other sports. He's definitely someone to look into more.

Is there anything new about yourself you'd like to share?

I have a dog, a really small lab, and his name is Gipper. I named him after the famous Notre Dame football coach Knute Rockne's famous speech "Win One for the Gipper," so that has some Catholic ties to it.

///

MAJOR LEAGUE SOCCER ALL-STAR REDISCOVERS BEAUTY OF CATHOLIC FAITH

Columbus Crew midfielder Eddie Gaven pursues soccer career with proper perspective.

July 25, 2012

Eddie Gaven is in his 10th season of Major League Soccer. His career includes an MLS All-Star Game appearance in 2004 and an MLS Cup victory with the Columbus Crew in 2008. These are impressive accomplishments for anyone, but what makes them even more so is that Gaven is only 25.

In 2003, the Hamilton Township, N.J., native was the youngest player up to that point to sign an MLS contract. He was only 16 at the time. While Gaven's soccer career was pursued with youthful zeal, his Catholic faith was left to decay.

The restoration of his faith started when his beloved game of soccer was briefly taken away from him. He was out with an injury, which left him with plenty of time to think about where he was headed.

While Gaven still plays soccer with great enthusiasm, he now realizes where his greatest treasure is: in the Catholic Church. He appreciates many things about the Church, but most especially Mass.

Gaven spoke with *Register* correspondent Trent Beattie about his soccer career and re-conversion in anticipation of the MLS All-Star Game, which takes place July 25 at PPL Park in Chester, Pa.

Most 16-year-olds would be happy to make the varsity team in high school. How did you get to sign with a major-league team at that age?

I was exposed to the Olympic Development Program, commonly known as the ODP, early on. Any kid can try out for the program, and I went for it. You start playing locally and then move on to state, national and even international play. I was fortunate to play on the national team for those under 14 years of age, or the U 14 Team, as they call it. That was an opportunity for some MLS coaches to see me, which led to a tryout, and then a contract.

Ultimately, I think it was God's grace that enabled me to play at a high level at such a young age. I had a God-given ability to play, and that's what made it all possible. You have to go back to God to see the source of any ability you have to do anything.

Then I took that ability and really worked with it. That was due to the guidance of my father, who played soccer four years at Rutgers University. He was my coach from the earliest days until I got onto the advanced teams. He taught me well and inspired me to really put everything I had into the game.

I would play every day — and while doing so would imagine myself playing in the World Cup against the players I'd see on TV. It was more than me just kicking a soccer ball in my own backyard; it was playing in a different place through my imagination.

When you finally did get to play against the best players in reality, what was that like?

It's a dream come true to play Major League Soccer. Some people don't like their jobs, and others don't even have jobs, so I'm incredibly blessed to do what I do and get paid for it. Not many people can say that, so I just want to be grateful for that and keep playing as long as possible.

I was able to play in the MLS All-Star Game in 2004, and that was one of the highlights of my career. I was only 17 years old at the time, and I was playing against those guys I had seen on TV. It was a lot of fun to play with such top-level competition.

The biggest highlight of my career so far was winning the MLS Cup in 2008. I had been traded by the New York Metro Stars to the Columbus Crew in 2006, and we actually ended up playing against my old team (after they'd changed their name to the Red Bulls) in the final. The whole season was really great for our team. From start to finish, we played very well.

While things were going well on the field, how were they off the field?

By 2008, things were going well off the field, but I couldn't say the same thing a few years before that. I was very much into soccer, not just as a career, but as an idol. I didn't take my faith as seriously as I should have, despite the fact that I grew up in a solid home. We went to Mass every Sunday and said prayers before meals, but in my later teen years, I just didn't take the faith that seriously.

I was caught up in the ways of the world, but what really got me out of that was an injury. I had to have hernia surgery and couldn't play soccer for about a month. This was the first time I could ever remember being without soccer, so while in the hospital and recovering at home, there was a lot of time to think. I started to see things more clearly and realized that while soccer is fun, it won't last forever. What will last forever is heaven or hell.

I read from St. Alphonsus Liguori that: "He who prays is certainly saved. He who prays not is certainly damned." Unfortunately for me, at the time I would have fallen into the second category of people. This was enough motivation for me jump-start my prayer life.

I picked up one of those blue Pieta prayer booklets, which contained the 15 prayers of St. Bridget of Sweden. There are 20 promises that go along with saying the prayers for a year, and so I prayed them every day for a whole year.

I found that as my prayer life grew, so did how seriously I took the faith. The more I prayed, the more I wanted to attend Mass, go to the sacrament of penance and live out the virtues in everyday life. This was in contrast to how I lived previously — not going to Mass or penance and just being overly concerned about soccer all day. The conversion was certainly tied to praying more and better than I had previously.

Here's a natural comparison that shows how reasonable prayer is. If you're interested in a girl and think there is potential for marriage, you want to talk with her. You want to spend time with her and communicate with her. What kind of relationship would it be if you had little or no desire to communicate? It would be a trivial relationship or no relationship at all.

The same is true with God. It's not enough to mentally acknowledge his existence; if you really want to love him more, you have to communicate with him. While communication is necessary in the natural order, it's even more essential in the supernatural order. There are certain graces God will only grant through prayer.

How did your spiritual life progress from your initial conversion to your married life today?

As a teenager, my mother wanted me to go to a Protestant youth group, where she hoped I would meet other young people who took their faith seriously. I didn't really want to go, but went just to please her.

Well, at this youth group, I met a beautiful girl who was very dedicated to her Protestant religion. As time went by and I considered the possibility of marrying her, I realized that we really needed to be on the same page spiritually — and at times, it seemed we weren't even in the same book.

We would discuss things a lot over the phone. I would tell her about the evidence I had found about why the Catholic Church was founded by Jesus Christ and why we believe what we do, and she would come back with arguments for being Protestant. We were both very much entrenched in our own sides, so it was a tough, drawn-out discussion.

Tears were shed and prayers were said, and, by the grace of God, Paula saw the light about the beauty of our Catholic faith. Today, she and I both know not only what the Church teaches, but why the Church teaches it. This is a huge blessing, and I really don't think we'd have the marriage we do today without the same beliefs. It just wouldn't work out.

What is your favorite part of being a father?

Our first child, a boy, is 13 months old, and I love to watch him grow. Every day when I come home various things change, so it's fun to see what he's interested in and what he can do that he wasn't previously able to do. He hasn't started using words yet, but he does make sounds and gestures.

The simplest things catch his attention, and he takes joy in them, so that's something we as adults can learn from. His innocence and joy for life are refreshing. It's easy to lose that simplicity as we get older — becoming more sophisticated and yet more unhappy — so we can definitely do well to imitate kids in their simplicity.

I try to be a good husband, father and worker by imitating St. Joseph, who is the perfect model we have for those three things. He did everything for Christ; his whole life was filled by grace, and he was completely united with the will of God. He's a model for any man who wants to grow in virtue.

What is your favorite aspect of Catholicism?

Well, three aspects really stand out. The first one is the Rosary, which is an incredible prayer or series of prayers. It has had a deep impact on my life and has renewed the faith in my heart. It's a very calming experience to pray the Rosary because you've come into Christ's presence through the heart of Our Lady.

The second one — Eucharistic adoration — is closely related to the first. You go from one type of Christ's presence that you can experience anywhere into another type that you can only experience in a sacramental way. That is, you've placed yourself before the tabernacle or monstrance in the church where Our Lord resides under the appearance of bread.

We usually go as a family to adoration once a week. This is in addition to attending Sunday Mass and then daily Mass as often as possible. Eucharistic adoration is an extension of the worship we give to Our Lord in the Mass.

That brings me to the third aspect of Catholicism that I appreciate so much: holy Mass. No tongue can express the power of the Mass because it's the same sacrifice as Calvary. We should see it that way and act accordingly, but, oftentimes, there's irreverence.

I grew up with the *Novus Ordo* Mass, unaware of the Latin Mass. However, when I started looking into the faith more seriously, I came across the Latin Mass, which was quite an experience to see for the first time. It was beyond anything I'd ever dreamed of. There's so much reverence in the Latin Mass, which I attend regularly now.

I'm very thankful to Pope Benedict for making the "extraordinary form" more widely available through his *motu proprio* five years ago. I enjoy sharing the Latin Mass with others and often invite teammates to attend with me. It truly is, as many have said before, the most beautiful thing outside of heaven.

///

MAJOR LEAGUE SOCCER PLAYER MOVES FORWARD IN FAITH

Danny O'Rourke of the Columbus Crew recommits himself to Christ amid life's difficulties.

April 2, 2013

Growing up in a Catholic family, Danny O'Rourke went to Mass regularly, but he didn't understand why he had to. Soccer was a greater concern for him, and it continued to be so during his years at Indiana University.

His impressive Hoosier tenure included three consecutive All-Big 10 selections (2002-2004) and two consecutive NCAA Championships (2003-2004). His collegiate career was capped off by being named a first team All-American and the nation's top player as a senior in 2004.

It wasn't until dealing with knee injuries early in his professional career that O'Rourke had the time to reflect on the meaning of the Mass and his relationship with Jesus Christ. For O'Rourke, Mass attendance now is no longer seen as an item on a checklist, but an encounter with the Lord of the Universe.

O'Rourke recognizes the Eucharist as the source of meaning and stability in a busy and confused world. He spoke with *Register* correspondent Trent Beattie as the MLS season was getting under way last month.

What are your expectations for this season?

There are always the goals of winning games, winning the division and winning the MLS Cup, but I'm not too big on those cliché goals. They sound good, but we're taking a more modest approach.

We're just trying to see how players will mix with each other, and we're trying to improve a little every day. That kind of approach doesn't make headlines, but it is realistic. You just take one little step at a time, commit to doing as well as you can for that day, and try to play as a cohesive unit.

How long have you known teammate Eddie Gaven?

We've known each other for almost seven years now. We were originally supposed to be traded when he played for the New York MetroStars and I played for the San Jose Earthquakes. That didn't work out, and now we've been on the same team since 2007.

It's awesome to have a teammate like Eddie, not only from a soccer standpoint, but from an overall human standpoint. He's a great player, but a greater man. He has an inspiring story, and I've learned a lot about being a Christian from him. We've attended Mass together, which we both have learned is a very Christocentric thing, not an impersonal one.

One of the things I admire most about Eddie is his dedication to prayer. He prays the Rosary every day, and he loves to go to Eucharistic adoration. In fact, he has introduced me to both of those forms of prayer. I really enjoy stopping by the church for adoration after practice. A million things are usually flying through my head, and adoration helps to calm me down and think in an orderly way.

The silence of the church is important, but even more important than that is the Person who is present there with you. Jesus Christ is in the tabernacle, always there for you and ready to hear you. It's amazing how blessed we are to have Our Lord in every Catholic church.

At the end of Matthew's Gospel, Jesus tells the apostles he is with them (and their successors) until the end of the world. This is true in many ways, but most particularly in the Eucharist.

Have you always taken the faith seriously, or did you have a notable conversion?

My story is similar to Eddie's. Growing up, my family would attend Mass, pray and do the other things Catholics do. However, I didn't have a really deep, personal commitment to what I was doing. There wasn't that core connection to Jesus that should have been there.

That changed when I had to deal with knee injuries in my first professional season. Not being able to play soccer for long periods of time gave me a chance to think about life and to pray more than I had before. Prayer is the essential thing. You can go through all the motions of what Christians should do, but continual prayer makes it personal and gives you the grace to have a better idea of what it is you're doing in the first place.

Another thing that really comes into play when you're injured is patience. I was used to doing everything pretty much on my own, with very little practical interest in what God wanted to do for me. The injuries were opportunities for me to let go and allow God to work though my life. Physically I was held back by injuries, but spiritually I was set free by them.

Aside from the knee injuries, have there been other tough times your faith has gotten you through?

Without faith, I would never have been able to get through the death of a Crew teammate, Kirk Urso, last August. He died unexpectedly of cardiac arrest, due to a congenital heart defect. He was only 22, so you just don't think something like that would happen, but it did. It's a reminder that you have to be ready to die at any time. You can't assume you have decades left, even if you're really young.

Kirk's death was very jarring. The only way not to be overwhelmed by it is to see it in an eternal context. Knowing that there is an afterlife makes hope possible and provides meaning to what happened. It helps you to get past all the superficial things that don't matter and to take your obligations to God more seriously.

We just had an exhibition game last weekend against the University of North Carolina (Kirk's alma mater). That was a great way to do something productive about a negative situation, because we publicly remembered him and raised money for heart research.

Do you find that being a professional athlete gives you a platform to influence people for the better?

People look up to pro athletes, so we have opportunities to use that for doing good things. One of the things I value most about playing pro soccer is my relationship with a boy named Evan. I met him when he was about 8, and I was in Houston at the time.

Evan and I seem to go through patches of illness simultaneously. I only have knee problems to deal with, but Evan has had three or four leg surgeries, and he has a gastrointestinal disease with a lot of bleeding. We talk often, and he has been a real inspiration to me. I've had to face tough competition on the field, but Evan has faced much tougher competition though illness. He's the strongest person I've ever met.

St. Paul writes in 2 Corinthians 12:10 that when he is weak he is strong. That sounds contradictory, but in light of faith, it makes sense. The only way you're going to be motivated to ask for God's help is if you realize you need it. Otherwise, you won't bother asking, and you'll remain alone.

This is why so many things we see as setbacks are actually blessings. Jesus didn't come to save the self-sufficient, but those who need saving. In our weakness, we know better where we stand with God, and it makes us cry out for help. The grace that follows makes us far stronger than we would have been on our own.

It reminds me of St. Peter, who is actually a good saint for soccer players because of his patronage for foot problems. He tried to do things on his own, but that always ended up in a mess. When he let go of his pride, acknowledged his insufficiency and humbly let Jesus set the agenda, then everything worked out as it was supposed to.

This isn't to say that the transition is always pleasant. However, weakness and strength go together perfectly, as long as you continually ask for God's help to be strong. Then you can move forward in faith.

///

DEFENDING THE BEAUTY OF THE CATHOLIC FAITH

Columbus Crew rookie soccer player Drew Beckie asserts his appreciation for the Church.

October 29, 2013

In an age when a number of young people leave the Church, professional soccer player **Drew Beckie** remains happily at home with Catholicism. The former All-Mountain Pacific Sports Federation First Team selection at the University of Denver enjoys the structure the Church provides amidst the troubles of life.

The Columbus Crew finished at 12-17-5 and out of playoff contention this year, but Beckie has learned about patience, balance and focus on the field. Helpful teammates are among those deserving credit for the soccer insights the 23-year-old defender has gained.

Off the field, Beckie has been reminded of the fragility of life, as his friends and family have dealt with flooding in Colorado. Memories of the early loss of his father have come to mind, but, more importantly, so has an overall faith context in which to place them.

Drew Beckie recently fielded questions about soccer, life and Catholicism from *Register* correspondent Trent Beattie.

What do you think of your first professional soccer season?

It was great to be welcomed onto the team right up front. We have a wonderful group of guys here on the Crew, so I'm blessed to be around them. From a results standpoint, however, it's been kind of a tough season. One of our starters, Eddie Gaven, went out with a knee injury in May, so we've missed his contributions. We finished at 12-17-5 and aren't in the playoffs.

However, I have learned a lot, especially about being patient. At this level of competition, there are always going to be guys who are a little better than you are as a rookie. They've been around longer and have more experience, so you can't get discouraged by any setbacks you might have while playing against them.

You just have to do your best every day and try to maintain an even balance. On a scale of 1 to 10, with 10 being the highest, it's better to be a 6 or 7 every time out than it is to be a 10 one day and a 1 the next. Every player in the league can have a spectacular game, and that's great, but what's better than one extraordinary performance is many good performances.

You mentioned Eddie Gaven. What is it like to have him and fellow Catholic Danny O'Rourke on the team?

It's great to be on a team that brings in strong men of faith. There are other Catholics in the league, but it seems as though the Crew has an overabundance of those who are willing to speak about it. Protestants usually do a better job of sharing their faith than Catholics.

Most of the athletes I've met in college and the pros are religious. You generally don't get to this level without some kind of hardship, and relying on faith in God is where most players go for support. Faith is a way to make sense of things and have an overall structure to life.

Then, once you're successful, you know you have to attribute that to the Lord. Despite the work you put in, you know that, ultimately, God is the one who gave you the talent, the ability to work with that talent and opportunities to display it.

You're originally from Canada, right?

I was born in Regina, Saskatchewan, and our family moved to the Denver, Colo., area when I was 3. Then we moved back to Canada and then again back to the U.S. I've been able to compete on the Under-17 Canadian National Team, but I currently have a green card to live in the U.S.

Even though I'm not officially an American, I do consider myself to be one. I've spent most of my life in the States, and I'm here now, so it just seems like I am a citizen. I know when the recent flooding occurred in Colorado, it hit very close to home. It's such an overwhelming thing when natural disasters happen. The damage to property can be difficult, but death is the most devastating to deal with, because it's so permanent.

You encountered a death in the family at an early age. How did that affect you?

My father died when I was 11, but he had been fighting cancer for four years leading up to that, so our family did have plenty of time to prepare for his passing. Father John Lager, a Franciscan monk and friend of the family, helped us in that preparation.

Encountering death is very challenging, but it can also be very beneficial. You can't help but think about heaven and what we're supposed to do in this life to get there. The darkness of death can really be a bright light if you treat it as such. You can see the beauty of Catholicism and the unbroken connection we have to those in the next life.

Death also helps you to understand the blessings you have in this life. When I would hear kids complain about their parents, I would get somewhat angry and think, "Don't they know that it's a gift to have both of their parents?" Ironically, I seemed to get that better than they did, even though I was operating with one less parent.

I can look back and still remember having my father coach my first soccer team in Denver. He didn't really know what he was doing, but just being together and playing together was the important thing. Later on, he and my mother would encourage me to have fun playing and put God first. Sports won't last forever, but God will, so we have to live according to that truth.

What are some of the things you enjoy most about the Church?

I really enjoy the Mass, which, unfortunately, can be misunderstood. Sometimes I hear stories about people who used to be Catholic, but they left the Church because the Mass is "boring" or they didn't get anything out of it. They thought of it as needless repetition.

Yet the repetition is one of the things I appreciate most about the Mass. All of life is filled with routines, so why would our faith life be any different? Should we be expected to make up our own worship as we go along or should we humbly receive what's given to us from the Church?

Sometimes loud bands and lively sermons are sought after in worship. I can understand the desire to get an emotional charge out of things, but that's not the goal of worship. Worship is about giving to God what is his due: our praise, honor and thanksgiving. It's clear from Luke 22:19-20 and John 6:51-59 that the Mass is the primary form of worship we're supposed to participate in.

Some people don't like the regular routine of the Church, but I do. The rituals of the Church draw us into the life of Christ and provide us with much-needed structure. I like how this structure serves as a base from which we can do charitable works. Those works are an extension of the love of God, not just isolated acts without reference to God.

I enjoy volunteering with Special Olympics soccer programs and with soup kitchens. When you help those in need, you also help Jesus himself, who is hidden among the poor. It's important to remember that everything we've been given in the Church is a free gift, so we're obligated to share it with others.

Do you have a patron saint?

St. Joseph is my patron. I have a plaque of him on my locker and also a holy card of him in my car. He's someone who is often overlooked, but if you think about it, no one, except the Blessed Virgin Mary, was closer to Jesus on earth. No one.

St. Joseph had the unimaginable honor of being the earthly father for the Son of God. That's a truly unique position in the history of mankind, and the fact that we honor Joseph as a saint means that he fulfilled the duties of the position. Because of this, anyone, but especially fathers, would do well to ask for his intercession.

After my own father's death, St. Joseph has been a father figure in my life, and so has Father Lager, who was recently appointed national chaplain of the Fellowship of Catholic University Students. Father Lager sees the importance of men who are strong in the faith, who can then lead others to Christ and the beauty of his Church. That's what life is all about.

///

SEEKING THE UNION OF SPORT AND FAITH IN PHILLY

Major League Soccer veteran Brian Carroll aims to balance competition with Christian charity.

August 7, 2014

Soccer has been a part of **Brian Carroll's** life as far back as he can remember. He and his two younger brothers, Jeff and Pat, battled against each other in almost every sport as they grew up in Springfield, Va., but they became particularly adept at soccer. This skillfulness resulted in all three of them playing the sport collegiately and professionally.

Brian Carroll finished his collegiate career early, exiting Wake Forest University after an All-American season in the fall of 2002 that nearly included a Hermann Trophy, college soccer's equivalent of the Heisman Trophy in football. He was selected 11th overall in the Major League Soccer draft by D.C. United in 2003, and the midfielder since has played in more than 300 professional games.

Despite his extensive experience, Carroll still finds the ideal, and oftentimes delicate, balance of athletic competition and kindness toward others to be a challenge. However, he has had help from late UCLA basketball coach John Wooden, MLS friends and, of course, the Catholic Church.

Brian Carroll, captain of the Philadelphia Union and father of two, recently spoke with *Register* correspondent Trent Beattie about the pursuit of athletic excellence while maintaining a well-rounded, Christ-centered life.

What do you think of the Union's season so far?

It's been a slow first half of the season, personally and collectively, but we've picked up the pace lately, and we are still in the playoff hunt. Last Friday, we tied a game with Eastern Conference leader Sporting Kansas City. That was a good indication that we're capable of more than our 5-8-9 record might suggest.

One thing that's always good to keep in mind, regardless of what your record might be, is to control what you can and let go of what you cannot. Your preparation is under your power, but the preparation of other teams is not, so there's no use in getting caught up in a concern over scores, standings, possible playoff brackets, etc.

I've been part of teams that played a fantastic game, maybe even the best they played that year, and yet, the other team was just a little bit better. Then there were times when you have an awful game and yet the other team was just a little bit worse. In the first case, you can't be frustrated about your great performance just because it wasn't quite as great as the other team's. In the second instance, you can't be too happy about playing an awful game; even though, yes, you did win it.

Instead of looking at it only from a numbers-comparison standpoint, it's better to look at it from a production standpoint. You try to produce the best soccer you can, and when you do that, then the great majority of the time, you'll win anyway. That's what UCLA basketball coach John Wooden found to be the case so many times in his unbelievable career. He cared about how well his own team played, regardless of how well the opponent might have played, and [yet] he also won a lot more games than coaches who were fixated on comparisons and results.

What do you enjoy most about playing Major League Soccer?

I really enjoy being able to take the God-given gifts I have and use them as far as they'll go. I've enjoyed the game from the time I was 5 to now, at age 33. Being able to play a sport continually for 28 years, the last 11 and a half of which I've been paid for, is a great blessing. I've always been able to maintain gratitude for being able to play soccer, and I'm even grateful for the gratitude itself, because, so often, we can take things for granted.

I also like being with the Philadelphia Union, specifically. It's nice to be back on the East Coast, to have enthusiastic fans (not only for soccer, but for the other sports in Philly) and to be able to live in a good suburb of the city. It's a good area, only an hour and a half from the mountains and beaches, where the beauty of creation is so wonderfully on display.

What are the most challenging things about Major League Soccer?

Professional soccer is a very competitive business. It's a do-or-die endeavor, where you're always trying to do your best, not only to compete against other teams, but in order to stay on your own team. If you don't produce, there's a line of guys nearby who'd be happy to take your position.

Considering that great competitiveness, it can be a delicate balance to establish solid working relationships with teammates. You have to maintain a high standard of play for yourself, but also try to help others to be as good as they can be. This is where treating others with charity is so important.

John Wooden's wisdom is helpful here and, of course, so is the broader perspective on life that the Church gives us. One of the guys who made this perspective clearer for me was Eddie Gaven. There was a three-year period from 2008 to 2010 in which we both played on the Columbus Crew as midfielders, and it was during this same time that we would talk about being Catholic and even go to Mass together.

Have you always taken the faith seriously or was there a specific time that you started to do so?

I come from an Irish-Catholic family and always remember the faith being a part of my life. In a similar way to being grateful for soccer, I've always seemed to have a steady interest in the Church. There wasn't a dramatic time that I left the Church or came back with a totally different perspective. I've just always seen being Catholic as an essential part of who I am.

We would go to Sunday Mass as a family, and I kept going to Mass at Wake Forest University. That was a time in life that you make your own decisions, and I found it pretty easy to go to Mass in college, even though I was living in a different state. I just knew that cutting off my relationship with God wouldn't bring happiness.

In addition to Mass continuing to be a regular part of life, soccer was as well. Despite the big changes, there were also big parts of life that I took with me.

Your experience of moving out probably helped your younger brothers when they left home.

I hope so, but I think we all helped each other out, though. I might not be at this level of soccer if I didn't have my younger brothers to compete with. I would play all kinds of sports with my brothers, Jeff and Pat, while growing up. It didn't really matter which sport, or even if we were inside or outside. We just always seemed to be competing in something.

As we developed, soccer became the sport we were most proficient in, so all three of us played in college and professionally. We've all played for D.C. United; I played with Jeff in 2006 and 2007, and then Jeff played with Pat in 2008, while I went to the Columbus Crew that year.

Now, Jeff is married with two kids and works at St. Bernadette Church in our hometown of Springfield, Va., as the marketing and development director. He also coaches the U-14 D.C. United Academy soccer team. My youngest brother, Pat, works for UPS and will be married to his college sweetheart later this year.

I will have been married for eight years on Dec. 30 of this year. My wife, Katie, and I have two children so far: one [age] 4, the other 2. Their ages can make going to Mass a big challenge, since they're barely aware of what's going on. I'm looking forward to when they can become more attuned to the importance of the Mass.

What do you enjoy most about family life?

Despite the challenges that 4- and 2-year-olds can present, I enjoy how much they bring people together. Family celebrations are made livelier and are renewed by additional members. People like to teach them things and also find out what they're thinking. Interacting with little kids like this is so different from interacting with other adults.

New children are always a blessing, and people are touched by how guileless they are. You think about the value of each human soul, and you also think about the value of being a part of the life of that soul. You see how much you're needed and how God wants us to function so closely together as a family under his Lordship. It's a beautiful thing to be united in faith like that.

///

OLYMPIC BRONZE MEDALIST TRANSFORMED THROUGH CRUCIBLE OF SUFFERING

Illness and injury help Mario Ancic realize identity as child of God.

August 8, 2012

If things had gone according to his original plan, **Mario Ancic** would have been playing tennis at the Olympic Games in London this week. However, his life took a different course than he expected.

The 6-foot-5-inch Croatian was riding high at the end of 2006. He was already an Olympic bronze medalist, a Wimbledon semifinalist and Davis Cup champion. He was ranked among the top 10 players in the world and was set to have an outstanding year in 2007.

However, just when things looked brightest, a mysterious illness took hold of Ancic, and he spent the next few years trying to overcome it. Initially, he saw his suffering as the worst thing that could happen to him. But he eventually came to see it as the best thing that God the Father could send him.

Ancic spoke with *Register* correspondent Trent Beattie about his trials and victories in time for the Olympic Games in London.

How did you start playing tennis?

As a little kid, I lived near tennis courts, and my older brother played tennis, so that's what I wanted to do as well. I played a lot on those courts, and tennis really became something I dedicated myself to completely.

That dedication paid off with some very impressive results, including a victory over Roger Federer at Wimbledon when you were only 18.

Not many people can say they've beaten Roger at Wimbledon, so you have to really have some things going for you in order to make that happen. One of those things for me was that it was my first Grand Slam tournament. When you're young, you tend to play more freely and fearlessly, so that helps.

Wimbledon's grass courts were also helpful, because they tend to favor the serve-and-volley game I like to do. This is one of the reasons Wimbledon is my favorite tournament in the world. It really matches well with how I like to play, which is also how my countryman Goran Ivanisevic liked to play. He won Wimbledon in 2001, so he had some good advice to give on how to play there in 2002.

What are your other top memories?

In 2004, I was able to reach the semifinals at Wimbledon, and then, later that summer, I won the bronze medal in doubles with Ivan Ljubicic at the Olympics in Athens. The summer of 2004 was very memorable for me, and I got a lot of confidence to take with me as I played more on the professional tour.

The greatest memory of my career was winning the Davis Cup with my teammates for Croatia in 2005. Davis Cup is similar to the World Cup for soccer, except that it's played in four rounds over the course of a year rather than in one month. We won the final round against the Slovak Republic, and the inspiration from that victory carried over into the next year, 2006, which was my best year overall.

Things didn't go too well in 2007, though, did they?

Everything had been going so well in 2006. I was ranked among the top 10 players in the world and was looking forward to what 2007 would bring. Little did I know that it would bring the toughest struggle of my life.

Early in 2007, I was feeling very tired at times, but I tried not to let it affect my game, and I kept on playing. I especially wanted to succeed in Davis Cup, where there is enormous pressure to represent your country well. However, I felt very sick during a Davis Cup match against Germany and was hospitalized. The doctors weren't sure what was wrong with me, so I couldn't get an accurate diagnosis. I was just very tired, with occasional nausea and fever, so I was forced to rest for long periods of time.

Nonetheless, I started to practice and even played matches before I was completely better. This wasn't the right thing to do, and it actually made the situation worse overall. I kept trying to come back over and over again, but it wasn't with enough rest behind me. I didn't want to deal with my illness, which turned out to be a bad case of mononucleosis.

Some guys on the tour have told me jokingly that I can be very hardheaded. This is true, so I think God used the mono to really talk to me. He was inviting me to take up my cross and follow him on a daily basis. This is not something I had thought of doing before, because my whole focus was on playing tennis well. I was willing to suffer in training for a match victory, but was unwilling (or even unaware) of how to suffer in life for a spiritual victory.

At some points, I was so weak that I could barely jog a short distance without losing my breath. I lost weight and had to spend more time resting. This was a big challenge for me because I was so used to flying around the world to play tennis. When you go from that to staying at home all day, sometimes in bed the whole time, it was almost unbearable for me.

I remember being very angry about the situation. I was irritated that God would allow this to happen to me. I asked, *Why me? Why now? Why this at such a young age?* I was only 22 when the mono started, and I was very committed to playing tennis. I had put a lot of work into it and expected to see more good things come out of it. I didn't understand why I was being prevented from playing the game I loved.

What was the turning point for you, as far as accepting the mono?

I can be very stubborn, so it took a long time for me to come around. The illness plagued me throughout 2007 and recurred in 2008. I pulled out of a lot of tournaments, including the Olympics. I remember literally having everything ready to go — I was all set — but just before departing on the plane, I felt so weak that I had to stay home and miss out on the competition.

That was a sad thing for me, because the Olympics are fun to play in, even for non-tennis reasons. You get to meet so many other athletes from other sports, and it's an inspiring thing to be a part of. I had been to the Olympic Games in 2000 and again in 2004, but a third time was not meant to be. Having opportunities like that taken away from you when your heart is set on them can be very discouraging, but if you take it in the right way, it can also be a blessing. That's the key: how you take it.

Two criminals died next to Jesus on the cross. The first one complained and wanted Jesus to take away his suffering. The second one accepted his suffering and spoke to Jesus (like we still can in prayer), and he was then told he'd be with the Lord in paradise. The outward suffering was the same for both criminals, but the difference was in their rejection or acceptance of that suffering. It's easy for us to ask for the suffering to be taken away, but sometimes that very suffering is what can draw us closest to God.

I was slowly going from being angry about the situation to accepting it, but it wasn't quite with the serenity I have today. I had been gradually realizing that I was more than a tennis player; I was a child of God — the God who was going out in search of his lost son. In the story of the Prodigal Son, it says that even when the son was still far away from his father, the father saw him, was moved with compassion and came running to him. This was true with me. Even though I didn't know exactly how to go back to God, I was seen by him and he led me back out of compassion.

What was one way God led you back?

One important way was through the writings of the saints. I began reading St. Augustine's *Confessions*, which really caught my attention. He reminded me of myself: someone who had strayed from God's plan for his life. He had a lot of worldly fame, but wasn't totally at peace. He explained his story so logically on every page that I was motivated to read the writings of other saints and also stories written about them.

St. Francis of Assisi's life really struck me as well. He was known as one of the holiest men around, yet he didn't share that same opinion of himself. He saw himself as a great sinner. Those of us who are much less holy than he was tend to think highly of ourselves, so his opinion of himself really moved me. When your standards are higher than just what your neighbor is doing, you aren't impressed by the good you might do. St. Francis measured himself by God's standard, so inevitably he would fall short of the ideal, even though he got closer to it than most of us do.

It's similar with Blessed Mother Teresa of Calcutta. She's well known around the world, but because her home country of Albania is very close to Croatia, she's even more popular in Croatia than in many other places. She was very humble, had a very low opinion of herself, but in a peaceful way. She was grounded in God's grace, so she was focused on what was important: serving Jesus in the suffering poor.

Ignatius of Loyola is another saint who has inspired me. He thinks so clearly and knows the importance of prayer. This is something I came to understand better — that prayer is not just a theoretical exercise, and Jesus' concern for our salvation did not end 2,000 years ago. His concern continues today, and prayer is a vital thing that connects us to his grace, which is just as alive today as it was many years ago.

How did your tennis career eventually end?

After I had attempted my 12th comeback in 2010, I returned to full communion with the Church. I had been an active Catholic earlier in life, but this time, it's better. I'm trying to live a Catholic life, not just from routine, but from knowledge and appreciation. I understand the Mass much better, which was due in part to Scott Hahn's book *The Lamb's Supper*. I used to go to Sunday Mass without much knowledge of what was happening. Now I go to Mass, not only on Sunday, but as often as possible during the week. When you know what happens in the Mass, you can't help but want to be present for that.

Once the mono had gone away by 2010, I was in a better frame of mind, which helped me with what I encountered next: back problems. The doctors presented me with surgery as an option, but it was risky, and even if it did work, they couldn't guarantee that I'd be able to play competitive tennis again. So I decided not to undergo surgery and knew my days of competing were over. It was still somewhat sad at the time, but there was a world of difference, as far as my acceptance of it.

In February of 2011, I made my retirement official, and today I look back on so many great memories with such joy, peace and appreciation. There were so many opportunities I had that most people don't get. I've played around the world on all the big courts, including Center Court at Wimbledon. I've played and had victories over all the top players, including Rafael Nadal, Andy Murray, Novak Djokovic and Roger Federer. In fact, I think Roger is the best player ever to play the game.

I think in one aspect of life or another, most people can say they were unable to do everything they had originally planned on doing. However, I can't help but be appreciative of what I was actually able to do.

Now you're building on your tennis experience by studying sports law, right?

That's right. Even before my illness and injuries, I was interested in law and studied the subject in Croatia. I got the rough equivalent of an undergraduate degree in law in 2008 and have worked in a law firm. Then I decided to pursue the specific category of sports law further. Even though I won't be playing competitive sports anymore, I wanted to build on something I already had personal knowledge of.

Columbia University in New York has one of the top-ranked law schools in the country, and they have a program for international students like me, so I thought it would be a good thing to take advantage of that. I'm starting classes later in August and expect to learn more about contracts, teams, unions and other things relevant to sports law.

New York City, with 8 million-plus people, is about two times the size of the entire country of Croatia. Obviously, there are some changes I'll have to get used to, but it's funny, because I already feel, in a sense, that I'm at home. One way that stood out for me was when I thought of how I'd be seeing the players on tour at the U.S. Open later in August. I thought of myself as the host to them, as if New York was my hometown.

I not only follow tennis, but other sports as well, including golf, baseball and soccer. There's the simple aspect of sports, but there's occasionally the added aspect of Catholic athletes as well. We've had some interesting stories of athletes in Europe who've become priests, and I know you have similar ones here in the U.S., such as the story of Father Joseph Freedy. You also have many other Catholic athletes, including Mark Teixeira, who plays baseball in "my hometown" of New York.

You've said that while you won't be competing on the Columbia tennis team, you will be practicing with them occasionally. What would you like to teach younger tennis players from what you've learned through your struggles?

One major thing I learned was not to plan too far in advance. It's easy to look ahead and think of all kinds of different things you'd like to do, but if you get too focused on things which haven't happened yet, then present opportunities can elude you. Instead of thinking of how nice it would be to do something way off into the future, it's more productive to choose smaller goals and take them on, one at a time.

I'd also say to enjoy the daily practices, not just for how they can prepare you for future matches, but also for the practices themselves. It is fun to win matches, but it's also fun just to hit the ball on the practice court. It's not necessary to have a pile of trophies in order to get some happiness out of tennis.

This reminds me of my uncle, who is a Franciscan priest. He was a missionary in Africa for many years, and when he came back, he told us fascinating stories of the people he encountered. They were often extremely poor, lacking in the most basic things. Some of them had no running water, no electricity, not even table salt. Just the basic things of life we take for granted they lived without.

While they lacked certain things we thought of as essential, they were very thankful for the Gospel being brought to them. We would use our lack of certain material goods as reasons for not accepting and living the Gospel, but they didn't do that. Oftentimes, the more things you have, the less time you have for God; and the less things you have, the more time you have for God.

There are so many blessings out there; we just have to open our eyes to see them. It takes more to get the attention of some people (like me), but God uses the exact tools each person needs to come to the realization that he is Our Father — and he has an indescribable love for us as his children.

///

PRO TENNIS PLAYER ACCOMPANIED BY OUR LADY OF GUADALUPE ON WORLD TRAVELS

Colombia native Santiago Giraldo Salazar is devoted to the Mother of God.

September 7, 2014

When Wimbledon and the U.S. Open are brought up in conversation, images of laser-beam winners hit by Roger Federer, Novak Djokovic and Rafael Nadal come to mind. One of the last topics to be associated with professional tennis is Our Lady of Guadalupe. Yet she has appeared at the grass courts of London and the hard courts of New York.

Well, sort of.

Santiago Giraldo Salazar, a professional tennis player from Bogota, Colombia, has been devoted to Our Lady of Guadalupe for years. He even considers her his "best companion" as he travels the world from tournament to tournament.

The 26-year-old, who spends part of the year living in Bradenton, Fla., keeps a scarf — much easier to travel with than a framed image or statue — with Our Lady of Guadalupe on it.

Salazar, currently ranked No. 31 in the world, spoke with *Register* correspondent Trent Beattie as this year's U.S. Open, held outside of New York City, was nearing its scheduled conclusion on Monday.

You reached the third round of Wimbledon this year, where you lost to seven-time champion Roger Federer, tying your best result in a Grand Slam. Why do you think you did well there?

The good performance at Wimbledon and other good results I've had this year have been because of the efforts made over many years and also because of a whole group of individuals that have been beside me. I've been through many matches and have been able to learn how to play the game better, which has resulted in a career-best ranking. To play in Wimbledon against Federer in the "tennis cathedral" of Centre Court is a very special moment, almost unique in my career.

Who did you think are the players most likely to win the U.S. Open this year?

I think that Federer (who has been my top tennis role model since I was young) was a great candidate. Andy Murray and Novak Djokovic are always dangerous, and you have to watch out for Kei Nishikori because he can give the big guys a surprise by beating them. Who knows, maybe next year I will be one of the candidates to win; but this year I did not go far. I lost in the first round to a good player.

What do you enjoy most about tennis, and what do you enjoy least?

I love tennis. I enjoy pretty much everything about it. I love to travel, to practice and, of course, to compete. What I do not like that much is maybe the lack of free time, because in order to play at this level, you have to be very dedicated. Yet I'm learning to become better at organizing and prioritizing my time. At the end of the day, I just reflect on all the good that tennis offers to me. That way, the little negatives don't affect what I do.

You've been to Mass in churches all over the world. What are some of the most beautiful churches you've been to?

There are great churches all over the world. Some of my favorites are obvious choices, like the Cologne Cathedral in Cologne, Germany, and Notre Dame Cathedral in Paris, France. There is so much grace, history and sacred artwork in these places. Sometimes you're in awe of what you see in them. They are very impressive, and they bring you closer to God, really. They get you to thinking about heaven, which is where our minds should be.

In addition to the obvious choices, though, some of my other favorite churches are in the least-expected places. God's grace operates everywhere, so you will sometimes be surprised by what good things you see when you are not expecting them.

Do you have a devotion to the Blessed Virgin Mary?

I am devoted to Our Lady of Guadalupe, or, as we say in Colombia, *La Virgen de Guadalupe*. I pray to her every day, and I carry a scarf with her beautiful image on it for all my trips around the world. She is my best companion because she makes me think of what matters most: the grace for all of us to become children of God. She is our spiritual mother who is full of grace, and she wants to have more spiritual children who live Christian lives here so we can live with her and her Son forever in heaven.

I also wear a crucifix on a chain, which brings similar feelings. I feel like I take a piece of God with me in each moment of my life because the image of his Son's unending love for us remains right next to my heart. Crucifixes are a testimony to the power of love, so I want that love to be with me always.

What are some of your favorite aspects of the Church?

I think that all the aspects of the Church are very special. I find beauty and grace in all of them, but I love holy Communion and the reflection afterwards to be most special. That is the most important time for anyone to have with Jesus because we are so close to him then. It is almost like Our Lady at the Annunciation: She accepted Jesus into her own body and soul, and, today, we can accept him into our bodies and souls, too.

Something good to do before receiving holy Communion is to make sure our souls are worthy of that grand honor. We can go to confession and let go of our sins so that Jesus will find a good home to live in. We wouldn't want a special guest to come into a dirty house, so we shouldn't want the Best Guest to come into a soul that is not clean.

Do you have a favorite Bible verse?

Yes, I carry my Bible with me on all my trips around the world, and something from Timothy, or Timoteo, is a favorite of mine. It is in 2 Timothy 1:7 and goes like this: "For God did not give us a spirit of cowardice, but, rather, of power and love and self-control." This is very refreshing and inspiring to read because it is a reminder of the strength we have from God.

The problems of life are nothing compared to the grace God wants to give us to conquer them, but we have to ask him for that grace. When we pray, we can get self-control and love, which is a very powerful combination. Prayer is what brings that strength to us, so I pray every day for it.

What do you think about having a South-American pope?

I am very excited to have a South-American pope. It is an honor that Pope Francis is Latin, so there is more thought given to how the Church is not meant only for Europe, but it is universal — for every country.

Pope Francis represents the whole Church with so much charisma and humility. He has a lot of energy, but he knows where it comes from: He lives out God's plan for him, and he is close to the people that he shepherds. He reminds me of John Paul the Great.

Juan Martin Del Potro, who won the U.S. Open in 2009, got to meet Pope Francis last year. It was easier for Del Potro to do that because he's from Argentina, but I still hope to meet Pope Francis one day. That would be more fun than winning the U.S. Open.

///

AMERICAN BOBSLEDDER HAS A GOLDEN DREAM

Catholic Digest, **February 2014**

American bobsledder **Steve Langton** believes God has a plan for him. This faith enables the 30-year-old Boston native to endure countless hours of training in preparation for the 2014 Winter

Olympics. The games, which take place in Sochi, Russia, will be his second—and perhaps his last—Olympic adventure.

Langton has achieved nearly everything that can he achieved in his sport, including 13 World Cup medals (four gold, six silver, and three bronze). The only thing that has eluded him thus far is an Olympic medal. The former NCAA track-and-field competitor hopes to change this in Sochi.

A business major at Northeastern University from 2002–2006, Langton knows that any reward will be preceded by an investment of talent. He spoke to *Catholic Digest* about his golden hopes in light of his faith in God's plan for his life.

What are your expectations going into the Olympics?

I hope that all my work and that of my teammates will come to fruition. At this level of competition, a lot of work is necessary, so you really hope it will be capped off by a tangible reward, hopefully a golden one. Whenever you see an athlete or a team on the medal stand, you can be certain that there have been many, many hours of preparation.

What are your top sports memories from childhood?

I'm the oldest of three boys, so there are many memories of us playing various sports with our father. Since we grew up in Boston, we also watched a lot of Red Sox games. They had some good teams throughout the 80s and 90s, but it wasn't until I was a little older that they won the World Series. Those victories were in 2004 and 2007.

Even more than baseball, though, I was a huge track-and-field fan. I followed American sprinter Maurice Greene. His winning the 100-meter sprint at the 2000 Olympics in Sydney, Australia, was a very memorable moment for me and my family. I was 17 years old at the time, and I was inspired to be a better sprinter myself.

I've been prenamed to the national bobsledding team, and my younger brother Chris might make the team as well. If we end up competing in bobsled events together, there will surely be some great memories. It's not often that brothers are on the same team like that.

It's easy to remain close to my brother Chris, since we train together, but I also continue to be close my other brother, Sean, and to my parents as well. In fact, I talk with both my mother and father every day. They are my biggest supporters.

Were you able to connect your faith with sports as you grew up?

In sports like baseball or football, you can compensate for a lack of natural speed, strength, or jumping ability. However, in track-and-field, that's not the case. You really need a good amount of natural ability to be able to compete at all. This makes it easier for you to realize that the talent you have comes from God, to the point that the connection becomes obvious.

Once you recognize the connection, you have to take what you've been given and put it to good use. In the parable of the talents in Matthew 25, it's made extremely clear that everyone is called to "invest" their talents and get more out of them. God wants us to use what he has given us to expand our horizons, but even more importantly to glorify him.

Did you come from a devout family?

My brothers and I grew up always attending Mass on Sundays with our parents. We went to St. Mary of the Annunciation School in Melrose, Massachusetts, and then to St. John's Preparatory School in Danvers, Massachusetts.

St. John's is an all-boys school, and I think that helped us to be better students and better athletes because we were focused on business. I've found that same concept to be true in bobsledding as well. It's a sport with a lot of travel, so having a meaningful relationship or being married is very difficult. I'm putting that on hold until after the Olympics, when I'll decide whether to go for competing in another Olympics or not.

How did you get started in bobsledding?

Throughout high school I was very much into running the 100- and 200-meter races. I enjoyed doing that, and I was even good enough to compete at Northeastern University in track-and-field. I was inspired watching the Olympics on TV with my family, but I knew that if I ever wanted to be a competitor, I'd probably have to find a different sport.

I'm the ideal height (6'3") and weight (235 pounds) for bobsledding, so that's what I ended up doing. Bobsledding is a very specialized sport, so most parts of the country don't have it available. However, I was fortunate that the Northeast was one of those places that did. I began competing in 2007 and have been doing so ever since.

Did your faith ever get you through a difficult time?

Within 12 months of the 2010 Winter Olympics in Vancouver, I had to have surgery on both my hip and my knee. I had really hoped to make the team, but two major surgeries made that look downright impossible. Despite the difficulty, I was still determined to give it my best shot.

I did what I could each day, gradually building up my strength. Amazingly, I was able to make the 2010 team. I was a little disappointed with our results once there, but the fact that I made the team at all was miraculous. In a tough and oftentimes dangerous sport like bobsledding, it's easy to be aware of the role that God has in things.

What are some of your favorite things about the Church?

I really enjoy going to Mass on Sundays because it's a way to press the "reset" button for the week and strengthen your relationship with God. Whatever your specific concerns are, you can take them to God and let him handle them. You're able to put aside all the happenings of the previous week and really focus on the things that matter most. Because of this, I always leave Sunday Mass feeling better.

I think being a practicing Catholic makes me a better athlete, because I see that, despite any setbacks, God always has a plan for my life. That fundamental belief about using one's talents wisely is accompanied by a trust in God's plan. Everyone runs into problems, but what you do with those problems is what matters. Faith in God through adversity enables you to draw closer to him.

Prayer is essential for a relationship with God. I pray in the morning and evening, and also prior to competition. I also pray informally at various points of the day, and I often use a rosary bracelet to pray at least a decade.

Do you have an overall philosophy of sports?

A lot of people try to come up with revolutionary training methods, but I think they're mostly unhelpful. You can tweak a few things here and there, but in the final analysis, there are only so many ways to train. If you focus on the basics and do those really, really well, then you're on the right path.

What is true with training methods is also true with the mindset you have, whether it's for sports or anything else. Instead of getting caught up in extraneous details or reinventing the wheel, it's better to stick to the basics. In reference to life in general, it's best to simply do what Jesus commands us to do. In John 14:15 he said, "If you love me, you'll keep my commandments."

Most of the time, it's easy to know what the right thing to do is, but the difficult part is actually doing it. That's why prayer is so important, because through praying we receive the love of God we need in order to do the things we ought to do. Prayer unites us with Christ, and we become empowered to do whatever we're called to do. This is why Philippians 4:3 is one of my favorite passages, as it is for many other athletes: "I can do all things in [Christ] who strengthens me."

God has a plan for each of us, but it's up to us to work with him on it. He expects us to invest what he has given us, and then we will see better where he wants us to go. God initiates things, but we need to respond. I hope that by preparing as well as I can, things will come out golden, but whatever happens, it's all about glorifying him.

///

SUMMER OLYMPIC HOPEFUL ASSISTS WINTER OLYMPIANS

Gymnast Matt Hicks is volunteering for the U.S.A. squad in Sochi.

February 7, 2014

Veteran gymnast **Matt Hicks** is finally going to the Olympics — the Winter Olympics. While it's not quite the realization of his childhood dream, it does come close. The 30-year-old Louisiana native is helping to ensure that America's athletes are taken care of while competing in Sochi, Russia.

Hicks still hopes to make the 2016 gymnastics squad, but for now, he is offering logistical help to his countrymen who are currently competing in hockey, skiing, bobsledding and other winter sports. Hicks sees his service as a means of helping athletes reach their God-given potential, which in turn, helps him reach his own.

Hicks, who is fluent in Russian, spoke with *Register* correspondent Trent Beattie before the 22nd Winter Olympic Games, which officially start on Feb. 7.

You're volunteering for the Winter Olympic team in Sochi. What exactly will you do?

I'll be the No. 2 guy in charge of volunteers for the American team. We'll be doing a bunch of problem-solving in order to make sure things go smoothly for the athletes. Anything that might come up, we'll be there to help out.

I will probably be using my fluency in Russian to help with translations, since I'm actually one of only two people from the group of volunteers who speaks Russian. I started learning the language in my teens because most of the great gymnastics coaches here in the States are from Russia. I thought it would be fun, not to mention useful, to learn their language.

I've been to Ukraine, the homeland of a former coach of mine, Rustam Sharipov, many times, but to Russia only once. That was in December of 2012. I got to do a lot of sightseeing then, but this time, it will be a lot of work — fun work, though. Outside of participating in the Olympics as an athlete, this is the most enjoyable thing to do from a work/career standpoint.

What do you think of the talk of boycotting the Olympics?

Some people have called for a boycott of this year's Olympics, like we did for the Summer Games in 1980. I'm not a fan of boycotting, though. That doesn't help the people it's supposed to. It only hurts the athletes and any chances they have for mending international wounds and promoting world unity. The games are one of the best means of engendering goodwill among nations, so to use them as a political punishment tool just doesn't seem productive.

You left home at 14 in order to pursue your Olympic dream. Was that difficult?

Yes and no. I moved two hours away from my home in Baton Rouge to Lake Charles, La., where there were better training facilities and coaching. Then, at age 16, I moved even farther away to Houston, Texas. There was a lot of value to these moves, since I was getting better and better at my sport. However, I don't think I ever lost the awareness of the fact that I was away from my family, which was tough.

I did have a "second family" of sorts, though, among the other gymnasts and coaches. The gymnastics community is fairly small, so we're a close-knit group. This "second family" experience was when I started to learn Russian, because my coach at the time, Vladimir Artemov, is from Russia. I thought that speaking the language of an Olympic gold medalist would make learning from him easier, and it did.

You seriously injured your back at age 18. How did that affect your outlook on life?

That injury was a real turning point in my life. I completed my flip correctly, but due to faulty boards under the floor exercise mat, I bottomed out on the concrete. There was too much "give" when I landed on it. That's when I fractured my L2 vertebrae in three places.

I went from being this hyperactive kid flying around the gym to someone who couldn't even walk without pain. I spent many hours alone, recovering. It was very painful, initially — not only from a physical standpoint, but also an emotional one. Sure, my back hurt, but my heart was in worse shape. I was suffering from not being able to work toward my Olympic goal.

Looking back, however, that injury was a great blessing — maybe one of the greatest in my life. I started to pray the Rosary and go to Mass on a daily basis. Going to Mass was about the only thing I did outside the house, and it was a humbling and enriching experience. It's not something I would have done had I not been injured, so you can see that sometimes things turn out better than they start.

It was also during this time that I was introduced to Padre Pio, a modern-day saint who was blessed with the wounds of Christ and who could bilocate. I was very impressed with this man who lived not long before I was born. That fact, in particular, really made me take a deep look at his life. Most of the time, the saints we hear about are from many centuries ago, which can make them seem out of touch. Yet Padre Pio lived among cars and airplanes and many other modern things that we have. That really got me to thinking about how holiness is meant for us today. It's not just for medieval people.

You also learned from Padre Pio how to use your suffering for a greater good.

Yes, that was a huge thing. I read books like *Padre Pio: The Wonder Worker*, and then I read a collection of his more personal letters. There was a wealth of information that guided me in my search for meaning amidst the suffering. I learned from Padre Pio about "suffering properly," which made the pain go from a major annoyance to a great gift.

I realized that everyone suffers in some way, that suffering is just a part of life in our world. No matter how hard we try, we will not be able to escape some sort of suffering; so the important thing to know is how to make good come out of it. This is done by uniting our suffering with the suffering of Jesus.

We become active participants in our own salvation and that of others when we are drawn near to Christ on the cross. Then we do what St. Paul wrote about in Colossians 1:24, "Now, I rejoice in my sufferings for your sake, and in my flesh, I am filling up what is lacking in the afflictions of Christ on behalf of his body, which is the Church."

Christ's suffering is superabundant, but it is "incomplete," in the sense that it is up to us to be drawn into it through our own suffering. It's not as if we sit back and admire what Christ did from afar, but, instead, we should see suffering for what it is: an opportunity to grow closer to him and to become more helpful to our neighbor.

A year after the back injury occurred, I was able to like the person I became. It was a trying time, but that's what made it all the better. It seemed like I was living as a Christian should live, amidst the trials of life. It's like in Sirach 2:4-6, where it says, "Accept whatever befalls you; in crushing misfortune be patient. For in fire gold is tested and worthy men in the crucible of humiliation. Trust God, and he will help you; make straight your ways and hope in him."

What are you doing outside of Winter Olympics volunteering?

I'm attending the Monterey Institute of International Studies in Monterey, Calif. I'm completing my master's degree in public administration, which I'd like to use one day by working for the United States Olympic Committee in Colorado Springs, Colo.

They have outstanding training facilities in Colorado Springs, which I was able to utilize during the four years I lived there. Once my competitive days are over, I'd like to be a part of the administrative side of things and help lead America's next generation of athletes. In the meantime, I'm still going to try one more time for the 2016 Olympic gymnastics team.

Helping the Winter Olympics athletes is a great mental preparation for that. You get to see what they go through and be a part of it. You're standing shoulder-to-shoulder with your countrymen in pursuit of athletic excellence. It's great to help others reach their God-given potential, which can only help each of us to reach our own.

OLYMPIC GOLD MEDALIST SHARES SOCHI EXPERIENCE

Bobsledder Curt Tomasevicz recounts his awesome adventures on the ice.

March 11, 2014

Curt Tomasevicz's illustrious bobsledding career includes three World Championship gold medals and one Olympic gold medal. However, the medal he appreciates most may be the bronze one he and his teammates won in Sochi on Feb. 23.

Because the competition was much greater this year than in years past, Tomasevicz sees tremendous value where others more cynical see only a third-best finish.

The Shelby, Neb., native's sights have always had a special character to them, looking beyond outward appearances to an object's deeper meaning. Tomasevicz has been interested in the importance of church architecture and liturgical practices since his days as an altar boy. He maintained that curiosity during his college days at the University of Nebraska, where he was a linebacker on the football team from 2000-2003. His curiosity for all things Catholic continued throughout his bobsledding career, which, after many triumphs, has likely come to a close.

Tomasevicz recently spoke of his athletic endeavors in light of his long-standing Catholic faith with *Register* correspondent Trent Beattie.

You competed for the U.S. in the 2006 Olympic Games in Turin, Italy, and in the 2010 Games in Vancouver, Canada. How did your Sochi experience compare with those in Turin and Vancouver?

Each year had a very different feel to it. In the 2006 Turin Games, I had only been competing in the sport of bobsledding for about a year and a half, so it was great to make the Olympic team that quickly. Just representing your country for the first time is an incredible experience, regardless of anything else that happens. From a competition standpoint, it was a wonderful learning experience to go up against the best bobsledders in the world. Curiously, though, the stands for the events were oftentimes half full, which was out of character for the Olympics. It was like the people in the area weren't aware of what was going on. One thing I was very aware of outside the games was the art, architecture and history of the area. Especially from a Catholic standpoint, there were tons of examples of this. There were just too many paintings, churches and stories of saints to count.

In Vancouver in 2010, it was almost like being at home. It was just above the border in Canada, the language was the same, and there were many American spectators. That's where we won the gold medal in the four-man event, so, of course, that was memorable.

This year in Sochi the experience was remarkable as well. Despite security, housing and cultural concerns going into it, the guys I was around had a rewarding time. Inevitably, there are going to be some bumps in the road with an event of such magnitude, especially when it's so far from your own country. Yet in our experience, any problems that came up were taken care of quickly.

What about the competition in Sochi?

It was awesome. From the time we won the gold in 2010 to when we just won the bronze, the competition had gotten so much better. In 2010, it was basically Germany vs. the U.S., but this time, any one of six countries could have won the gold. Germany, the U.S., Latvia, Russia, Switzerland — even Great Britain — were all contenders. We won the bronze by three one-hundredths of a second in a very competitive field, so we're very happy about that.

Bobsledding is not a very popular sport in the U.S., so how did you first get involved in it?

I knew in my senior year [at the University of Nebraska] that I wasn't quite NFL material, but I still wanted to compete in something. That's when I was introduced to bobsledding, which turned out to be what I'd use over the next almost decade to develop my God-given abilities.

How does your faith affect your performance as an athlete?

I wouldn't be the athlete I am today without my background, where I learned self-discipline and developed the ability to maintain composure when competitive situations are tough. Everything around you might be going crazy, but when you've maintained a prayer life and sacramental life, you can be secure in what you're doing.

Was your Catholic faith always a part of your life?

Yes. Most of the town of Shelby is Catholic, so the faith has been there for me from the start. When your life is centered around the Church, like it was for me in Shelby, it gives you the solid foundation you need. You can trust your neighbors, who are more like extended family than strangers who happen to live near you. Then at the University of Nebraska, the Catholic players had the opportunity to go to Mass before every football game. This was a much-appreciated gift, since college games are usually on Saturdays. It wasn't as if we were obliged to go to Mass, like we would be on a Sunday, but the opportunity to go was still offered to us.

My faith also played a role in my academic minor, which was astronomy. The Church has a long history of supporting science, especially astronomy. A Catholic from Poland, Nicolaus Copernicus, first developed the idea that the earth rotated around the sun, which is known as heliocentrism. Blaise Pascal, Gregor Mendel (a priest) and Louis Pasteur are some other remarkable examples of Catholics who have made valuable advances in science. It's easy to see that if you take creation to be a good thing, which the Church does, then studying that creation is also good, as long as it respects the laws of God and dignity of man.

What are some other aspects of the Church you appreciate?

I'm grateful for how the Church has consistently kept its moral teachings over the centuries. Some people want the Church to become more liberal, but there's priceless value in the Church's conservative character. Yes, the specifics of what we know on a natural level can develop, but that serves to strengthen, not diminish, the Church's message about our basic human dignity. One example of this is in embryology, where the advances in ultrasound have shown more and more clearly that the unborn child is just that — a child, a magnificent creation of God that is owed respect. That's what true science gives us: a greater, more vibrant understanding of what it means to be human.

Another thing I'm grateful for, especially in light of my Polish heritage, is the pontificate of John Paul II. I was born in 1980, so he had always been the leader of the Church for me. He knew the importance of young people, and he had the ability to communicate very well with them. This was formative for me as I grew up and learned more about being Catholic.

A third thing I'm grateful for is the Church's architecture and the other ways it uses material objects to point to God. I was an altar boy at Sacred Heart Church in Shelby from third grade through high school, and I would ask questions about the incense, the colors of liturgical vestments and other things. The liturgy is not hastily assembled; it's methodically planned out, with every material aspect having a spiritual meaning. All these objects are "housed" in the church-building structure, which itself has meaning. Ideally, it is a vehicle for promoting the teachings of the Church, so you have stained-glass windows and other things that reveal the life of Christ in a beautiful way that anyone can understand.

What are your plans now that the Olympics are over?

Well, there are about 15 different directions my life could go, but one thing I do know is that my days competing in bobsledding are probably over. I've traveled the world and done everything that can be done in the sport — in some cases, many times over. I'm grateful for that, and, now, I'll most likely be transitioning into something new, at least somewhat so. It may be coaching. I'll be getting away soon and spending time in solitude, thinking about my future. Growing up in a small town helps you to understand the value of silence and reflection, so I plan on using those gifts — and my tattered prayer book — to discern where God wants me to go. The future may include pursuing a Ph.D., getting married or any number of other things.

One thing I will do for sure is travel back to Europe. I'll be going to Italy this summer with my mom to see some of the same things I did at the Olympics in 2006. We'll also go to other parts of the country and other countries as well. That should be a great cultural — but most of all, spiritual — experience.

///

OUTLAWING THE NATURAL LAW

A world-renowned Catholic doctor warns
of the new assault on human dignity and talks about
prayer's medical "side effects," his debates with
Jack Kevorkian and how to prevent Alzheimer's.

January 7, 2011

Dr. Vincent Fortanasce knows the field of medicine as well as anyone. He has studied psychiatry at Yale, neurology at the University of Southern California and orthopedic rehabilitation at Rancho Los Amigos Hospital, one of the top rehab centers in the country. He has spent decades treating thousands of patients, including world-class athletes and celebrities.

Many people have become familiar with Fortanasce by reading bestselling books, the most recent of which is *The Anti-Alzheimer's Prescription*, released in 2008. Others know him from his shows on bioethics for St. Joseph Radio Presents. He fought against California's pro-embryonic stem-cell research Proposition 71 and has debated assisted-suicide advocate Jack Kevorkian.

Over the course of his 30-plus years in medicine, Fortanasce has seen immoral practices such as abortion legalized, but now has an even greater concern — immoral practices being made mandatory. His warning: Natural law may be outlawed if those who care about it do not fight.

You went from high-level athletics to the medical profession. You seem to have always been interested in the workings of the human body.

Yes, I've been interested in the workings of the human body all my life. My father encouraged that in me. He was a New York state handball champion and my Little League coach in 1952 on Long Island, which was one of the first Little League teams.

My father even helped me to coach my own sons for their Little League teams in the 1980s.

My own childhood interest in sports carried on to college, when I attended Seton Hall University and played third base on their baseball team. I also won a gold medal in weightlifting at the 1961 Junior Olympics and was an alternate member of the 1964 U.S. Olympic team.

I actually studied for the priesthood for about five years, but did not continue with that. Instead, I studied psychiatry, and in doing so, I realized that I was more interested in how I liked physical medicine more than mental medicine. That's what led me into neurology and orthopedic rehabilitation. The way physical things affect how our minds function is a fascinating thing.

What can you tell the skeptic who thinks that the Church's teachings on the dignity of human life are somehow inconsistent with modern medical science?

You simply cannot be a scientist without believing in God. How can our marvelous universe — and within it, the human body, which is so intricate — how can these things even exist without a Creator? It's just not possible for such amazing things to come about from mere chance. There has to be a Supreme Being, and this Being cannot contradict himself. He would not reveal something to us which would go against the natural world he created.

The Church's teachings on the dignity of human life fit in exactly with medical science. In fact, we would be in a bad position if we didn't heed the Church's teachings on human life. That's where a lot of the world is today, because they won't let the Creator into his own creation. We do have free will, but only in conforming our will with the will of the One who created us can we function physically, mentally and spiritually as we ought.

There are even physical benefits to prayer and forgiveness, for example. It's God's way of rewarding us through our human nature, of spurring us on to do more good. If we're petty and negative, that has a negative physiological correspondence to it which harms our bodies. On the other hand, being magnanimous and positive also has a physiological correspondence, but in that case, it's beneficial to us.

When we pray, there is a specific response from the body. It starts in the neocortex area of the brain with a willful decision to pray. Then a series of events occurs, including activity in the frontal inferior gyrus, or the "optimistic center" of the brain. This slows down adrenaline production and leads to relaxation of the nervous system. Blood pressure decreases and our muscles relax. Simultaneously, the part of the brain called the hypothalamus is engaged. This produces dopamine and seratonin, or the "feel-good" neurotransmitters.

When these two neurotransmitters are abundant, our stress reactions change. Exterior stressors do not elicit panic, but an "it's okay" reaction. Panic would correspond with overproduction of adrenaline, which, as we saw, doesn't happen when praying.

This gives scientific backing to James 5:13, which reads: "Is any one of you sad? Let him pray."

Yes, prayer is a gift from God which enables us to gain a foretaste of impassibility of the saints in heaven. Nothing can harm a soul in heaven, and in a certain way, although not exactly the same, nothing can harm a soul on earth that prays consistently. This is due not only to invisible realities, but also to material ones that occur physiologically. God constantly works through secondary causes, so this shouldn't be a surprise to us.

Depression is correlated to low levels of serotonin and dopamine, which is the basis of anti-depressant drugs. These drugs artificially increase serotonin and dopamine levels, thereby relieving depression. Studies have shown that prayer can do the same thing, and without any negative side effects. Along with exercise, prayer vitalizes the "optimistic center" of the brain and enables us to deal well with the challenges of life.

Health care has been a topic of much discussion recently. What are some of the basic principles that should guide our views and decisions in this matter?

This is my real specialty: medical ethics. What we have to do is keep the doctor-patient relationship in the forefront. That's what medicine is all about: treating and healing human beings. The problem comes in when organizations like health maintenance organizations (HMOs) operate; they are most vigilant about the costs. This leaves the doctor-patient relationship to deteriorate.

We don't need far-away, number-crunching bureaucrats to make decisions for us that limit treatment options. What we need is to have caring, compassionate doctors who take the time to treat patients as individuals. Patients are not burdens or costs that need to be dealt with or even dispatched; they're human beings with dignity that need to be accepted and treated as such.

We should not reward individual doctors on the basis of not giving patients care. This is what HMOs do: The doctors who cost them the least get the highest bonuses at the end of the year. This is obviously not how health care should work; doctors should not be getting bonuses for frugality in treatment, but bonuses for effective and compassionate care.

Another problem is that organizations which have been reliable in the past are now failing us. For example, the American Medical Association has lost its soul. The AMA is now led by those unwilling to reason about morality and commonsense science. They endorse [human] embryonic stem-cell and cloning research, which means the destruction of innocent human lives. This is exactly the opposite of what medicine is about. We're called to heal, not to kill, and physicians — especially Catholic ones — need to stand up and do something about it. The National Catholic Bioethics Center's website has opportunities for us to do just that.

Are there any specific bioethics issues that need to be addressed more than others?

A commonsense question to ask in health care is: "What is best for the patient?" With children specifically, the question is: "What is best for the child?" We can list all kinds of things that are good: no diabetes, no allergies, no cancer, etc. The next question becomes: "Should we treat the child before birth or after birth?" I believe the AMA leadership will say that it's best to do so before birth and that we should use pre-genetic selection and eugenics to do so.

This is immoral because pre-genetic selection uses in-vitro fertilization techniques, part of which is the abuse of multiple embryos. The embryos that have genetic predispositions to specific diseases are destroyed — murdered — because they don't meet the eugenic standards. The healthy ones are implanted, and then we have kids with "good genes."

What makes this especially dangerous is that, unlike embryonic stem-cell research, there will be actual results, or healthy babies. So we have to ask why we can't do something that will produce a good. No evil can be done for a possible good, but that will be difficult to convince people of when they see the good in front of them but not the evil that has been done in the lab to the human embryo, or humans in their most vulnerable stage.

I believe that the biotechnology industry will use the AMA to *force* the use of pre-genetic screening. This will be done under the banner of "compassion for children." Those who object will be labeled as cruel and could be jailed for noncompliance. There is legal precedent for this with Jehovah's Witnesses, who object to blood transfusions. Anyone who objects to "compassion for children" could be jailed, which includes faithful Catholics. This is outlawing the natural law, plain and simple.

Through eugenics it is possible to have people who are stronger, more intelligent, etc., but we have to ask ourselves, "Do these traits make us better humans or somehow more *human*?" Instead of increasing brains or brawn, how about increasing compassion? Instead of heavy-handedly manipulating genetics, we should be enhancing compassion through the way we treat each other. We should be teaching children the immense value of the Golden Rule: "Do unto others as you would have them do unto you."

What are some of the best resources for the layperson to read that integrate sound science with Church teaching on life issues?

Believe it or not, one of them is my own book *Life Lessons From Little League*. In the book we explain how conscience is formed, how you can help a young person understand how he fits in with the rest of society. For example, if you just punish a kid for throwing a bat, he might not necessarily learn from it. But if you explain to him why throwing a bat is dangerous, how it can injure someone else, etc., then he makes the connection with himself and how he should treat others. The Golden Rule applies here.

When we have a solid moral foundation to draw on, all the challenges that come with new medical techniques are really

284 /// FIT FOR HEAVEN

quite simple. It's when there's no foundation, or a shaky one, then all the problems come in. Abortion, embryonic stem-cell research, assisted suicide and the like may be seen as "necessary evils" or even as goods. This is what happened in Nazi Germany and what has happened in our own country with abortion specifically, and we're headed in that direction with the other issues.

Wesley J. Smith writes very well, and one of his books is called *Culture of Death: The Assault on Medical Ethics in America*. There are also shows I've done on pre-genetic selection and other important topics for St. Joseph Radio Presents.

You've debated assisted-suicide proponent Jack Kevorkian. What stands out in your mind from these debates?

Jack Kevorkian was really after people at the end of life whom he called "useless," people whom he thought could be made useful by donating organs. Criminals on death row and Alzheimer's patients fit into this category of people no longer considered as people, but merely as animals. They would die anyway, Kevorkian thought, so why not make use of them?

This is done through "medicide," or killing people to make medical use of them, which is what the Nazis did. When German doctors were asked how they could participate in the Nazi eugenic projects, they gave the same answer in three parts. The first reason was the Jews were not people, the second reason was they would die anyway, and the third was that we should make use of them.

It's not okay to kill people with Alzheimer's, but we can take away some of the steam from people who think it is okay by reducing the number of Alzheimer's cases. Simply by postponing the onset of the disease by five years through my program, we can cut in half the number of people who have it.

Before reading your book, **The Anti-Alzheimer's Prescription,** *most people probably would not have thought of Alzheimer's disease as being largely preventable. What are the fundamentals of that prevention?*

The basis of the book is what we call the D.E.A.R. Program. The "D" is for diet, "E" for exercise, "A" for accentuating brain reserves, and the "R" is for rest and recovery.

Diet is very important for preventing Alzheimer's and for being healthy in general. We should be eating foods high in antioxidants, omega-3 fatty acids and folate. That means fresh fruits and vegetables, fish, lean meats, nuts, whole grains, olive oil and dairy products. Then the proportions of what we eat, and what we eat first, is important as well.

Exercise is also important, in that it helps to build a stronger, smarter brain by increasing brain mass and capacity and increases the body's metabolism. Aerobic and anaerobic exercise help to reduce stress and incidence of hypertension, diabetes and depression.

In addition to a physical workout, we need to give ourselves a mental workout, which accentuates brain reserves. No matter how old we get, we can continue to rewire our brains by growing new neurons and dendrites. This can be done by learning new things, such as a foreign language, or for men, learning your wife's birthday.

Stress is a big problem today, and if it goes unchecked, it can actually mean the destruction of the brain. We need to learn how to rest and relax, sleeping more and simply enjoying life. The serenity prayer is valuable here in learning what we do have control over and what we don't — and also what we should be changing and what you should not. Most of us will find we need to meditate more, enhance our other religious practices, listen to good music, laugh and actually enjoy things rather than constantly thinking about what we have to do next.

The D.E.A.R. Program greatly helps to reduce the chances of Alzheimer's and encourages overall health and enjoyment of life. We'll be filming a 12-part series for EWTN later this year, which is related to the program. It centers on the connection between faith and health, the neurochemistry of the soul, or what I call "grace-amine."

Do you have a patron saint?

Yes, my patron saint is St. Anthony of Padua. In fact, all six of my children are named Anthony. That is, all of their middle names are Anthony.

///

THE HEALING OF A FOOTBALL PLAYER'S WOUNDED HEART

Former quarterback finds peace of soul in the Mass, priesthood and intercession of St. Joseph.

April 27, 2012

The 49th World Day of Prayer for Vocations will be celebrated this Sunday, April 29, with the theme "Vocations, the Gift of the Love of God." This theme is very close to the heart of **Father Joseph Freedy,** director of priestly vocations for the Diocese of Pittsburgh.

There was a time when such a concept was distant from his heart, which had been set on worldly goods. He was a standout quarterback in high school and at the University of Buffalo. Thousands cheered him on and looked up to him, but his heart remained restless. Despite his earnest attempts to the contrary, he could not find happiness in the noise of the world.

Happiness would be found where he had not expected it: in the Mass. After reading The Lamb's Supper: The Mass as Heaven on Earth by Scott Hahn, what was once seen as a burdensome routine was revealed to be just what Joseph Freedy's heart was seeking. His understanding of the Mass was so changed that he went to the seminary. On June 21, 2008, he was ordained a priest.

Father Freedy spoke with *Register* correspondent Trent Beattie.

You recently got back from a silent retreat. Would you recommend such a retreat to others?

Absolutely. Blessed Teresa of Calcutta always said that prayer is "God speaking in the silence of our hearts and us listening." With the amount of noise in our world today, it really is necessary at times to get away from it in order to be able to connect with God on a deeper level. His voice most often can be heard not in the noise of the world, but in the silence of the heart. In Psalm 46, the Lord says, "Be still and know that I am God." Then in the New Testament we see that Jesus is frequently going away to a solitary place to pray.

Sometimes when I start my annual retreat, which is required for priests, it takes a couple days to settle down and get into it. It can be a struggle initially, but by the time it's over, the feeling I have is often one of wanting to stay there forever.

There are many types of retreats out there, but I find that I am disposed best to receive the grace the Lord desires to give on a silent retreat. There's a time for faith sharing and fellowship, but there's also a time to be silent and allow the Lord to be the only voice speaking in our hearts.

It's about getting closer to the Lord and allowing him to speak to your heart. A retreat is basically an extraordinary manifestation of what we should be doing daily in prayer.

Did you want to be a priest as a young boy?

I was raised in a solid Catholic home in which we regularly had incredible priest friends over for dinner. For us, priests weren't just people you'd only see at Mass, but you'd also see them around the house with your family. As a young boy, I was fascinated by these men and impressed with their exciting lives. Unconsciously, I looked up to them as one would do with an uncle. The call was there from a young age, but it was latent.

Then football came into the picture.

In western Pennsylvania, football is a very big deal, so playing wasn't anything out of the ordinary. My two older brothers played the game, so I followed suit.

However, I took football too seriously, building my whole identity around it and using it as a means to fill an interior void. I dealt with a lot of insecurity growing up. I had a great family, so I don't know why that insecurity was there, but from seventh grade through high school and even into college I wanted, even needed, to be the kid I thought everyone wanted me to be.

Religion was put on the back burner, and I tried to overcome the insecurity with praise and acceptance from everyone around me. I was a standout player in high school and then played at the University of Buffalo. During high school and into the first couple of years in college, partying was common for me as well. That was another thing I used in an attempt to fill the void within me.

However, something that helped to lead me into growing up and becoming a man was taking on the responsibility of leading the football team in college. I was not the starting quarterback initially, but because of a series of injuries to the guys ahead of me, I assumed the starting position for the 1999 season. Being the leader of a football team in Buffalo, where the sport is also taken seriously, was a way to start looking beyond myself and become more serious about life.

What were the other things that enabled you to do that?

In college, I got caught up in the garbage of the party scene, but through becoming the starting quarterback and being in a serious relationship with a girl for a few years, the Lord helped to pull me out of some of that.

Then, a third thing that helped me grow up and really changed my life forever was reading a great book when I was home from college for Christmas break. My father would always have a Bible on the end table, along with another book. He would read from them before going to work each morning. Well, the book he happened to have there when I was on break was *The Lamb's Supper* by Scott Hahn.

The opening paragraph really caught my eye because of how it related to my own life. It basically said that, on the one hand, nothing is so familiar to Catholics as the Mass, yet most of us don't know what is beyond the surface of the memorized prayers. That really described my experience. I had attended Mass all my life but had never really looked beyond the outward appearances. Once I did look beyond them, I was drawn in by what was there.

My heart began to be filled with peace, joy and love. It was similar to St. Augustine's experience, in that he had looked all over for happiness, but, only years later, realized that it was right in front of him. It was right there all along. My heart's deepest longing would be satisfied in the Mass like I had never thought possible.

What did you do next?

After reading *The Lamb's Supper*, I went back to school and wanted to go deeper into my faith and share what I had learned. I went to a group called Fellowship of Christian Athletes, but, at the time, I found many of the ideas the group discussed to be in opposition to what I was taught as a Catholic.

Then I went before the Lord in the Blessed Sacrament and asked him what to do. I spent a lot of time with the Lord, wrestling with him as far as what his plan for me was. On the one hand, I was beginning to be so much happier than before, but, on the other hand, I was at first very reluctant to really let go of my own designs on life and pursue the priesthood.

I met with a vocations director, and he gently encouraged me to surrender to God's plan for my life. God knows what's best for us infinitely better than we do, so the intelligent thing to do is let him guide us.

After you surrendered to this call, you studied at the Pontifical North American College in Rome. What was that like?

It was an incredible experience. My first year there (2005) was the year Blessed Pope John Paul II died. There was his enormous funeral, which attracted attention from around the world. Then we welcomed our new Holy Father, Pope Benedict XVI. What a blessing both men are to the Church.

During my time there, I got to see that the city of Rome is saturated with grace — so much history, so many saints, so many visible testaments to the Christian faith. It was a great faith-building experience I'm so grateful for.

I also got to travel outside of Rome, and it was really an eye-opening thing to witness the truly universal character of the Church. Regardless of where you are in the world, it is one Catholic Church we belong to.

What do you appreciate most about the priesthood?

I could talk for an hour about this. The thing that's most amazing is acting *in persona Christi* — or "in the person of Christ." This is what occurs in confession, when the priest says not "Jesus absolves you," but "*I* absolve you." It also occurs in the Mass, when the priest says not "This is Jesus' body," but "This is *my* body."

The priest is the mediator between God and men, which is an unbelievably beautiful and profound thing: God is calling me to do this. It's so great that it's difficult not to cry when thinking about it. Sometimes I have cried even while acting *in persona Christi* because I'm struck with the love God has for his people. The humility of God to allow mere men to act in the person of the Only Begotten Son is an amazing thing.

To know that my hands have been anointed to bring the body and blood of Christ to the world and to forgive sins — what an indescribable blessing. The gift of the priesthood is overwhelming. I've been ordained for almost four years now and have never had an unhappy day as a priest. Praise God for that.

You're currently the director of priestly vocations for the Diocese of Pittsburgh. What are some of the challenges you face in that position?

I've been doing this for two years now, and it's an incredible joy. There are challenges, though, to building a culture of vocations. Perhaps the biggest one is convincing young people that God is alive and real and has a perfect plan for our lives. He has prepared a vocation for each and every one of us from all eternity.

It's the concept expressed in Jeremiah 1:5: that before God formed us in the womb, he knew us. Our lives are not accidents, but perfectly prepared and provided for by God. I'm so content knowing that I'm doing what I was born to do, and I want others to know that contentment as well by helping them to realize their own calls.

What advice do you give to young men who are discerning a call to the priesthood?

There are three essential things I mention, and all of them lead us closer to God. The first is prayer. You simply have to pray every day; otherwise, you're not going to have the grace to do God's will.

292 /// FIT FOR HEAVEN

Praying as a child in need of his father's help is what enables us to live our daily lives in peace.

What I tell young men regarding a possible priestly vocation is to pray over the calls recorded in the Bible. That is, meditate upon the call of Abraham, of David, of Jeremiah, of St. Peter, of St. Paul. Look into the history of how God calls men to his service and pray about whether this is something God is calling you to as well.

The second thing that is incredibly helpful is Eucharistic adoration, which can be seen as a specific form or occurrence of prayer. It's talking with Jesus in his direct presence. The same Jesus who walked the earth 2,000 years ago is still with us today in the Eucharist. Prayer before the Lord is something very special.

The third essential thing is to stay close to Our Lady. John Paul II wrote that all vocations occur with a Marian disposition at the Annunciation. In other words, we may not have been planning on a specific calling, but when we know God is calling us, we have to be receptive to that and put it into action with love.

There is also a book I like to recommend to young men discerning a priestly vocation. It's called *To Save a Thousand Souls* by Father Brett A. Brannen.

Do you have a patron saint?

St. Joseph is my patron. He was the most chaste spouse of Our Lady and the foster father of Jesus. How amazing is that? As the protector and head of the Holy Family, he is a prime example of what a man in general, and what a priest specifically, should be. This is explained in the book *The Life and Glories* of *St. Joseph* by Father Edward Healy Thompson.

St. Teresa of Avila had great admiration for St. Joseph and said that anyone who was having trouble praying should take him as a guide. She received many benefits from him and wanted to share his powerful intercession with everyone else. I understand her desire because, like the Holy Spirit, St. Joseph is often overlooked today. If we learned more about St. Joseph and became more devoted to him, we would come much closer to being the men God called us to be. We would be totally dedicated to Jesus and Mary.

///

LOU HOLTZ ON MARRIAGE, HIS CATHOLIC FAITH AND NOTRE DAME

Register *"In Person"* interview
with the Hall of Fame coach.

September 26, 2012

As college football nears the midpoint of its 143rd season, **Lou Holtz** is among the many taking it in. The 75-year-old ESPN analyst has seen more than his share of games, mostly from the sidelines as a head coach. He coached a total of 388 games at six Division I schools.

Holtz is best known for his years at the University of Notre Dame, between 1986 and 1996, which include an undefeated national championship season in 1988. What is less known, but no less important to him, are the experiences that prepared him for the Notre Dame years.

One of the things Holtz prizes most is the education he received, fittingly enough from the Sisters of Notre Dame, while in grade school in East Liverpool, Ohio. He also appreciates the more than half century he has spent with his wife. And, most important of all, he appreciates being Catholic.

Holtz recently explained this and other things to *Register* correspondent Trent Beattie.

You've spoken glowingly of the religious sisters who taught you in grade school. How did they influence your life?

The Sisters of Notre Dame at St. Aloysius Grade School influenced my life tremendously. This was due to the fact that they encouraged you always to make sure that God is the focus of your life, and they didn't allow you to do anything except to the very best of your ability.

When this is passed on to you in your formative years, I can't begin to tell you how important it is. I owe the good sisters so much for what they taught me and will be forever grateful for their selfless dedication.

In high school you asked God to make you a great athlete, but you were guided into coaching instead. Do you think that if you'd become a great athlete, you never would have become a great coach — and that maybe coaching was a way for you to become more selfless?

I used to pray that God would make me a great athlete, and he never did. Yet he put me in the coaching profession, where I've experienced 45 years of being involved in great games and competitiveness and having a positive influence on other people's lives. Had I been a great athlete, I'm not sure I would have even gone into coaching. I may have turned out feeling that my life ended when my athletic career ended, as happens so many times with various athletes.

I do know this: God does answer your prayers, but it's not always in the way you expect. God knows what's best for us, though, so there's no need to worry when things don't go how we originally wanted them to go. We just have to be willing to make changes and go a different route sometimes.

What are your top memories from Notre Dame?

Impossible to answer. Every single day being there was very special because there were so many opportunities to encounter and live out the Catholic faith. Mass and confession were always available, and you could pray the Rosary at the Grotto of Our Lady of Lourdes, which is a smaller-sized replica of the original in France.

If I had to give some top memories, though, I guess they would be having three of my four children graduate from that fine university and then one of them getting a second degree from the law school. Just being on campus and being able to represent Notre Dame through football are great memories, but I think the statue they built of me and dedicated in 2008 has to rank up there as well. That was a very humbling experience.

You've been married for more than 50 years. What do you value most about marriage?

I appreciate my wife, Beth, so much. She has been there through good times and bad, and no one has been more supportive of me. Her loving attention and candor have helped me more than I can say. We've always done things as a team, not just me going my own way. That's essential if you want your marriage to work, and ours has for many years. It has been more than 50, thanks be to God.

You've stated that if something wouldn't bother you on your deathbed, it shouldn't bother you right now when it actually is happening. Has that belief brought more peace of mind to you?

That's a great perspective to live life with, similar to the serenity prayer. It's helpful for anyone, but maybe in a special way for coaches. Coaches can get too focused on results and winning, so it's good to step back and let go of things a little bit. I just try to change the things I can, accept the things I can't, and pray I have the wisdom to know the difference between the two.

I follow three rules: Do the right thing, do the best you can, and always show people you care. You've got to make a sincere attempt to have the right goals to begin with, then go after them with appropriate effort, and remember that you can't really achieve anything great without the help of others.

Another way of seeing it is that anything great you do achieve will be for others, in the sense that helping other people realize their potential is what achieving is all about. It's not a one-man show; it's about contributing to the good of the team. That's how you have to see it.

Our perspective in life is so important, and this was reinforced by my experience with the New York Jets in 1976. That was one of the best coaching jobs in the country at the time — and, yet, I didn't take advantage of it because of my own attitude. I came into it seeing problems instead of opportunities, and this prevented me from getting the most out of the team.

Everyone goes through adversity in life, but what matters is how you learn from it. I like to say that life is 10% what happens to you and 90% how you respond to it. I did learn from the Jets experience, and it really helped me in subsequent years with other teams.

You've stated there's nothing the Catholic Church teaches that you don't believe. Do you think many people are rudderless, in that they accept only some Church teachings and not others?

I think life is a matter of choices and that wherever we are, good or bad, is because of choices we make. If you choose to do drugs, drop out of school, join a gang or have five children out of wedlock, you're choosing to end up in prison or in poverty, and that is not a result of choices I made, but of choices you made. We need to get back to holding people accountable for their choices, and that includes people in the Catholic Church.

I think the Catholic Church is infallible when it comes to religious principles [on faith and morals]. That's what I was taught by the Sisters of Notre Dame growing up, and I believe that to this day. Do I agree with the practical decisions of Church leaders on some things? Certainly not. But, by the same token, I try to follow the Catholic teachings. That's what brings meaning and lasting happiness to life.

///

GERRY FAUST ON MOTHER MARY AND HIS DAYS AT NOTRE DAME

January 6, 2013

With their defeat of USC on Nov. 24, the University of Notre Dame football team finished the regular season undefeated for the first time since 1988.

This has garnered the team even more attention than usual, bringing to mind past Fighting Irish records and coaches. **Gerry Faust** is one former coach who has many stories to tell from his days at Notre Dame. After an extraordinarily successful career at Archbishop Moeller High School in Cincinnati, he was catapulted directly into the head coaching job at Notre Dame in 1981.

Faust learned from his football experiences at Notre Dame in large part because of his devotion to the Blessed Mother. He spoke with the *Register* prior to 12-0 Notre Dame's Jan. 7 game with the University of Alabama (12-1) for the national title. At press time, the game had not been played.

What do you think of this year's squad at Notre Dame?

What's not to like? They've played very hard and have done very well. It's been a tremendous season, and they're looking to continue that success on Jan. 7 against Alabama. Everyone would like to be undefeated the whole way through a season and win a bowl game, but it doesn't happen all that often.

A good number of your teams at Archbishop Moeller High School in the 1960s and '70s were undefeated. What made them so successful?

We had a great coaching staff, great kids, great parents and an outstanding school. The staff was interested in the kids, the kids were dedicated to their schoolwork and play, and the parents oftentimes sacrificed to keep their kids in a Catholic school. The principals and administration at Moeller were also great. The main thing underlying all of that was the Catholic identity of the school. We were Catholics first, and everything else grew out of that.

You coached U.S. Speaker of the House John Boehner in the late 1960s at Moeller. What do you remember about him?

John came from an outstanding family with 11 brothers and sisters. It was one of those large Catholic families that you don't see as often today. It was a great family, and they had an influence on John, because he was an excellent person and football player. He was an unselfish player as a linebacker and long-snapper. He was into the good of the team, which isn't surprising when you have a large "team" at home.

I enjoyed coaching John in the late '60s and remember him well. We've kept in touch over the years, as I've done with many of my players. I'm very pleased to say I know John, not because he's speaker of the House, but because he's a good Catholic man. He still has the team-centered mentality in which ego is sacrificed for the good of others. He's a family man, someone dedicated to the dignity of human life in all its stages, and someone who wants to see our country do better.

Most high-school coaches don't go directly to head coaching positions in college. How were you selected as head coach of Notre Dame in 1981?

Growing up in Dayton, Ohio, I wanted to attend Notre Dame more than any other school. As it turned out, I wasn't quite good enough to make their football team, so I attended the University of Dayton and loved it. I started at quarterback in my junior and senior years, but Notre Dame never left the back of my mind. In fact, my coach at Dayton was a former Notre Dame coach.

After graduating, I taught and coached at Chaminade High School in Dayton for two years. Then I was offered the job as head football coach of a new Catholic high school in Cincinnati, Archbishop Moeller. Over the years, 26 of our Moeller kids would end up playing for Notre Dame. That's an amazing number of players to come from one high school.

In 1977, I actually wrote a letter to Father Edmund Joyce, executive vice president of Notre Dame, telling him that if he ever needed a head coach, I'd be happy to help him out. Father replied that they weren't in need of a new coach then, but he did thank me for sending so many great young men to Notre Dame. Notice he said they were not just great players, but great young men.

I went to the Notre Dame spring game in 1980 with my wife, Marlene, and our three kids. Before the game, we went to the Grotto, which was very crowded. When enough room opened up, we knelt down at the railing and prayed to the Blessed Mother. Then I got up and lit eight candles — seven for my family and also one for me, that I would get to coach one day at Notre Dame. I promised that if I became head coach there, I would visit the Grotto every day.

Head coach Dan Devine stepped aside after the 1980 season, and I was offered the job. I was told it would be the toughest job in America, but I said it would be the greatest job in America. I was thankful to be there, and every day I was at Notre Dame I went to the Grotto to pray to the Blessed Mother, just as I had promised. Even to this day, every time I go to South Bend, Ind., I stop at the Grotto to thank the Blessed Mother for interceding on my behalf with Christ, her Son.

People sometimes wonder why we ask for Mary's prayers. It's similar to what happened to me as a child. I would ask my dad for something, and he would say, "No." Then I asked my mom, who in turn asked my dad, who then say, "Yes." Sometimes mothers have a way of getting things for their children that they otherwise would not have gotten. Our imperfections are overlooked when our intentions are presented to Christ by his immaculate Mother.

You had a good but not spectacular record at Notre Dame (30-26-1). There's pressure at Notre Dame to be spectacular, though.

There is pressure. I knew that going in, and our teams experienced that. They wanted to win so much for Notre Dame, which added more pressure, and that hurt them at times. About 17 of the losses in my years at Notre Dame were by eight points or less, so sometimes it was mental mistakes at key times rather than just being outplayed.

After beating LSU twice in the previous four years, including when they were ranked No. 6, we played them at home at the end of the 1985 season. It was a close game, and we were about to go ahead in the fourth quarter. Our QB, Steve Beuerlein, threw a pass to Tim Brown, who had his hands on the ball, but looked to see the opening for the end zone. The ball tipped off his hands, and then LSU intercepted it, eventually winning the game 10-7.

After the game, I was told Tim was in the locker room crying. He blamed himself for the loss. When I got to Timmy, he was very upset. He told me that if he made that catch, we would have won. I told him the loss was my fault, that if I had made a few better calls during the game, he wouldn't have been in that tight position at the end of the game. I decided to step down as head coach, and, shortly after that, I went to Father Joyce. He was very much into the good of Notre Dame football, but also felt badly for me. When I resigned, he thanked me and actually hugged me. We both had tears in our eyes.

What was your favorite moment at Notre Dame?

When people ask this question, they usually want to know if it was running through the tunnel for my first game. My favorite football memory was in fact not from any of the games. It happened on the very first day of spring practice in 1981. We opened the practice to anyone who wanted to watch, and 5,000 people showed up. It was such a large crowd that we had to get the police in there just so we could get onto the field and practice.

Even though it was cold, cloudy and rainy that first day, I was just thrilled to be there. The team would usually run onto the field together, and I was with the kickers at the south end. I ran out in front of them and pointed to the sky in gratitude. I said, "Dear Lord, dear Lady, I can't thank you enough for this opportunity."

This might sound overly dramatic, but just then the clouds parted enough for the sun to shine on the famous golden dome of the Main Building on campus. Atop of the dome is a very large statue of the Blessed Mother. You could see her from the practice field, and there she was, brightly greeting us at practice. My prayers had been answered.

Sometimes I wondered why I would be allowed to get my dream job at Notre Dame but then not do so well there. Also, being fired later on at the University of Akron wasn't what I had planned on either. I prayed about it, and I think the reason these things happened was so that people will relate to me better. When I speak at men's groups and other events, they can understand my situation, the ups and downs of life. That gives me more credibility, because they know I'm a real human being.

I have also learned that adversity doesn't have to get the upper hand on you. As long as you have faith, family and friends, you can get through anything. Faith is the most important thing, then family, then friends — or even just one friend. You don't have to be the most popular; you just have to have one friend, someone to share things with. You can be a friend to anyone, regardless of how they might respond to you. You always have the ability to give. ...

This brings to mind my early days back at Archbishop Moeller High School. I would pray before the statue of the Blessed Mother and Christ Child for three things: one, that the Moeller football teams would win games; two, that I would meet a great Catholic woman to marry; and, three, that I would be the head coach at Notre Dame. All three things happened — due to the Blessed Mother interceding on my behalf with her Son.

///

FORMER LSU FOOTBALL PLAYER GAINS THE RIGHT PERSPECTIVE ON LIFE

Ben Domingue discovers 'Catholics aren't crazy' and is now a Fellowship of Catholic University Students missionary in Texas.

November 5, 2014

When **Ben Domingue** went away to college in 2009, he also fell away from the practice of his Catholic faith. Football became the central focus of his life, and he engaged in the worldly pursuits that frequently surround and influence bigtime college sports.

While Domingue's LSU Tigers were playing well on the field, he was drifting farther away from God off the field. It wouldn't be until his junior year that the Lafayette, La., native started journeying back to the Catholic Church. The week before LSU was to play Alabama in the 2012 BCS National Championship, Domingue, who was a center on the team, had a powerful encounter with Jesus Christ through suffering humanity.

Domingue, who is now a missionary with the Fellowship of Catholic University Students (Focus), spoke of his dramatic conversion with *Register* correspondent Trent Beattie, as the 14th-ranked LSU Tigers prepare to take on the 4th-ranked Alabama Crimson Tide this Saturday in Baton Rouge.

Did you grow up in a devout family?

I grew up in a Catholic family that went to Mass every Sunday, prayed grace before meals and said the Rosary once a week. We did all the right things, but I didn't know why we were doing them. To me, it was about rules; I didn't have a living relationship with Jesus Christ.

I did have good relationships with my three older brothers and father, though, as shown in our competition in all kinds of sports. My father wouldn't let us win just to be nice; he was always trying to make us better and would go all-out on the football field or basketball court or wherever else we were.

My father was (and is) a big New Orleans Saints fan, and my brothers thought very highly of LSU football. When they were college age, LSU Tigers' football was a big deal to them, so it became a big deal to me. I was in seventh grade at the time, so from then on, football was my favored sport, and playing for LSU was the big goal.

You achieved that goal in 2009, when you made the LSU football team as a walk-on.

From when we started workouts in June of 2009, LSU football was everything to me. It was what I based my identity on and what gave me purpose in life. I stopped going to church and made football my religion. I was so thrilled to make the team that year, and I fell into a mindset common on a lot of college football teams: a worldly, gladiator-like, pagan type of life. This is how I lived for three and a half years in college.

How did you come to know Jesus in a personal way?

I remembered two people asking who Jesus was to me. They spoke of needing a Savior for our sins, but that didn't register with me. It's like what Venerable Fulton Sheen said: The one thing in the world you don't gain knowledge of by doing is sinning. Put in another way, the more you sin, the more you're blinded to the evil you're engaged in. You're so close to and invested in sin that you don't see it for what it is.

The week before the BCS National Championship game in January of 2012, I was on Bourbon Street in New Orleans at night. I left a place I shouldn't have been and saw a pimp, a prostitute, a drunkard and a homeless couple. The sight of them struck me as pathetic, and I thought, "These people are so broken and messed up; they can't even help themselves. They need a Savior. *Oh*, I guess now that whole Jesus thing makes sense for them."

Then I heard the Lord speak to me interiorly, "Ben, you're just as broken as these people are; only your circumstances are different. I blessed you to be a blessing. Where are you?" Those words cut me to the heart. I knew if I was going to be honest with myself, I really wasn't content. I was hollow inside and was chasing after things in order to fill a need to be loved.

Later that week, Stephen Rivers, who was then a quarterback for LSU, and James Hairston, who was then a kicker for LSU, asked me to go to Mass with them that Sunday. They knew I was Catholic, but I don't think they were aware of how far down the road of iniquity I was.

I had stopped going to Mass regularly, but would still go on Christmas and Easter out of mere social convention. However, that Sunday, which was one day before the National Championship game, I went to Mass for a spiritual reason for the first time in a long time.

Something about the Mass was different: I think the newlyfound knowledge of my sins humbled me and opened me up for Jesus to come inside. I wasn't completely given over to him at that point, but I was starting to get there.

How did you get there?

Over the next several months of 2012, I had bits and pieces of true doctrine given to me here and there, but the most pivotal thing was at the Easter vigil in 2012. My sister-in-law (my second-oldest brother's wife) became Catholic, and they were passing out this book called *Rediscover Catholicism* by Matthew Kelly. I loved how the Eucharist was explained. I thought, "If the Eucharist is the body, blood, soul and divinity of Jesus, then Catholics aren't crazy."

All those outward gestures and actions Catholics do finally made sense to me. We kneel in the presence of Jesus in the Eucharist. We bow to altars on which the sacrifice of the Mass takes place. We shut up and pray after we have received Jesus in the Eucharist. We actually make visits to Jesus in the Eucharist even when Mass is not occurring.

That discovery led me to read more and pray more. I deepened my knowledge of the Catholic faith through books like *Treasure in Clay* by Fulton Sheen and *The Fulfillment of All Desire* by Ralph Martin. I saw how the truth of doctrine wasn't boring; it was the most fascinating thing there is, when you apply it to the lives of people.

Truth is what we are all looking for; it's what makes us really happy, and we can't attain the fullness of truth unless we pray.

How did you become a Focus missionary?

Before Focus, I went back to playing football. I was about to enter my senior year, but this time around, I was going to do things differently. I had an encounter with Jesus, and I knew he had to be shared with others. I wasn't going to continue my errant ways; I was going to make it known I was a full-blooded Catholic.

My rejection of worldliness and acceptance of Catholicism didn't sit well with some of my teammates, who had known me as "one of the guys." That didn't matter to me, though, since I had become contented on a deeper level. I previously thought happiness was found in outward things, but I learned that it comes from being in touch with the beginning and end of all things — in other words, with God.

I also got in better touch with some fellow Christians. In my senior year, I roomed with Stephen Rivers, which was a great blessing. He had been raised in a Catholic home like I had, but he had actually understood from an early age why Catholics do the things we do. It wasn't just a bunch of rules for him; he knew that Jesus was the center of our lives.

We prayed the Litany of St. Sebastian (a patron of athletes) every night and prayed the Rosary every morning, offering each decade for different groups of players on the team — the offensive line, defensive line, kickers, etc. It was awesome to grow closer to Jesus in my senior year through my friendship with Stephen. Even though I didn't get to play that year as much as I had hoped to, things were very good with me.

Then you were prepared for working with Focus.

In the first half of my senior year, I met with Jacob Ardoin, a Focus missionary at LSU. We were talking about how, since Jesus is real, we need to tell people about him. Then Jacob said I should become a missionary with Focus, like he was. I thought about it and really liked the idea, but I quickly ousted it from my mind, since I had job offers to consider.

Eventually, I did interview for the position and was accepted. Before my talk with Jacob, I had been looking to line up a job in the secular world, so I wondered what kind of offer I would get from Focus. I asked how much I would be paid, and the answer came as a surprise. I was told that I would not be paid anything, and, furthermore, I would be assigned by someone else to go to any one of a number of college campuses across the country; and further still, I would have to go on a dating fast (no girlfriend) for a year. I thought, "That is the stupidest job offer I have ever heard of. Who would ever want to do something like that?"

I wanted to reject the whole thing outright, but I thought more of how much Jesus meant to me. I went on a retreat, and the guy next to me (a self-proclaimed atheist) said he was giving God one last chance. If something didn't happen on this retreat, he would be done with God. When they had a Eucharistic procession and brought Jesus by, the guy next to me was crying. He knew he was in the presence of God, and God was speaking to his heart.

Then I heard Jesus call me: "Come follow me, and I'll make you a fisher of men" by bringing people closer to their Savior. I realized that even if I had to raise my own salary, go to an unknown place and forego dating for a year, it was more than worth it. The intention of those three aspects of Focus is to get the missionaries closer to Jesus. They're like modified versions of poverty, obedience and chastity from the religious life.

What kind of work do you do now?

Now I work at the University of Texas at Austin, with an emphasis on assisting athletes. Focus has a program called Varsity Catholic, which seeks to help athletes in their specific struggles. I think athletes have a tougher time in college than non-athletes, because there are so many demands on their time, and people have high expectations for them. Playing well, signing things, getting people tickets to games, etc. Athletes are looked up to, which in a sense is unreasonable, because they're just as human as anyone else.

As I enter my second year with Focus, I am enjoying what I get to do. There's nothing better than bringing the love and forgiveness of Jesus Christ to hurting humanity. I have experienced that love and forgiveness myself, so it's wonderful to help others experience it, too. I know what college students go through, and I also know what college athletes go through, so it's easy to take that knowledge and put it to good use. All things work together for the good for those who love God, right?

I wouldn't be able to do the work I do without the spiritual support of the Church. I go to Mass, do a Holy Hour of Eucharistic adoration and pray the Rosary every day. I also go to confession at least twice a month, and I rely on the intercession of my patrons: St. Sebastian, St. Joseph, Blessed Pier Giorgio Frassati, Venerable Fulton Sheen and St. Michael the Archangel. You can't beat a team like that.

There's no better team to be on than God's. If you're on that team, you're guaranteed a championship, and it's one that can never be taken from us — not even by Alabama [smiles].

///

RICE UNIVERSITY KICKER MAINTAINS HEAVENWARD TRAJECTORY

*Despite losing his mother to cancer,
James Hairston sees the enduring power
of the mystical body of Christ.*

December 23, 2014

In 2006, at 13 years of age, **James Hairston** lost his mother to skin cancer, but he gained a more mature perspective on life. He realized how important human beings are, that tomorrow is not guaranteed to anyone and that our actions here should have heaven as their final aim.

This line of thought was further refined at Jesuit College Preparatory School of Dallas, where Hairston was inspired, through the *Spiritual Exercises of St. Ignatius*, to see life in its proper order and adjust his behavior accordingly. He knew that, no matter what path he chose, God should be given all the glory.

With this principle in mind, Hairston pursued a goal of playing college football. True to the traditional Jesuit framework, he made outwardly visible his inward devotion by making the Sign of the Cross before every kick.

After kicking for three years with the perennial powerhouse LSU Tigers, Hairston graduated early with a bachelor's degree in finance. He then enrolled at Rice University to kick for the Owls this season and to pursue a master's degree in statistics.

As the Owls (7-5) prepared for their game against the Fresno State Bulldogs (6-7) in the Hawaii Bowl on Christmas Eve, 21-year-old James Hairston took time out to speak with *Register* correspondent Trent Beattie.

You started your collegiate career at LSU. Did you have a smooth transition to Rice?

Yes, the transition has been very smooth for at least three reasons. One, there are awesome guys on the football team here. Two, school has been great from an academic and social perspective. Three, I've been able to live and interact with my mom's side of the family here in Houston.

My mom's sister, Shelley, and her husband, Mike, have been great hosts. They've opened up my mom's side of the family to me in a way that I had not known previously. Growing up in the Dallas area, I didn't have an immediate connection to my cousins in Houston, but I'm happy to say that my time here at Rice has changed that.

What do you expect in the Hawaii Bowl against the Fresno State Bulldogs?

Even though the Bulldogs have a losing record overall, some of their losses are to teams like USC, Nebraska and Boise State [combined 28-9 record]. Plus, they have a winning record in their conference, so they are a good team. It should be a good game against them on Christmas Eve, as long as we don't get too relaxed in scenic Hawaii.

You played in a BCS National Championship in your freshman year at LSU. What do you expect from the top teams this year?

This year will be a little different, since there are semifinals before the final game, but we might be blessed to see some of the best collegiate football ever. Alabama has reclaimed the No. 1 spot and is the favorite going into their semifinal game against Ohio State, even though the Buckeyes have also been playing very well recently. I've met Nick Saban and know that he has a very well-coached team, with a lot of player leadership, so I expect big things from them. With that said, Oregon and Florida State, who play in the other semifinal, are also very impressive, so it will be entertaining to see them play.

Because their efforts often decide the outcome of a game, kickers have a lot of pressure on them. Do you have any rituals that offset the pressure?

I pray the Rosary before every game, which is super helpful in calming me down and helping me focus. I've been devoted to the Blessed Virgin Mary since my own mother died. I was 13 at the time, and I remember thinking very clearly how, from then on, Mary would be my mother.

Earlier this year, a little kid walked up to the barrier next to the field during a game and asked, "No. 5, how do you kick the ball so far?" I responded, "The Blessed Virgin Mary." He was puzzled, so an adult nearby said to him, "That's Jesus' mother."

I also make the Sign of the Cross before every kick. That small but important gesture has been with the Church for centuries, and I use it now to thank God, to remind me of what's important and to give a good example. Not everyone has the opportunity to play in front of thousands of people, so you have to be grateful for that, but also keep the game of football in perspective and make sure you carry yourself in a way worthy of a Christian.

Did your mother's death make you think deeply about what really matters in life?

My mother's death brought with it the realization that tomorrow is not guaranteed, so you should make the most of the opportunities you have each day. You can't just sit back and hope good things will happen; you have to choose a goal and pursue it with determination. You won't always get the results you want, but you have to keep doing the things you're capable of and making the best of whatever might occur.

More than anything, though, my mother's death helped me to see that the ultimate questions of life are not just a hobby or matters of private interest. They are what we should all be concerned about,

312 /// FIT FOR HEAVEN

because, before we know it, we will be facing Jesus as judge after our deaths. As our Savior, he wants us to get to heaven; as our judge, he knows, by a simple review of our lives, if we have wanted the same thing.

You visited the grotto at the University of Notre Dame shortly after your mother's death and then revisited it earlier this year. What was that like?

When I was 13, my father and I went to a Notre Dame football game and then to the grotto. That was a special thing for me, considering my new appreciation for Mary and also the faith and football traditions surrounding Notre Dame.

This year, after we played Notre Dame, I barely had time to get to the grotto again. A man named John Shaughnessy helped me to get there and back to the team bus on time. That brought back a lot of memories, and it was a very special event because it involved so many aspects of life that are dear to me.

You also use a sacramental, on a daily basis, that was given to us by Mary.

Yes, I wear a Miraculous Medal around my neck, and it is sometimes a great conversation piece. Earlier this year, I met Victor Saenz, a Rice grad student, because of the medal; he saw me wearing it on the bus and then introduced himself. He studied philosophy at Notre Dame and is now pursuing a doctorate at Rice, so he has plenty of interesting ideas on the natural law and theology.

I also use a brown scapular, which was given to me in August by Father T.J. Martinez. He died of stomach cancer in November, but despite being only 44, he was able to accomplish so much during his life. He earned five graduate degrees, including one from Harvard, and established Cristo Rey Jesuit, a school in southeast Houston for low-income families. They started out with around 80 kids five years ago and now have around 500.

Father Martinez was an inspiration to me and many others. He reminded me to use this life as a preparation for the next life or, in other words, to be actively and persistently Catholic. He had a saying that "We do the difficult things first and the impossible ones soon after."

One sure way to make the impossible possible is through Marian consecration. I recently read the popular book *33 Days to Morning Glory* and made the consecration at the suggestion of Father Tony Lackland, the pastor at All Saints' Church in Dallas. He has been a huge help to me in my faith journey.

Do you find certain aspects of the Church to be challenging?

I like how the Catholic Church teaches us what Christ lived and died for. We are challenged by the Church to live thoroughly Christian lives, which is not an easy task. However, in the Church, we receive the grace to do this. We have all seven sacraments Christ gave us, and we have a rich tradition of prayer and self-sacrifice. To see this lived out, we need only to look at the extensive list of saints who have been completely dedicated to Christ, even to the shedding of their own blood.

The source of all grace is Christ, which can be summed up in one portrait I have in my room. It is of the Sacred Heart of Jesus, shown burning with love for mankind. Because true love is always followed by suffering, a cross and a crown of thorns are depicted in the portrait as well.

Christ's self-sacrificing love is made clear in a most amazing way in the sacrament of confession. Where else can you be forgiven of your sins after baptism like you are in confession? There's no doubt; because you hear the merciful words of Christ through the mouth of the priest: "I absolve you from your sins in the name of the Father, and of the Son, and of the Holy Spirit." Without absolution, life is a great burden. With absolution, life is a great joy.

Life being a joy reminds me of my best friend, Stephen Rivers, whom I played with at LSU. I'm sure it's funny to see us playing football together, because it's almost like we become little kids. It's especially striking to see Stephen, who is 6 foot 7 inches, jump up and down after making an exciting play.

I got to meet Stephen's older brother, Philip, and he helped me to remember that I should enjoy the game of football. Anyone who plays in college or the pros has to take what he does seriously and put a lot of effort into it. However, having no sense of humor and having no fun actually make you a worse player. Enjoying something helps you do it better, and so does laughing at yourself, because then you're freed from unreasonable expectations, and you just play like a kid would.

Do you know what field you'll go into after completing your master's degree?

I'm not sure what I'll do yet. It might be investment banking, oil and gas or commercial real estate. Whatever it is, I already have so many positive experiences to take with me because I've met so many great people in high school and then at LSU and Rice. I've been repeatedly blessed in so many ways that I can't help but see the mystical body of Christ vibrantly. We are connected in ways so profound that we won't be able to understand them until we get to heaven.

///

A GOD GREATER THAN GOLF

Dominican Brother Peter Hannah shares how his life changed from putting to preaching.

August 8, 2013

If things had gone according to the dream of his youth, **Dominican Brother Peter Hannah** would have been playing in this year's PGA Championship. The tournament, which runs Aug. 8-11 in Rochester, N.Y., showcases the best players in the game, and it is the final leg of professional golf's four major tournaments (the other three being the Masters, the U.S. Open and the British Open).

While the PGA Championship was something Brother Peter had hoped to play in one day, God, as they say, had other plans.

Instead of focusing on golf, Brother Peter's mind is now intent on the feast of St. Dominic, Aug. 8. The founder of the Dominicans inspired Brother Peter, 35, to join his order and become a priest. Brother Peter is currently a deacon, and he is scheduled to be ordained to the priesthood on the feast of the Visitation, May 31, 2014.

Brother Peter recounted his conversion story to *Register* correspondent Trent Beattie in time for the feast of St. Dominic.

How did you start playing golf?

I remember seeing the beautiful green golf courses on TV as a child, but it wasn't until the summer after eighth grade that I started playing. There was a neighbor friend my age who was also interested in golf, and we were on the greens many hours over that summer. There was something about the beautiful courses, clean air and the atmosphere of respect for an ideal of sportsmanlike conduct.

That, combined with a desire to get lower and lower scores, was a marvelously addictive experience.

It almost seems like a religious experience.

Yes, I didn't realize it at the time, but, eventually, I came to treat golf as a replacement religion. When there's a spiritual void, something has to fill it, and oftentimes that something is sports. It's easy to make recreation a religion these days, and men in particular tend to fall into this trap.

Were you raised in a devout family?

I was raised as a Presbyterian Christian in Monterey, Calif. We would go to church as a family every Sunday. However, like most young people, I didn't consciously engage in my faith. Then, in high school, I went through a rebellious phase, where I grew so interested in golf that I lost interest in attending church or giving God a place in my life.

My consuming interest in golf stayed with me through my first years of college at the University of California-San Diego. I was able to play on their traveling team and represent the school at golf tournaments. I even had the desire to play professionally. I put the emphasis on desire, because, after my tenure at UCSD, I would have had to, at best, play on mini tours before getting a chance at the regular PGA Tour. I was a decent player, but definitely not good enough to go straight onto the tour.

What are some of the most important things you learned from your UCSD years?

When I first got to UCSD, I was happily swept up in athletic, academic and social activities around campus. I did my best with golf and grades, and, on the social end, I chose to join a fraternity to establish bonds with other young men my age.

There are good aspects to fraternity life. You can get to know other people, learn organization and leadership skills and raise money for charitable causes. However, the other side of that two-edged sword is the partying atmosphere, which encourages many destructive modes of behavior. The drinking, drugging and denigrating attitudes toward women are staples of that partying life.

By my junior year, I was starting to become disillusioned with fraternity life, and I wondered if there might be something more satisfying. Like many contemporary people, I imagined that if I were to commit to any religion I'd want to study non-Christian ones first.

Before I could do that, however, my father recommended *Mere Christianity* by C.S. Lewis to represent Christianity, and I finished it in three days. It was amazing how Lewis offered answers to questions I had but couldn't even articulate. I realized, with the help of grace, that Jesus Christ was not just a nice man, but God become man. After being convicted by reading Lewis' masterpiece, I realized that Christ was categorically different than other major religious figures, such as Buddha or Mohammed. To believe in Christ was to believe that he was the Son of God and to follow him completely. I was so convicted that I lost interest in studying non-Christian religions.

How did that change you?

Becoming a committed Christian changed everything for me. I became more optimistic, began reassessing many of the habits I'd acquired in fraternity life, and eventually lost my immoderate attachment to golf. I discovered that only by offering God first place in my life could I treat golf in a balanced and healthy way.

I went from reading C.S. Lewis to reading G.K. Chesterton, the first person I came across who wrote of the Catholic Church as if it were a distinct entity. Previous to Chesterton, I had read and heard of Christianity only in general, amorphous terms, but now I was reading of the Catholic Church as the vehicle Jesus Christ established to spread his teaching.

What happened next?

I graduated from UCSD with a degree in history in 1999 and then pursued a master's degree from St. John's College in Annapolis, Md., which is a Great Books school. [The books are called "great" because of their role, for better or for worse, in shaping Western culture.] We covered classics from thinkers such as Aristotle, St. Augustine and St. Thomas Aquinas, right up to modern-day works from Alexis de Tocqueville, Charles Darwin, Karl Marx and others. I enjoyed hashing out ideas with my classmates, who ranged from devout Catholics to committed Protestant Christians, to agnostics and atheists.

Actively considering so many ideas from so many different authors really helped to refine what I believed in. Even though St. John's is not a Catholic school, I became increasingly Catholic in my ways of thinking. I found myself able to defend the Catholic position on certain issues much better than I could the classic Protestant position.

While attending a Mass I was invited to by a Catholic friend, I had quite an experience. When the priest elevated the Host, it was like a lightning flash of inspiration. I was kneeling there, with hundreds of people at the Sunday Mass, and I thought, "If what the Catholic Church teaches about the Eucharist is true, this is the most astonishing and beautiful thing that I have ever seen. If the Catholic Church is right about the Eucharist, then I must become Catholic, since God is manifesting himself here in a way he isn't in other Christian communions."

While still in Annapolis, I decided to give the Lord one hour of prayer per day. The Episcopalian church I went to was locked on the morning I resolved to begin the daily hour. But the Catholic one had a little side chapel set aside specifically for prayer — what I would later learn is called "perpetual adoration." Within about two months after frequenting this chapel, I came to believe in the real presence of Our Lord in the Blessed Sacrament.

Once this happened, I was on my way to being received into the Church in the upcoming summer. Only six months after this, I discerned a call to the priesthood.

How did you decide to become a Dominican?

As I began discerning religious communities, I realized that, though I deeply valued contemplation, I wasn't called to be a monk; and, though I very much liked engaging the world in an active way, I needed a strong contemplative element in my life. The Dominicans had the perfect balance of these qualities, in my mind.

Having grown up on the West Coast, I knew that part of the country was in great need of evangelization. That led me to be a part of the Western Province of Dominicans, and it influenced my choice of a religious name. My full religious name is Brother Peter Junípero. Blessed Junípero Serra was the Franciscan friar and priest responsible for founding the chain of missions along California's coast. The mission he began — to bring the Christian faith to California — I very much identified with and wanted to take up again, as it were.

One simple way we friars evangelize is by wearing our white Dominican habit. I was actually in the grocery store recently and ran into some guys at the checkout stand who were wearing sweatshirts bearing the name of my fraternity. After greeting them and telling them we were members of the same frat, they stared back with somewhat dumbfounded looks. After one of them got over his initial shock, he asked, looking at my white Dominican habit, "What's with the getup?" I explained who I was briefly, and he shot back in an only semi-joking manner, "Whoa. You give me hope."

Have you found the habit to be a plus, in general, when it comes to evangelization?

I've been approached countless times in public when wearing the habit and have gotten into sometimes extensive conversations about all sorts of spiritual subjects: religious life, Christian moral teachings, prayer, how celibacy and poverty can be paths to spiritual freedom. So many people today are hungering and thirsting for a trusted person to talk with about the Catholic faith. Much of what they've heard is formed by the media, so I see wearing my habit and offering myself to anyone who has questions as a very simple and easy way to evangelize and present a clearer picture of the faith. It's being that "visible sign" John Paul II and Benedict XVI so frequently exhorted us religious to be.

St. Thomas Aquinas valued recreation in the overall context of the Christian life. If he played golf, which PGA player do you think he would play like?

I see similarities between St. Thomas and Ernie Els: fairly large-framed, steady and plodding. They share a cheerful disposition, but with an underlying strength. There's a calm confidence about both of them. They work hard and can bowl over the opposition through sheer, steady perseverance.

What about another Dominican saint, Vincent Ferrer, and St. Dominic himself?

St. Vincent Ferrer was known for being a very charismatic preacher, "on fire," you could say. He would travel around Western Europe preaching about repentance and living a virtuous life. The corresponding golfer for Vincent Ferrer, in my mind, is Seve Ballasteros. He was always full of fire and passion, and you never really knew what to expect from him on the course.

St. Dominic was also a passionate preacher, but he was very disciplined. His work did have a set pattern, as he methodically set about to bring people back to the truth. That makes me think he would play golf like Jack Nicklaus, who had an inward intensity and fire, combined with outward discipline. Nicklaus could be very intimidating to his opponents but retained an ever-gentlemanly disposition, even amidst fierce competition.

A Catholic life lived to the full can combine this inward intensity — in prayer, striving after virtue, sternness in the face of falsehood and anything that threatens human dignity — with an outward gentleness and meekness. This is a combination St. Dominic had, and one that we would do well to imitate. We need men and women who, out of love for God and neighbor, desire to bring others into the fullness of good that Jesus Christ wants us all to have.

///

RAISING THE BAR IN EVERY AREA OF LIFE

Belmont Abbey College's high-jumping president calls for excellence and virtue on and off campus.

November 7, 2013

As a two-time NCAA Division I All-American and National Champion high jumper, **Bill Thierfelder** had long been accustomed to raising the bar in a literal sense.

Now, he does so in a metaphorical way by promoting excellence and virtue in every aspect of life. In fact, each light post at Belmont

Abbey College is adorned with a banner reading "Excellence & Virtue," serving as a reminder of what every member of the Belmont Abbey community is called to embody.

Thierfelder has frequently spoken about his insights into a virtuous life in classrooms, boardrooms, meeting halls and training facilities across the country.

Now, for the first time, he is imparting this knowledge through a book, from TAN/St. Benedict Press, called *Less Than a Minute to Go: The Secret to World-Class Performance in Sport, Business and Everyday Life*.

He recently spoke with the Register about his new book, pursuing virtue and the state of Catholic higher education.

Why did you write your new book, Less Than a Minute to Go?

That's a great question, since I really had no time to write it, and I have never considered myself a writer. Being president of a college is almost a 24/7 job, and my wife, Mary, and I have 10 children, so spare chunks of time are few and far between. (We are still praying for the gift of bilocation!) Add to that the fact that I'd never written a book before, and you're talking to one of the least likely candidates for the job.

I never thought I'd write a book, but friends would encourage me to get one out. They wanted me to share, in a written format, some of the insights I'd gained over the years. I can't claim any credit for those insights; that credit goes to the Holy Spirit. However, I did see the validity of my friends' point. A book would be a great way to reach beyond the immediate Belmont Abbey community to share great things with others.

I knew if I wrote a book that I would donate all of the royalties to Belmont Abbey College. The final validation for writing the book came when St. Benedict Press asked me to write it and then offered to donate all of their profits from the book to the college. Unlike larger schools, we have a very small endowment with which to support our operations, so the opportunity to bring in funds for the school was an important consideration. Not only would I be able to share helpful insights and techniques with others in a new way, but I would at the same time be able to help support the college.

It was a sometimes arduous path, as I often stayed up until 3am writing. Then, on what was supposed to be our family vacation, I wrote all day and night. Without the encouragement and editorial advice of my entire family, including my 6-year-old, Matthew, it would not have been possible. In fact, by making it a family affair, it brought us even closer together.

The book isn't only for athletes, is it?

The book is filled with examples of how athletes from various sports perform at the highest levels, but it shows how anyone, at any level, can significantly improve their performance. On the deepest level, it is also a book about how to be truly happy in this life and the next. The book shows how world-class performance and virtue are not mutually exclusive and why we will be most successful and happy when pursuing both.

Sport is a wonderful metaphor for illustrating how virtues are developed and strengthened over time. It provides an environment that can reveal insights about how our bodies, minds and souls work. While the book may be a great aid to anyone looking to improve athletic performance, it also offers tips and advice for improving other areas of life.

The first section of the book, [about] preparing the mind to win, helps us to see ourselves and others more clearly and avoid the ways of thinking that can hurt our performances. The second section, [focusing on] making peak performance a common occurrence, shows how and why peak performances happen. The third and final section,

[on] playing with a passion that never ends, shows how sacrifice is essential to our success and happiness in this life and the next.

A recurring theme of the book is that, ultimately, what we do is far more important than what we say. We hope people's words will match their actions; but in the end, the way you really know them is by what they did, not by what they said. Having given us life and free will, God is essentially asking us, "Do you love me?" Our response to that question comes forth very clearly by the way we choose to live our lives.

Do you find that, despite the many problems in sports today, virtue is slowly working itself into that world?

Most athletes are very good people, the kind of people you would treasure as friends. Examples include Mike Sweeney, Jeff Suppan and many others you have interviewed for the National Catholic Register.

The problem is that the vast majority of the media tends to focus exclusively on the athletes who practice vice. It leads us to believe that all athletes are terrible individuals with no morals or virtues. As fans and spectators, we should expect and demand more from the media and those athletes who choose to live lives of vice. After all, we are the ones paying to support their careers.

Do you find that most students appreciate the Catholic environment at Belmont Abbey?

Definitely; even those members of the community who are not Catholic appreciate it. As a Benedictine abbey and college, we welcome each guest as we would Christ himself. This permeates the entire campus — whether you're in the classroom, the basilica, the library or the gym. We strive for balancing life intellectually, spiritually, socially and athletically. The warmth of our Catholic [college] home draws people from all walks of life who desire to double their talents by seeking the truth and living in response to it.

Many of our full-time students are already solidly grounded in the faith, while some are still on a journey to deepen their faith. One really fascinating fact about Belmont is that nearly all of our evening students are not Catholic. This might seem strange, until you consider that North Carolina has a relatively small percentage of Catholics and that it is the only Catholic college between Virginia and Florida.

Why would so many non-Catholics seek out a Catholic school when so many other private and public institutions are available to them?

I think our appeal to non-Catholics occurs for two reasons, both of which are inextricably linked to our Benedictine identity. Following the Rule of St. Benedict, we receive each visitor as we would the person of Jesus himself. This welcoming attitude resonates well with the Southern tradition of hospitality.

Another reason for our appeal to non-Catholics is that we have a love of Scripture, as expressed in the practice of *lectio divina*. For over a millennium, this love motivated the Benedictine monks to preserve the Bible by painstakingly reproducing it by hand, one copy at a time. This reverence for the written word of God is obviously very attractive to Protestants, who witness the monks praying Scripture (the Divine Office) every day.

What are your biggest challenges at Belmont Abbey?

The greatest battles are always spiritual. The devil has us on his radar, [which means] we will continue to fight the good fight for religious liberty, the sanctity of marriage, the right to life and the teachings of the Catholic Church as applied to colleges, found in Pope John

Paul II's apostolic constitution, *Ex Corde Ecclesiae* (From the Heart of the Church).

The other significant challenge is not having an endowment that [would help] make first-class Catholic education and formation available to more students. My hope and prayer is that this book will help to bring attention to the good work being done by our amazing faculty, coaches and monastic community at Belmont Abbey College.

I have often said, "I don't believe in accidents." I believe in divine Providence. If you're reading my words right now, it's no accident. God is calling you to look, discern, pray and to say, "Maybe I'm supposed to be [at Belmont Abbey College]. Maybe I'm supposed to be contributing in some way to what God is calling that place to be." And I'm hoping that you're going to come and join us.

What is the current status of Belmont Abbey's battle with the Obama administration over the HHS mandate that would force organizations such as your own to pay for abortions, contraceptives and sterilizations?

There have been many other stories in the news recently, so the HHS mandate is not getting the attention it once did but still deserves. The battle continues, and the Becket Fund for Religious Liberty has just refiled our lawsuit in response to the recent actions by the Department of Justice.

This remains a serious issue that will require all of us banding together in order to win. The martyrs of the Church are the standard-bearers for us in this fight. They gave up every material possession — even life itself — for what they believed in. It may not come to that for us, but if necessary, we need to be willing to follow the examples of St. Thomas More and St. John Fisher and be ready to answer with our lives.

///

BUILDING STRENGTH THROUGH VIRTUE

SportsLeader program gains in popularity and importance among coaches and teams, including Michigan State's Rose Bowl-bound football squad.

December 31, 2013

Ask Lou Judd about the state of athletics, and you might get an earful. The 41-year-old father of six is passionate about stemming the tide that would place sports above everything else. He has maintained this outlook since 2004, the year he joined SportsLeader, a virtue-based mentoring program for coaches.

Judd has seen positive results from SportsLeader, both on the field and off the field. Among the most visible on-field outcomes are found with the Michigan State University football team, which won the Big Ten Championship this year and plays in the Rose Bowl on New Year's Day. Off-the-field stories showing the effectiveness of virtue-mentoring are numerous, but they all have the same theme: Virtue equals strength.

Judd spoke with *Register* correspondent Trent Beattie about the past, present and future of the Louisville, Ky.-based SportsLeader program.

How did you get started with SportsLeader?

In 2004, Paul Passafiume, a businessman and junior-high football coach in the Louisville, Ky., area, and Joe Lukens, a former Ohio State University football player and current businessman in the Cincinnati area, both saw a need for a virtue-based training program

328 /// FIT FOR HEAVEN

in athletics. A win-at-all-costs mentality had become more common and was harming youth development. Sports had become almost a deity.

Paul and Joe joined forces and started what is now called SportsLeader. They brought me on board that first year, and we launched a program for high-school students. Because it was explicitly Catholic, the public schools didn't allow it, so we came up with a broader one that is compatible with Catholicism but not overtly Catholic.

Catholics know the theological virtues of faith, hope and charity; and the four cardinal virtues of prudence, justice, temperance and fortitude. We extended the list of virtues to include things such as humility, patience and magnanimity. Because the school year is usually 36 weeks long, we identified 72 virtues so that one could be learned each week during a two-year period. With this framework, a high-school student would be exposed to the same virtues two separate times during four years.

How is the SportsLeader program implemented?

We have three pillars to our program: virtue, mentoring and ceremony. *Virtue*, which comes from the Latin word for "strength" or "manly excellence," is what we're all about. Our central motto is: "Virtue equals strength." This is vitally important to teach, because the word "virtue" can sometimes have an out-of-reach or less-than-appealing ring to it. When you get right down to it, though, virtue is at the very core of what it means to be a capable, productive and content person.

Mentoring is the main vehicle through which the virtues are passed along. We recognized early on that coaches have a uniquely important role in forming young people, so coaches are the ones we train. They receive all the information and methods for instilling virtue in their players.

Ceremony is a vehicle through which the virtues are reinforced. We gather the players of a team and their fathers, near the beginning of a sports season, in a jersey ceremony. Each father shares a story of his son living out a specific virtue, tells his son he loves him (and why he does so), and then gives him a jersey and a hug.

A second aspect of the ceremony is what we call "Letters to Mom." Each player writes a letter to his mother expressing love and gratitude to her. The players and their mothers gather, and each player reads his letter out loud to all present. Then he gives his mother a rose.

The high-school version, which includes all 72 virtues, is also the one we started to use in colleges. Then there's a simpler version for grade schools that is based on the three core virtues of charity, humility and courage. We still have the mentoring and ceremony aspects for younger athletes, but it's easier to teach just a few basic concepts to them.

How has the program been received?

Very well. Young people want to be guided and formed by knowledgeable adults, and this is a great way to do that. Coaches have a pivotal role in youth development, even more than parents, teachers and clergy, in many cases.

As a kid, you don't choose your own parents, teachers or clergy, but you do choose to be part of a team that is guided by a certain coach. Because young people want to hear what coaches have to say, we train the coaches on how to impart the virtues. This has worked extremely well.

What are some examples of SportsLeader being used successfully?

There are so many examples, but maybe the most visible one is the Michigan State football team. We met with Head Coach Mark

Dantonio in 2011, and he wanted to start the mentoring part of SportsLeader. We did that, and even went beyond the basic structure of our mentoring program.

The team's strength coach, Ken Mannie, took on, not just six or seven guys in a small group, as is the usual practice for each coach of a team, but he would actually mentor the entire team. He did this on an individual basis throughout the year, by being demanding but caring. He had high standards for his players but was there to help them live up to those standards. The team would communicate and share concerns with each other after workouts led by Ken. He regularly handed out cards with encouraging messages on them. Players collected the cards and kept them in binders.

This year, the Michigan State football team won the Big Ten Championship and is playing in the Rose Bowl against Stanford on New Year's Day 2014.

So there's no basis to the fear that virtue will make teams less competitive?

No, not at all. If your team is much more talented than mine, then yes, yours will probably win, no matter how virtuous mine is. However, if our teams are basically equal in talent, the more virtuous one will win. That is, the team that plays cohesively, that sacrifices, that perseveres in the face of adversity — that's the team that will come out on top in a matchup that is otherwise equal. This is true of football, basketball, baseball or any other sport.

How many schools currently use the program?

About 130 currently use SportsLeader, although that's a little misleading, because the number of participating teams within each school varies. Some schools have all their teams onboard, while others have a few or one team. We've worked with Chris Ledyard, athletic director of Franciscan University in Steubenville, to bring the program to all of his teams, making Franciscan the first university to have comprehensive implementation.

Most of the schools we serve are in the Midwest and Northeast, such as Rice Lake High School in Wisconsin, Archbishop Moeller in Ohio and Tyburn Academy in New York. We are in other areas across the U.S. and Canada, though, and we're actually in the first phase of bringing SportsLeader to the entire Archdiocese of New Orleans, so that's very encouraging.

Aside from great teams, what are the benefits of SportsLeader?

It's important to remember that Sports Leader is not just about sports. Yes, you will develop stable, reliable athletes through the program, but, more importantly, you will develop stable, reliable human beings. Virtue carries over into other areas of life.

One way this is shown is though Bruce Scifres, head football coach for Roncalli High School in Indiana. He has taught his players about prayer, instructing them to "Take God with you on every play." He has told them that from when the huddle breaks to when the play starts they have just enough time to say a short prayer: "Lord, be with me on this play"; "Jesus, strengthen me"; "Come, Holy Spirit." These are just a few of the aspirations that cannot only help someone play better, but the very practice of prayer itself is starting to become a habit.

When the player encounters a situation in school that could lead to a fight, he can say a short prayer instead of indulging in reckless thoughts and then actions. Before a job interview, he can say a short prayer instead of letting nerves get the best of him.

A major area of concern in schools today is bullying, and SportsLeader is the answer to the problem. When you have an entire football team onboard with the program, bullying just doesn't exist. The players won't engage in it, and if they see it happening to someone else, they won't allow it. Athletes tend to set the moral tone for the entire school, so when the football team in particular doesn't approve of something, it won't happen.

Do you plan on taking the program to professional sports?

Our focus now is on K-12 and college, but we would like to be in pro sports at some point in the future. We've already talked with Mark Chipman, owner of the Winnipeg Jets, Eric Sutulovich, special-teams coach of the Atlanta Falcons, and Joe Lombardi, quarterbacks coach of the New Orleans Saints. While these men endorse our program for young people, there is no current plan to implement it on pro teams yet.

What we are about to implement is a specifically Catholic version of SportsLeader, which we'll use in Catholic schools. This will be similar to what we started with in 2004, but it will be expanded, in part through the help of Chris Willertz, who joined SportsLeader in June 2012.

Have you implemented Sports Leader with your own family?

Yes, I'm the coach of my 10-year-old son's soccer team, and we use the program. Just like other coaches, I teach the team about a specific virtue each week. My son comes home and repeats the definition and the accompanying story to his younger siblings. All the kids who can talk are constantly talking about virtue. That's something that warms a father's heart. They have their minds on the right things already.

///

FORMERLY TROUBLED BASKETBALL PLAYER NOW THRIVING ON GOD'S TEAM

Florida priest Father Richard Pagano finds joy in conversion and evangelization.

February 27, 2014

At one time, **Father Richard Pagano** believed lasting happiness was to be found playing basketball. The point guard, who played hoops at a New Jersey community college, thought running down the court, escaping defenders and maneuvering past a much taller center for a finger-roll basket was the greatest thrill in life.

Many knee injuries later, Father Pagano started to see things differently. He gave up his desire for worldly glory and replaced it with one for God's glory. After his dramatic conversion, he discerned a call to the priesthood and entered St. Vincent de Paul Regional Seminary in Boynton Beach, Fla., in 2008. He was ordained on May 18, 2013, at the historic Cathedral-Basilica of St. Augustine.

While Father Pagano's enthusiasm has carried over from his days on the hardwood floor, it's now being channeled toward a radically different end.

The 31-year-old Diocese of St. Augustine priest recently spoke of his journey from the basketball court to the sanctuary with *Register* correspondent Trent Beattie.

Did you grow up in a devout family?

I came from a difficult family situation. My parents divorced when I was 2, so my mother, sister and I moved in with my mother's parents in upstate New York. My uncle and aunt (my mother's siblings) lived with us as well, since they were 20 and 18 at the time. Some of my greatest childhood memories were of church and family. We would regularly go to the seemingly huge parish of St. Catharine of Alexandria in Blauvelt, N.Y. We were going to "God's house," as my mother described it, and following that, we would have big family gatherings at my grandparents' house. Their house was a Grand Central Station of sorts: lots of people, lots of activity and celebration. I loved that.

Tell us how you first got involved in basketball.

I remember shooting hoops at the age of 5 with my uncle on a rim that hung from the back of my grandparents' garage door. Those are my first memories of a basketball, and I look back with gratitude on them.

As I got a little older, I played all kinds of sports, especially the team and contact ones. I would play football with no pads, and an all-out, very aggressive version of basketball. I slowly became more disciplined, though. I would spend hours dribbling around the driveway and playing pick-up games in the neighborhood. As a guard, I developed a reliable jump shot, then a keen floor vision, then an ability to penetrate defenses.

Things were going great with basketball in high school, but I was taken in with the partying that is all too common for young people. I made the varsity basketball team as a junior, but was cut halfway through the season because of my off-court behavior at a tournament in Kentucky. The coach said my actions were inconsistent with the school's expectations of a varsity player, and he was right.

Was that a wake-up call for you?

Unfortunately, being cut didn't really motivate me to improve my behavior. I was still a wild young man without a serious purpose in life. The highest purpose I could find was in basketball, so I rededicated myself to the sport at Bergen County Community

College in Paramus, N.J. Things were going very well, but by that time I had been playing in pain for four years on a bad leg. I was told it was just a sprain, but never had an MRI, so all that time I was basically tearing up the cartilage in my knee.

Well, my knee finally gave out completely, and my basketball career seemed finished. I then moved back to Palm Coast, Fla., and, despite the recommendation of my doctor to stay off the court after knee surgery, I was suckered into playing pick-up basketball. Then my other knee gave out, and my basketball career really was finished completely. The most pathetic part of the scene, though, was that my "friends" who coaxed me into playing that day were all laughing as I was writhing in pain on the ground. They really got a kick out of my injury.

So when did you start to see that your life had a purpose beyond basketball?

I was in the hospital rehabbing my second knee surgery, and no one came to visit. My "friends" were amused at my predicament, and, because of my wild ways, my family didn't want to have anything to do with me. I effectively pushed everyone I loved away [because of] my lifestyle. I was buried in darkness and lies, isolated in my sin. I was empty and needed a Savior. It was in that time of great need that I prayed with humility for the first time in my life.

Before then, I would occasionally ask God for things, but there was no desire to do God's will; it was all about my own selfish interests. Now that I needed physical, emotional and spiritual healing — and then a true purpose and direction in life — I laid bare my soul and asked what countless souls have asked through the centuries: "Jesus, I am doing everything wrong. I need your help."

The very next day, I saw a Bible on my table. I'm not sure how it got there, since I hadn't seen it before, but I started reading it, especially Proverbs and Ecclesiastes. Those books really spoke to my heart, to my need for redemption and purpose. The serenity prayer was printed in the Bible, so I started praying that every day. There was also a Seven Sorrows prayer card inserted in the Bible, so I began a devotion to Our Sorrowful Mother. That blossomed into a daily Rosary; and Our Blessed Mother's concern and guidance brought about a new reality: My life was finally making sense. I went to confession and Sunday Mass and, eventually, made weekday Mass and Eucharistic adoration regular practices. Step by step, I was becoming more immersed in God's grace, and I became freer and freer to do God's will. I saw more clearly that my worldly desires were empty and futile and that God's way was the only way that would bring me true happiness.

I've always been comfortable talking to groups of people, so I wasn't shy about sharing my newfound faith. I would preach to fellow students at the Daytona Beach Community College and hand out Bibles to them. My friends and family were suspicious of my actions, since they were so used to me being a wild guy. They couldn't believe that I had really been transformed by God's grace. I was so on fire with the faith that I could not put down the Bible, the *Catechism of the Catholic Church* and the works of my new best friend: Pope John Paul II. I fell in love with John Paul II's life and ministry.

At one point, I was asked, along with my fellow students, to make a presentation on a world leader from recent or distant history. Well, of course, I chose JPII. When I proposed my topic, my teacher said I could not present on him. I asked why, because others were doing presentations on religious leaders. She would not even entertain my question, but I went ahead and presented on JPII. Up until then, I had an A in the class; but the final project on JPII brought me down to a B. That is the grade I am most proud of in my entire academic formation!

How did you discern a call to the priesthood?

Providentially, my pastor at Santa Maria del Mar in Flagler Beach, Fla., Father John Tetlow, was also the diocesan vocations director, so he helped me to discern God's call. I was blessed to see that God was calling me, not out of my own worthiness, but out of my unworthiness. The fact that the priesthood was an unmerited, gratuitous gift was made perfectly clear, and it remains that way for me today.

Everything I had been searching for is now present to me. I have deep meaning and purpose to my life that I love to share with others on a daily basis. Since each day is different, there are so many adventures in the life of a diocesan priest. I get to be with my spiritual children at the most important moments of their lives: baptisms, weddings, funerals and many places in between. Celibate intimacy brings great and lasting joy, since joy is not dependent upon physical pleasure. Joy is a state of soul that comes when self is left behind and the service of neighbor in the love of God is embraced.

Does your past help you in your present ministry?

While I wouldn't recommend worldliness to anyone, I did learn things from my past experiences that help me today. When I went to a maximum-security prison to preach, I was able to get the attention of inmates by reciting lyrics of certain rappers they admired. They couldn't believe I knew what was so familiar to them. After I got their attention, I was able to preach to them the saving truth of the Gospel from a perspective that the light always shines most clearly in the darkness.

What advice would you give to young basketball players and young athletes in general?

I would say: Never invest your time and effort into something for the purpose of attaining human glory. Human glory is fleeting, so seeking after it is a life committed to "chasing after wind." If glory comes after the investment of your life in Christ, that's fine, but always remember it is his glory that is to be revered. Refer your praise back to God, who is the author of all human gifts and who shares his glory with us. You'll never find fulfillment in a game or another worldly pursuit, but only in the glory of God.

///

CANADIAN PRIEST HELPS EWTN VIEWERS GET IN COMPLETE SHAPE WITH NEW SERIES

Father James Mallon, who will be a featured speaker at this weekend's EWTN Family Celebration in Vancouver, B.C., hopes to encourage springtime renewal with Cross Training.

April 2, 2014

The world's confusion about what it means to be human is the motivation behind **Father James Mallon's** latest media venture. The 44-year-old priest of the Archdiocese of Halifax, Canada, wants to lend a hand to those who have misconceptions about the human body as it relates to the soul. Too many people, he believes, have been taken in by a dualism that seeks to separate the physical from the spiritual.

Father Mallon wants to emphasize that God created each of us as a united body and soul, a fact not even the grave will have the last word over. Despite separation at death, our bodies will rejoin our souls before the Last Judgment. In the meantime, the pastor of St. Benedict parish in Halifax points out that we can use our bodies to know, love and serve our Creator.

Father James Mallon spoke of his new EWTN series, *Cross Training*, which made its debut March 6, with *Register* correspondent Trent Beattie.

What was the inspiration for the Cross Training series?

There's a real crisis of anthropology in the world today. Many don't know what it means to be human. Instead of seeing themselves as embodied spirits, as *being* their bodies, they consider their bodies to be extraneous to their true selves. They think they merely "have" a body that will be discarded or exchanged. This explains why so many people believe in reincarnation today. A biblical anthropology, on the other hand, shows that we are our bodies and that we cannot exchange our bodies as we would our clothing.

Even before the recent Facebook announcement about having 50 different gender options, there was a pervasive confusion about what it means to be a male or a female. If I am not my body, and choice rules the day, I can define my gender exactly how I want, and my embodiment has absolutely nothing to contribute to the matter.

Even though the Church has an accurate and beautiful anthropology, it is not uncommon even for Catholics to be in the dark about it. The resurrection of the body might be the best example. I run into Catholics all the time who are shocked to hear that the bodies of the blessed in heaven will be raised and reunited with their souls.

Cross Training is meant to show that, as human beings, we are embodied spirits and that our bodies are not secondary to who we are; they are an essential part of who we are. Therefore, everything physical has a spiritual dimension and vice versa. This impacts questions of human sexuality, bioethics and how we address the question of health. This latter topic is addressed in *Cross Training*.

How is Cross Training *different from your past series on* EWTN, Dogmatic Theology?

The major difference, from a production standpoint, is that *Dogmatic Theology* was made by the John Paul II Media Institute for showings at individual parishes. We had no intention of broadcasting it, but we were approached by EWTN to do that. *Cross Training*, on the other hand, was made from the beginning with the intention of being aired on EWTN.

From a content standpoint, there are some obvious differences. *Dogmatic Theology* uses the oftentimes obsessive concern people have for their pets today as leverage for teaching basic truths of the Christian faith. *Cross Training* taps into an aspect of our culture — the fitness craze — to give a Catholic perspective, but it has a very different approach.

I was the only host for the first series, whereas I'm one of four hosts for the second series. The other three hosts are Ronnie Lunn, coordinator of youth ministry here at St. Benedict parish; Marilyn Cipak, a registered dietician; and Corey Robinson, a former member of the Canadian National Wrestling Team.

Each of the hosts brings a different perspective to the show. Ronnie has a personal trainer and power-lifting background, so he goes into detail about different muscles and other aspects of physical fitness. Marilyn specializes in proper eating, and Corey has a powerful conversion story, not to mention an advanced athletic background.

Each of our 13 *Cross Training* episodes focuses on a different topic, but all the episodes are centered on the truth that we as human beings are embodied spirits. Some topics covered are motivation, stress, patience, vital rest and outdoor life. While each episode has a different topic, they are all presented in the same basic format that includes a nutrition, exercise, prayer and book component.

We wanted to make sure that we explain the proper motivation for physical health. One can pursue it out of vanity, the appearance of being fit; or he can do it as an end in itself, which negates the spiritual dimension of the human person. The purpose of replacing junk food with healthy food is not simply to lose weight or to be a good machine; it is done in order to love God completely.

It's interesting that you include nutrition, because the topic of gluttony seems to be one of the most neglected in the Church today.

The world today sees nothing wrong with disciplining oneself for the sake of athletics. Engaging in an austere nutrition and exercise regimen for the purpose of winning an Olympic medal is seen as a noble venture. Do the same regimen with a spiritual purpose, however, and the world wants to lock you up as insane. We see the material benefits of the former and not for the latter, so the world assumes that something must be suspect in it.

Yet the Church has a long history of corporal austerity for a higher purpose.

We can go all the way back to New Testament times, when St. Paul wrote of an imperishable crown. In 1 Corinthians 9, he stated that athletes exercise discipline in order to win a perishable crown, but we Christians exercise discipline to win an imperishable crown. Then he wrote, "Thus, I do not run aimlessly; I do not fight as if I were shadowboxing. No, I drive my body and train it, for fear that, after having preached to others, I myself should be disqualified."

We spent about nine months filming and editing the *Cross Training* episodes. It was a lot of work and a lot of laughs, and it was all volunteer — no money was made by any of us — but when all the episodes were completed in December, we could look back with some satisfaction. Now, we hope that many viewers will reap abundant benefits from the series.

How did you discern a call to the priesthood?

In my youth I never, ever considered becoming a priest. I believed in God, but my daily life didn't have a vital connection to what that belief should mean. My family moved from Scotland to Canada when I was 13, and I proceeded to get into the trouble that many teens do.

When I got into serious enough trouble to attract the attention of the police, my father forced me to go on a weekend retreat. That was a life-changing weekend for me because I really experienced God's love and got closer to him. The only problem was: Once the retreat was over, I didn't know what to do. Since there was no one to disciple me, what I gained from the retreat didn't have a chance to blossom.

In my late teens, I met a young Protestant lady who became my girlfriend for a few years. She would ask me questions about what I believed. Her questions led me into searching for an answer to what it actually meant to be a Catholic, and I slowly discovered the riches of our Catholic faith.

On Easter Sunday of the first year of my undergraduate studies at Dalhousie University in Halifax, I had a profound experience in which it was made very clear that God wanted me to become a priest. It was unmistakable, and yet I basically said to God, "Thanks, but no thanks." I didn't want to embrace the call. It took me a whole year to accept the call, and I'm glad that I finally did so. I love my vocation to the priesthood.

Now that all the Cross Training *episodes have been completed, what activities fill your calendar?*

Aside from the typical duties of a parish priest — which I love to do, by the way — I've been traveling around to speak, mostly about parish revitalization. We need to change our model of pastoral care from one of maintenance to one of making missionary disciples. We can't be content with doing general upkeep; we need to train and equip parishioners to take the graces they're given and go into the world to share them with others.

A natural outgrowth of my favorite speaking topic is a new book that will be released later this year. It's called *Divine Renovation: From a Maintenance to a Missional Parish*. Long before the book comes out — on April 5, to be exact — I will be speaking on the topic of the family and the New Evangelization at the EWTN Family Celebration in Vancouver.

When discussing the renewal of the Church, some people have talked about changing our theology. We don't need to change our theology; we need to start living it. That requires that we change our own attitudes and ways of living, which is always more difficult than trying to change others or changing things outside of ourselves. We have to remember, though, that there is nothing quite as wonderful and beautiful as the Catholic faith lived to the fullest.

///

SAN DIEGO BASEBALL CAMP HAS CHRIST AT ITS CENTER

MLB All-Star Mike Sweeney will lead the innovative clinic this summer.

May 11, 2012

Mike Sweeney's Catholic Baseball Camp, to be held July 24-26 at Cathedral Catholic High School in San Diego, is not your average baseball camp. In addition to the customary fielding, hitting and base-running, this camp will include daily Mass, confession and praying the Rosary.

Participants will learn not only how to become great baseball players, but great human beings as well. Contrary to what some think, the two are not incompatible, the camp's originator and leader, Sweeney, explained.

"The reason I started the camp was to share the integration of two of my loves in life: baseball and the Catholic faith. Of course I value playing baseball, but, more importantly, I set a tremendous, unsurpassed value on Catholicism," Sweeney said.

The five-time All-Star was part of generically Christian baseball camps during his days with the Kansas City Royals from 1995 to 2007, but he wanted to put together a more complete presentation of the Gospel message.

"At the other camps, we played baseball all day and then, at the end of the day, we talked about Jesus. I loved being there, but felt like I was diluting the message to fit the Protestant mindset, because those who ran the camps were Protestant. It was like presenting half of what I should have."

Sweeney put more thought into the other things he should have presented during his later playing years with the Oakland Athletics,

Seattle Mariners and Philadelphia Phillies. After officially retiring in March 2011 and taking care of other business last summer, he was finally able to bring everything together. The plan for a Catholic baseball camp was finalized at a Lenten retreat this year, and a website was launched shortly thereafter.

"At this camp we'll not only talk about Jesus, but actively encounter him all day, starting in the Mass, where he's present in a unique and unsurpassed way. We'll also have a priest hearing confessions, we'll study the Bible, pray the Rosary and associate specific Bible verses with baseball," the 38-year-old father of four explained.

"For example, in Hebrews 12:2, it says we should keep our eyes on Jesus. If we do that from morning until evening, then we're able to live the day correctly. By analogy, if we keep our focus on the baseball from the beginning of the game until the end, then we're able to play correctly. Even during a game, the focus is still Jesus; but from a physical-mechanical standpoint, the focus is the ball."

Training the Tongue

Another interesting aspect of the camp is how Sweeney has assigned each inning of the scrimmage games a unique theme. There's the "friendly first," in which everyone gets a chance to hit, regardless of how many outs there are. This is followed by the "silent second," in which everyone is supposed to remain quiet, thereby learning to tame his tongue in the spirit of James 1:26.

"Using our tongues for blessing and not cursing or other inappropriate utterances is essential to becoming a truly Christian person," Sweeney said. "What can be helpful in learning to do this is when you stop talking altogether for a specific period of time. That way you're able to silently reflect on whether it's really necessary to verbalize something you might want to say later on. Then you're able to see how many things were better left unsaid, and then you'll be able to pray and focus on the right things to say."

Speaking of the right things is a key part of the camp as well. Sweeney will share his personal testimony, as will two-time All-Star Mark Loretta, who is currently a special assistant for the San Diego Padres.

"I want to talk about how being a member of the Catholic Church gives me a security that nothing material can," Loretta said. "If you put your hope in the things of this world, you're bound to be disappointed, but if you trust in Jesus and do what he tells you to do, then everything will work out fine.

"This was the Blessed Virgin Mary's message at the wedding feast of Cana. She told those there to do whatever he [Jesus] tells them to do. Can't get better advice than that. We want to include Mary's message in the camp, in part by praying the Rosary. Each camper will receive a special rosary whose beads are actually little baseballs, and we'll pray the Rosary as a group on the field. It's a way of showing the boys that rosaries are not your grandma's jewelry, but a powerful sacramental that they can use as well."

Loretta is grateful for the chance to contribute to the cultivation of authentic Catholic masculinity in his own back yard.

"I'm thankful to Mike for allowing me to be a part of this," he said. "It's great to be able to help out right here in San Diego. I was living and playing here in 2005, but was unexpectedly traded to the Boston Red Sox. I eventually made my way back, so it's great to be back home and contribute here."

Philip Rivers

Another area athlete who appreciates the opportunity to speak to camp participants is Philip Rivers of the San Diego Chargers. While the All-Pro quarterback is not known for his baseball skills, he is a strong supporter of integrating faith and sports.

"I grew up playing baseball, and, in fact, baseball was my favorite sport from the age of 8 to the age of 12," he said. "I didn't play it in high school, though, and instead focused on football. What I'm going to do is talk about how much being Catholic means to me, how it makes life's battles easier, and how it actually makes me a better athlete."

Rivers is aware of the relatively small window of time professional athletes have in order to use their public platform for good. However, he admires how Mike Sweeney continues to do this even after his retirement.

"Mike had a great major-league career. He used baseball then to share the Catholic faith, and he's still using it now," he said. "I really like that about him. He never stops thinking of ways to use what he's given to glorify God. He's very good at planning things like camps, thinking through what needs to be done."

Having a plan before embarking on any activity is something Rivers strongly advocates, and he sees the camp itself as an opportunity to pass this message along to the kids. "You can't just float out somewhere and hope things work out okay," he said. "You really need to have a foundation in whatever you do, and the ultimate foundation is Jesus Christ. He gives us everything we need through his Church, so in sports or anything else, we can prepare best by first making use of those things. I'm very happy to be supporting a Catholic camp like this one."

Rivers is also a supporter of Miles Christi, a religious order that is sponsoring the camp. A priest from the order, Father Martin Latiff, is scheduled to offer Mass each morning, to hear confessions and to give a blessing at the end of the day.

"I'm going to be there for spiritual assistance," he said. "I want to help the campers realize that the disconnect between sports and faith is not necessary. You really can integrate the two."

Father Latiff believes that playing sports can be a great opportunity to evangelize others. "You can use baseball or any other sport as a vehicle to bring people closer to God. Anything you do you can do for God, and that includes sports. What matters is pleasing the heart of Christ. You can do this in baseball, just as in any other area of life."

Just the Beginning?

Sweeney is in complete agreement with this sentiment, which he will share with others through his camp. "It is an athletic camp, but it's more than that," he said. "It's also a retreat, in a sense. Where else can you get top-notch instruction and be able to participate in the sacraments at the same time? Such an exciting prospect has drawn campers from all over the country. Colorado, Texas, Illinois, Michigan and Florida are some of the places campers are coming from."

Not surprisingly, Sweeney has received requests to conduct camps in many of these states. While he doesn't have the time to organize them all, he does want to offer a blueprint for such camps.

"I wanted to created a template for how a Catholic baseball camp should run. I can offer it to those interested, then have them draw the local instructors and sponsors. I can fly in and offer my services for the camp itself, but the locals have to be the ones who do all the pre-event organizing."

The post-event results are something Sweeney looks forward to as well. "We'll see the good effects of these camps here below, but will only know the full effect in eternity. We want to help the boys become better players by learning from the All-Stars, but also want to encourage them to reach for the stars, in the sense of looking to higher realities outside the material world. We want them to hit a home run for Jesus."

///

LOOKING INTO THE MYSTIQUE OF NOTRE DAME FOOTBALL

Excellence transcends the football field for the famous Fighting Irish, and this commitment to quality incorporates a strong component of Catholic faith.

January 4, 2013

The University of Notre Dame is second to none when it comes to rich football tradition.

This is made clear by glancing at the records of just three of the school's coaches, the legendary Knute Rockne, Frank Leahy and Ara Parseghian. They have a combined 287 wins, 40 losses and 18 ties at Notre Dame (an .857 winning percentage), along with nine national championships.

And it will add another title in 2013, if this year's unbeaten Fighting Irish squad can overcome the powerhouse University of Alabama team in the Jan. 7 BCS Championship Game in Miami.

Notre Dame's excellence doesn't end on the football field, however. In fact, its football team's athletic achievements may even pale in comparison with its academic ones. Since 1962, Notre Dame has graduated an amazing 98.74% of its football players in four years, the highest mark in the nation.

Holy Cross Father Willy Raymond said this has not happened accidentally, but by design.

"Notre Dame has a long history of high academic standards," said Father Raymond. "The school was established in 1842, and the football program only came along 45 years later, in 1887. There are plenty of other sporting teams and, of course, plenty of academic disciplines that most people are not familiar with. Yet football is the

350 /// FIT FOR HEAVEN

most common way the average person knows about the school. That's the entry point, but there is so much more beyond it."

Father Raymond related how head football coach Frank Leahy put together a successful program in the 1940s and 1950s, but at a price, according to some administrators.

"Frank Leahy was a great coach," Father Raymond acknowledged. "His teams won plenty of games and four national championships. However, there was a feeling among the school's administration that he was independent of them. They wanted him to realize he was part of the university and that football came after academic and spiritual pursuits."

Continued Father Raymond, "Father Theodore Hesburgh, who was the university's president from 1952 to 1987, set out to put football in its rightful place. This brought about enough tension for Coach Leahy to resign in January of 1954, even though he had two years left on his contract.

"The two men had their differences, but would eventually reconcile before Leahy's death, in 1973. Father Hesburgh was even present with Coach Leahy during the last two days of his life."

The Ara Parseghian Era

Some thought after Leahy's departure from Notre Dame in 1954 that the football program itself had seen its last days of success. "The emphasis on academics would not allow Notre Dame to recruit the top athletes, they thought," Father Raymond explained. "The football team didn't do too well for a decade after Leahy left, but that turned around with the hiring of Ara Parseghian in 1964.

"During his tenure, the program posted a record of 95 wins, 17 losses and four ties, with no loosening of academic standards. The belief that you can't have both top students and top athletes was proven false."

Parseghian was thoroughly aware of the importance of recruiting young men who were skilled both physically and mentally.

"The coaching staff knew that Notre Dame was first and foremost an institution of higher learning," the 89-year-old Parseghian told the Register. "The central purpose of attending the school was to become educated in a specific discipline. Football was strictly secondary. Contrary to what some might think, this really did help us. Players like Joe Montana were great not from a sheer physical standpoint, but primarily because of their minds."

When a player's mind was not on academics, he was certain to hear about it from the coaches.

"If someone didn't attend class, we were all over him," Parseghian noted. "There was no tolerance for taking schoolwork lightly. Most of the time, this wasn't an issue, though. When you have rigorous entry requirements to begin with, chances are very good that you'll do well once you're attending the school. The pre-entry screening process was very helpful."

Something else that proved helpful for Parseghian's teams was spending the night before home games at Moreau Seminary, located on the other side of St. Joseph's Lake on campus.

"The first year I was at Notre Dame, 1964, we found that the seminary was spacious enough to house the football team, in addition to the seminarians who were already living there," he recalled. "I was pleased with this, because the atmosphere of the seminary was so tranquil. It was very conducive to getting a good night's rest."

The next morning, the entire team, Catholics and non-Catholics alike, would attend Mass and receive a blessing from a Holy Cross priest. Blessed medals were handed out to players and coaches as well.

Parseghian, who is not Catholic, appreciated this spiritual component to Notre Dame football: "There was always an underlying spirituality to whatever happened at Notre Dame. That was one of the main reasons I enjoyed being there so much."

Parseghian chose to stay in South Bend despite offers to coach in professional football. He found the area to be a great fit, especially considering his children's ages at the time. "It was perfect for my family. The spirituality, the smaller town, the dedication to learning — it all came together so well. It was better to be there than to have gone to a larger city, which would have been necessary if I had accepted a position in pro football."

Summed up Parseghian, "I appreciate my years at Notre Dame, not just from a professional standpoint, but from a family one as well."

A Player's Perspective

Anthony Brannan, a linebacker at Notre Dame from 1996 to 2000, also has a great appreciation for his experience in South Bend. The dedication to academic and athletic excellence impressed him, but most impressive was the spirituality encompassing his collegiate years.

"The academic standards at Notre Dame were very high, from gaining admission to attending classes to actually graduating," Brannan remembered. "On the recruiting trip, you're likely to talk with more advisers than coaches, and once you're in school, the coaches made sure you attended classes. I recall seeing assistant coaches at classroom doors to make sure we players were there. It wasn't just support staff, but the coaches themselves who were present."

It was clear to Brannan that playing football came second to earning a degree. However, excelling at football was also expected, a reality he enjoyed. "In my first year on the squad, I had the opportunity to play for Lou Holtz, who was upbeat, energetic and goal-oriented. He was very much into the game and wanted to get the best performances out of his players."

Brannan remembered that Holtz's perspective didn't end on the football field: "He took it all into context. Before games, he would say, 'Gentlemen, remember who you're playing for: Our Lady on the Golden Dome (there was a large statue of the Blessed Virgin atop the Main Building on campus) and Our Lord.' That was just one example of how spirituality was to be found nearly everywhere on campus or at university-related events."

Impressed by Knute Rockne

Holy Cross Father Paul Doyle will be among those hoping the Fighting Irish do well against the University of Alabama Crimson Tide for the national title. Father Doyle is the home-game chaplain for the team, which is appropriate, considering how he learned of the university in the first place.

"My father was attending Mount St. Mary's in Emmetsburg, Md., in the 1920s," Father Doyle explained. "At the time, Knute Rockne was doing a fine job of coaching at Notre Dame, which brought a lot of attention to the school. That impressed my father, and he was determined that his future children would attend Notre Dame. My three brothers and I ended up doing just that.

"I was also ordained a Holy Cross father and spent my first nine years in parish ministry. Then I returned to campus and have been here ever since." In fact, Father Doyle doesn't even leave campus for road games; he lets another priest take care of the team away from home.

On campus at the Basilica of the Sacred Heart, Father Doyle offers Mass the morning of home games, with all the players and coaching staff present. At the end of Mass, the Litany of the Blessed Virgin Mary is prayed, a relic of the true cross is venerated, and team members receive a blessed medal of a saint.

"The traditions surrounding Notre Dame football have largely remained unchanged," Father Doyle said. "We've had Mass for the team on game days since the 1920s at least, and the medals have been a part of it for as long as I can remember. We give inexpensive oxidized medals of a different saint to the players and coaches before every game, along with a short catechesis on the saint. We explain why that particular witness of God is relevant to them today."

Father Doyle said he tries not to repeat a saint within a four-year cycle, so everyone will have a new medal to add to his collection each week. While this year's squad is just under 50% Catholic, players and coaches tend to cherish the medals, regardless of their religious affiliation.

Broader Perspective

In the locker room just before the game, Father Doyle leads the team in prayer. An Our Father is prayed, and Our Lady of Victory is invoked. The whole team is blessed, and, shortly afterward, they take to the field with a sense of purpose and a perspective that extends beyond football.

While the best-known aspect of the University of Notre Dame is its football team, the school is not devoted to the sport at the expense of its founding principles. The academic and spiritual components of student life are generally seen as superior to, and also helpful for, athletic pursuits.

Success on and off the field are interconnected in South Bend, and most fans remain steadfast in their loyalty to the nation's best-known Catholic college. Football unites them, but something greater than the game unites them even more.

Father Doyle believes the major unifying principle is tied in with the founding of the school itself.

"It ultimately goes back to the purpose behind the school's origin — to recognize not just the laws of nature, but the Author of those laws; not just the history of nations, but the Lord of those nations; not just the truths of philosophy, but ultimate Truth Itself," Father Doyle said. "No one has done this better than Our Lady (translated 'Notre Dame' in French), so it is fitting that the school is named after her. The mystique of anything good here in South Bend is inevitably associated with Our Lady."

///

ATHLETIC CLERGY USE SPORTS FOR THE GOOD OF SOULS

Hockey, marathons and baseball are among favored athletic activities.

August 26, 2013

Some people think of the priesthood as the death of any enjoyment of life. No wife, no children, no sports, no fun. It's all dreadfully serious business for priests, the thinking goes. Such thinking itself, according to notable clerics, must go.

"Certainly the priesthood is serious business. You can't get any more serious than eternal salvation," said Bishop Thomas Paprocki of Springfield, Ill. "However, everyone needs to step away from their responsibilities from time to time in order to recreate, and the clergy are no different."

Aside from providing much-needed recreation, Bishop Paprocki, who has completed 19 marathons himself, has found athletics to be very helpful in drawing others to Christ. He uses time spent running to pray (often on a 10-bead finger rosary) and to mentally assemble homilies and articles that are often introduced by sports stories.

"I've used sports many times to begin a discussion, especially with the young," the national chaplain for LIFE Runners explained. "St. Ignatius of Loyola said that you should meet someone where he's at in order to bring him where you are. You make the effort to see things as your audience does and then connect that perspective with what you're delivering. You build on what's already there, and for many young people, what's already there is sports."

Sports have been there for Bishop Paprocki since his youth in Chicago. As one of seven boys, he played everything, from hockey (a family favorite) to soccer and baseball. Yet, despite having a ready-made team on hand and a great enjoyment of sports, he didn't consider himself to be a gifted athlete as a young man. Instead of letting this get in his way, however, it was motivation to improve.

"Even though I had six brothers and a real appreciation for sports, I certainly wasn't the best at any sport I played in," Bishop Paprocki admitted. "I think that made me work for things and become a better person overall. Instead of taking sports for granted, I realized how much effort can be needed to learn them, and I understood the setbacks people encounter. This has helped me pastorally, because I can use my own challenges to connect with and help others."

Bishop Paprocki has found fear, frustration and failure to be among the most common difficulties people encounter. He has taught that fortitude, faith, family, friendship and fun can be the solutions: "The challenges we face in sports are so similar to the ones we face in other areas of life. Sports give us, especially when young, the opportunity to learn how to overcome problems on a smaller scale. Then we can take what we've learned and transfer it to the bigger world beyond sports."

"I've written about this topic in a new book called *Holy Goals for Body and Soul: 8 Steps to Connect Sports With God and Faith*. I wanted to give readers some practical ways to live faith-filled lives through the lens of sports. There is so much to be learned from sports, not only for the sake of playing them better, but for living better, God-centered lives."

Plowing Ahead

Franciscan Father Gregory Plow, who has competed in 11 marathons, including one with Bishop Paprocki, recently took his running skills to a whole new level. Not content with traditional 26.2-mile races,

Father Plow, who is the coordinator of household life at Franciscan University of Steubenville, Ohio, decided earlier this year to enter his first ultramarathon.

The Wild Idaho Ultramarathon, which took place on Aug. 3, extended 53.4 miles, up and down the mountainous terrain of the Boise National Forest, under midday 90-degree heat. Not surprisingly, there were a mere 22 participants and only 17 finishers.

"It was by far the toughest thing I've ever done physically," Father Plow related. "We started at 6:00 in the morning, and, because of the continuous elevation differential and pit stops, I didn't finish until just after midnight: 12:07, to be exact. I was the last one to finish, but I did finish."

Finishing strong was a central theme for Father Plow, who suffered in the heat during the day, and, because of the temperature decreasing to the 40s at night, later approached hypothermic conditions. His hands became chalk white, indicating blood had gone from his upper extremities to his major organs in order to keep them functioning.

This slow shutdown was first noticed at the 38-mile checkpoint, where Father Plow met up with an aid-station volunteer who had completed an ultramarathon himself. The volunteer, an experienced ultramarathoner named John, offered his jacket — and his companionship — to Father Plow, accompanying him to the end of the race.

"I was really struck by John's generosity and his personal sacrifice, which helped me to finish strong. I was reminded of how all the apostles abandoned Jesus on the way to the cross — that is, all of them, except John. It was a tremendously moving experience, not just from a social standpoint, but from a spiritual one as well."

Prayerful faith in Christ was on Father Plow's mind from start to finish. He offered the first 48 miles of the race for each of the 48 campus households in Steubenville. Miles 49-52 were offered for those who will be awarded the Spirit of St. Francis Scholarship, and the remaining distance was presented to God in thanksgiving.

"My fellow friars were thankful I made it through the race, and most of them thought I was crazy for entering it in the first place. It was gut-wrenching, to be sure, but it was also thrilling to be in it, especially because of its greater purpose," Father Plow concluded. "I wanted to encourage holiness of life for students already at Franciscan University, and I wanted to enable incoming freshman to attend the school, despite their financial difficulties."

Father Plow, who is the chaplain for the Steubenville chapter of LIFE Runners, said he will not be competing in the Wild Idaho Ultramarathon or any similar ultramarathons again. However, he won't rule out shorter or less elevated ultramarathons, and he is scheduled to run in a standard one on Sept. 15.

Vocation Pitches

Father Larry Young is a diocesan priest whose athletic background includes baseball, backpacking and canoeing. In 2010, he recruited other priests and some seminarians to form the DC Padres, a Washington-area baseball team. Father Young plays and manages the squad as they compete against local high-school varsity teams, with the purpose of promoting vocations to the priesthood.

Most of the DC Padres have played high-school baseball, and about half of them have played on club or intercollegiate teams at the university level. Players on opposing teams and spectators in the stands have taken notice that this is not about washed-up baseball players retreating to slow-pitch softball, but still-fit players continuing in fast-pitch hardball. As Father Young said, "It is real baseball that we play against high-school teams. We're throwing and hitting fastballs out there. It's incredibly fun."

Because of the primary obligations of priests and seminarians, Father Young's team has only been able to play eight games in the past three years, yet they have a respectable 4-3-1 record, after winning their game on Aug. 25. "We would like to play more games, but, so far, that hasn't been possible," he said. "We just try to make the most of the games we have played, and we look forward to maybe one day playing in even larger venues."

Each game, which is played at a minor-league stadium around metro Washington, includes a short vocation talk at the end of the third inning. One of the DC Padres gives his own personal testimony to the crowd, the largest of which so far was around 1,000 people. While no team-influenced vocations statistics are kept, Father Young hopes the talks — and his team's play —will encourage the thought of the priesthood in spectators' own discernment.

"People see us out here as normal, red-blooded American men enjoying our national pastime,"

Father Young observed. "We enjoy sports as much as anyone else, so we like to let young men know that a vocation to the priesthood doesn't mean you'll somehow have to give up every kind of recreation you formerly enjoyed.

"We want young men to see that it is a manly thing to be a priest and that Our Lord calls men to imitate him by laying down their lives in the service of his Church. One active and enjoyable way to communicate this message is through baseball, which we use not only to throw hardball pitches, but as a platform for a vocation pitch. We've found that sports and spirituality can easily go hand-in-hand."

///

BRINGING THE CHURCH INTO THE WORLD OF SPORTS

Ray McKenna, the head of Catholic Athletes for Christ, is enthusiastic about the missionary mandate.

February 14, 2014

Ray McKenna thought he was the only one in professional sports ministry experiencing anti-Catholic bias. In his volunteer work with Baseball Chapel, a Protestant group, he would hear things about the Catholic Church that weren't true. He initially ignored the slights in the hope of obtaining a greater good: bringing athletes closer to God.

Yet, as time went on, McKenna discovered that his anti-Catholic experiences were shared by many, including five-time Kansas City Royals All-Star Mike Sweeney. "Mike and I met in the mid-1990s, while he was still in the minor leagues. I learned as we spoke over the years that he had experienced many of the same things I had in baseball: a strong Protestant outreach that, despite some of its pluses, had glaring minuses."

Both McKenna and Sweeney attended a "nondenominational" Protestant ministry conference at which the Catholic Church was virulently attacked. A well-known Major League Baseball player who had been raised Catholic, but left the Church for a Protestant denomination, was now throwing out distortions about the Church to anyone who would listen.

"That was the most heartbreaking moment for me," McKenna recalled. "I had heard negative things before then, but in that presentation, the Church's positions were so distorted that you couldn't even recognize what he was talking about. It was then that I really started to think in earnest about starting a distinctly Catholic organization in pro sports."

In 2006, Catholic Athletes for Christ (CAC) was born. The nonprofit organization started serving players in Major League Baseball, then expanded to the National Football League and other professional sports. Further participants include Olympic and collegiate athletes, and, most recently, high-school athletes.

CAC's outreach to Catholic high-school students, or "Cathletes," is a venture spearheaded by Bishop David O'Connell of Trenton, N.J., and Bishop Thomas Paprocki of Springfield, Ill. It is the first fully Catholic program of its kind, bringing a sound and detailed theology of sports into the world of high-school athletics.

Recent Vatican Meeting on Sports

"Sports, no matter what level, are a great way to spread the truth about Jesus Christ," McKenna said. "Sports are very much a part of today's culture, and, since Pope Francis has spoken of engaging the culture, evangelization through sports is a natural fit for us."

Last Oct. 21, McKenna attended the Pontifical Council for Culture's meeting on "believers in the world of sports," the fourth such meeting held in the past 10 years. It was during this event that McKenna and CAC board member Linda Del Rio, the wife of Denver Broncos Defensive Coordinator Jack Del Rio, were able to meet informally with Pope Francis.

McKenna said the meeting was "an amazing experience. It was so brief, yet so long. We only had a few moments with the Holy Father, but it was such a moving experience that it seemed to last forever. Linda handed Pope Francis a football that was signed by Denver Broncos players. He explained that he liked football, too — namely, the soccer variety."

McKenna saw the Vatican event as part of a continued recognition and confirmation of the importance of sports in the areas of catechesis and evangelization. He believes that because sports should be a means of teaching and living the Catholic faith, it was rewarding to have that ideal widely acknowledged and promoted by the Church.

While the Church can trace sporting references back to the writing of the New Testament, the philosophy and theology of sports have become more refined, especially since the first half of the 20th century. McKenna loves to share a 1946 Pope Pius XII passage on the meaning of sports:

"Sport, rightly understood, is an occupation of the whole man, and while perfecting the body as an instrument of the mind, it also makes the mind itself a more refined instrument for the search and communication of truth and helps man to achieve that end to which all others must be subservient, the service and praise of his Creator."

A few weeks after his Roman journey, McKenna, back home in the Arlington, Va., area, presided over the CAC's third annual Courage Awards on Nov. 13. At the ceremony, professional soccer-player-turned seminarian Deacon Chase Hilgenbrinck was honored for his "bold and courageous testimony regarding his Catholic faith, both within and outside the world of sports."

Retreat Moves Players Forward to Christ

Less than a week after the Courage Awards, McKenna was off to Malibu, Calif., for the annual CAC Baseball Retreat, which took place Nov. 19-21.

The annual retreat is one of the most-appreciated aspects of CAC for Mike Sweeney, who serves as chairman of CAC's Athlete Advisory Board. He sees the event as a way of bonding with like-minded, faith-focused men: "One of the most appealing things about Ray's group is its yearly retreat in Malibu. Baseball players and other athletes, their priest-chaplains, and even Catholics in the entertainment industry, go to this great event."

Sweeney sees the retreat as a "very rewarding and spiritually-nourishing environment" to be a part of. He has received spiritual nourishment from presenters and has also given spiritual nourishment himself. At the 2013 installment, Sweeney provided food for thought through a dynamic presentation on the Blessed Virgin Mary's role in the lives of Christians.

"If you want to see how to fulfill the will of God, look no further than Mary," Sweeney said. "She is the first Christian, the ideal Christian and the Christian who brings Christ to all Christians. She has such an exalted position because of her humility in accepting and carrying out God's will. We can learn so much from her life, which was a continual devotion to Christ. As the saying goes, 'No Mary, no Jesus. Know Mary, know Jesus.'"

"It's important to realize that Jesus Christ founded the Catholic Church," the former Royals first baseman emphasized. "The Catholic Church is the home of those who want to follow Christ to the fullest. It's more than just picking the correct group, though; it's about being a living member of the body of Christ. It's about the intimate union we have with Our Savior in the Eucharist, when we literally have the blood of God Incarnate running through our veins. It's not possible to be closer to Jesus in this life."

This closeness is something that has appealed to Sweeney since his days in the minor leagues. While most other Catholic players away from home for the first time seemed to slacken in the practice of their faith, Sweeney was drawn even closer to the Eucharist. As others stopped going to Mass and confession and sometimes started attending Protestant worship services, Sweeney went out of his way to get to a Catholic church at least every Sunday.

"I was personally drawn to the Eucharist in a way that made it easy for me to make the sacrifices necessary to get to Mass on Sundays," Sweeney said. "I would wake up early, take a cab to a church and get fed by God through the Scriptures, but even more so by the Eucharist. It would be a good number of years later that the Mass was more readily available to players, who then became more aware of how much it meant to them."

Sweeney is appreciative of McKenna's efforts to bring the sacraments closer to players. "CAC has been instrumental in bringing the Mass to a majority of MLB stadiums. That used to be nonexistent, but now it's very common. It's much easier to be a practicing Catholic in professional baseball these days, and that is due mostly to Ray McKenna."

Extending Brotherly Love

Another baseball player who has benefited from the expansion of CAC is Philadelphia Phillies pitcher Justin De Fratus. The 26-year-old California native met McKenna at spring training in 2011 and has grown in his faith ever since.

"When I first started in pro ball, you'd think everyone on the team was either a Protestant or just nonreligious," De Fratus said. "You wouldn't even know who the Catholics were. In the past three years, however, I've come across more and more guys I didn't know were Catholic. It's been a very pleasant revelation to me that there's a Catholic community in baseball."

That community has extended beyond the baseball field for De Fratus, who attended the annual Malibu retreat in 2012 and 2013. These experiences have been meaningful to him in part because of Mike Sweeney's presence: "Ever since I saw the *Champions of Faith* DVD in 2007, I've been a huge fan of Mike's. He's been an inspiration to me, not so much from a baseball standpoint, but from a spiritual one. Yes, his playing career was outstanding, but more impressive is the way Mike strives to live his Catholic faith."

Living that faith has become easier for De Fratus, who is now very much aware of the blessing it is to have like-minded friends in the world of sports: "It is a relief to know you're not the only one trying to do God's will. The sacramental presence provided by CAC has been a huge support, and I'm thankful that Ray McKenna has been key in bringing this about. He always seems to be occupied with serving athletes in one way or another."

Following a full schedule ending last year — including Major League Baseball's winter meetings in December — McKenna has plenty of projects to undertake in the first half of this year. Among them are the annual NFL Combine Mass, the inaugural NFL Retreat, a new-and-improved website and a more extensive catechetical training plan for professional athletes.

With McKenna's heavy schedule, does he have any regrets? "Only that I didn't start CAC sooner."

BACK APPENDICES

///

QUOTES FROM POPE FRANCIS ADDRESSING YOUTH IN ST. PETER'S SQUARE IN JUNE 2014

"Sports in the community can be a great missionary tool, where the Church is close to every person to help them become better and to meet Jesus Christ."

"[To belong to a sports team] means to reject all forms of selfishness and isolation—it is an opportunity to meet and be with others, to help each other, to compete in mutual esteem and grow in brotherhood."

"Put yourselves in the game, in the search for good, in the Church and in society, without fear, with courage, and enthusiasm."

"Don't content yourselves with a mediocre 'tie.' Give the best of yourselves, spending your lives for that which is truly valuable and that which lasts forever."

///

QUOTES FROM POPE BENEDICT XVI'S MESSAGE TO CARDINAL STANISLAW RYLKO REGARDING THE INTERNATIONAL SEMINAR ON SPORTS, EDUCATION, AND FAITH IN NOVEMBER 2009

"Sports have considerable educational potential in the context of youth and, for this reason, great importance not only in the use of leisure time but also in the formation of the person. The Second Vatican Council listed sports among the educational resources which belong to the common patrimony of humanity and facilitate moral development and human formation (cf. *Gravissimum Educationis*, no. 4). If this is true for sports activities in general, it is particularly true for sports in parish youth centers, schools and sports associations, with the aim of assuring the new generations a human and Christian formation."

"Through sports, the ecclesial community contributes to the formation of youth, providing a suitable environment for their human and spiritual growth. In fact, when sports initiatives aim at the integral development of the person and are managed by qualified and competent personnel, they provide a useful opportunity for priests, religious and lay people to become true and proper educators and teachers of life for the young."

"In our time when an urgent need to educate the new generations is evident it is therefore necessary for the Church to continue to support sports for youth, making the most of their positive aspects also at competitive levels such as their capacity for stimulating competitiveness, courage and tenacity in pursuing goals."

"As I recently had the opportunity to recall, it should not be forgotten that "sports, practiced with enthusiasm and an acute ethical sense, especially for youth, become a training ground for healthy competition and physical improvement, a school of formation in the human and spiritual values, a privileged means for personal growth and contact with society."

///

QUOTES FROM ST. JOHN PAUL II'S HOMILY FOR THE "JUBILEE OF SPORTS PEOPLE" IN OCTOBER 2000

"Because of the global dimensions this activity has assumed, *those involved in sports throughout the world have a great responsibility*. They are called to make sports an opportunity for meeting and dialogue, over and above every barrier of language, race or culture. Sports, in fact, can make an effective contribution to peaceful understanding between peoples and to establishing the new civilization of love."

"*Playing sports has become very important today*, since it can encourage young people to develop important values such as loyalty, perseverance, friendship, sharing and solidarity... Sports have spread to every corner of the world, transcending differences between cultures and nations."

"At the recent Olympic Games in Sydney [in 2000] we admired the feats of the great athletes, who sacrificed themselves for years, day after day, to achieve those results. *This is the logic of sport*, especially Olympic sports; it is also *the logic of life*: without sacrifices, important results are not obtained [and neither is] genuine satisfaction."

"In Corinth, where Paul had brought the message of the Gospel, there was a very important stadium where the "Isthmian Games" were held. It was appropriate, then, for Paul to refer to athletic contests in order to spur the Christians of that city to push themselves to the utmost in the "race" of life...With this metaphor of healthy athletic competition, he highlights the value of life, comparing it to a race not only for an earthly, passing goal, but for an eternal one—a race in which not just one person, but everyone, can be a winner."

"*Those that sow in tears shall reap rejoicing*" (Ps 125:5). The responsorial psalm reminded us that persevering effort is needed to succeed in life. Anyone who plays sports knows this very well: it is only at the cost of strenuous training that significant results are achieved. The athlete, therefore, agrees with the Psalmist when he says that the effort spent in sowing finds its reward in the joy of the harvest: "Although they go forth weeping, carrying the seed to be sown, they shall come back rejoicing, carrying their sheaves" (Ps 125:6).

"[Christ] is, in fact, *is God's true athlete*: Christ is the "more powerful" Man (cf. Mark 1:7), who for our sake confronted and defeated the "opponent", Satan, by the power of the Holy Spirit, thus inaugurating the kingdom of God. He teaches us that, to enter into glory, we must undergo suffering (cf. Luke 24:26,46); he has gone before us on this path, so that we might follow in his footsteps."

///

QUOTE FROM VENERABLE POPE PIUS XII'S *SPORT AT THE SERVICE OF THE SPIRIT* IN JULY, 1945

"Sport, properly directed, develops character, makes a man courageous, a generous loser, and a gracious victor; it refines the senses, gives intellectual penetration, and steels the will to endurance. It is not merely a physical development then. Sport, rightly understood, is an occupation of the whole man, and while perfecting the body as an instrument of the mind, it also makes the mind itself a more refined instrument for the search and communication of truth and helps man to achieve that end to which all others must be subservient, the service and praise of his Creator."

///

SAINTS FOR SPORT

Various saints, regardless of the athletic capabilities they may have had on earth, are sufficient for our petitions involving athletic competition. A saint does not need to have hit in the Major Leagues in order to help a Major League player or coach. Veteran Major Leaguer Willie Bloomquist invoked Saint Rita of Cascia in his time of need, while World Series-winning manager Jack McKeon relied upon the help of St. Therese of Lisieux.

However, there are some saints who had athletic or military backgrounds, which makes them particularly fitting for athletic intercession. It can be very inspiring to think that Venerable Solanus Casey, for example, used to play baseball. This very holy man lived in the United States and knew about the New York Yankees, Detroit

Tigers, and Chicago Cubs, which makes the universal call to holiness more real for us. Everyone is called to be a saint.

Saint Michael is an archangel who led good angels in a victorious battle against Lucifer's rebellious crew. Saint Michael is often pictured as a soldier with a sword and shield, standing over a defeated dragon. His victory over evil spirits makes him a powerful intercessor He has the word "Saint" before his name, not because he's a man, but because "saint" comes from the Latin word meaning "Holy."

Saint Paul was initially a persecutor of Christians and was even part of the stoning of Saint Stephen. However, Saul, as he was then known, had a dramatic conversion experience on the road to Damascus, was baptized and took the name Paul. His often-quoted letters make up a large part of the New Testament and contain athletic references such as 1 Corinthians 9:25: "Every athlete exercises self-control in all things. They do it to receive a perishable wreath, but we [do it for] an imperishable [one]."

Saint Christopher is a third century martyr who is best known for carrying the Christ Child across a river. "Christ-bearer" is actually what his name means. Medals bearing his image are worn by many people, especially travelers and athletes. Because of changes to the liturgical calendar in the 1960s, a common misconception arose that he had been "demoted" or removed from the Church's list of saints.

Saint Stephen was a deacon whose preaching of the Gospel led to him becoming the first martyr of the Church. Many Jews, including the future Saint Paul, did not take his words as an invitation to eternal happiness, but as blasphemy. Stephen's stoning to death is described in the Acts of the Apostles, and his name means "Crown of Martyrdom."

Saint Sebastian was born into a wealthy Roman family in the 3rd century. He was appointed an officer of the Roman army by Emperor Diocletian, who was unaware of Sebastian's Christian beliefs. During the emperor's massive persecution against Christians, Sebastian visited them in prison and brought them supplies. He helped to covert soldiers and a Roman governor to Christianity and was martyred for being a Christian.

Saint Artemius Megalomartyr was a military leader under Constantine and an Arian heretic who persecuted Christians, including St. Athanasius. However, through sincere prayer, Saint Artemius saw his errors for what they were and became a faithful son the Church. He was accused of destroying pagan idols and subsequently tortured and martyred.

Saint Ignatius of Loyola was a Spanish noble who entered the army in 1517. Four years later he was seriously wounded and brought to a hospital. It was here that he read biographies of saints, which led him to ponder the mysteries of God and rededicate himself to the Church. Saint Ignatius founded the Society of Jesus, or the Jesuits, and became well-known for his preaching and his monumental book, *The Spiritual Exercises*.

Saint Andrew Bobola was a 17th century Polish Jesuit priest whose missionary efforts were rewarded by entire villages coming back to the Catholic faith. He helped the sick during an outbreak of the plague. He was captured by the Cossacks, dragged by horses, hacked with knives, and skinned alive and beheaded for being a Catholic.

Saint John Bosco was a 19th century priest who put on shows similar to those found at circuses and fairs, and at their conclusion, he would share the homily he had heard earlier that day at Mass. He ministered to young people, including through a hospice chaplaincy and through helping orphans and especially tough boys, with whom he would play sports and other games.

Blessed Pier Giorgio Frassati was a layman devoted to the Mass and Eucharistic adoration. However, he also enjoyed sports and outdoor activities such as soccer, skiing, and mountain climbing. He used the material means at hand for helping others, especially the sick. During one of his visits to the sick, he contracted polio and died in 1925 at age 24. His body is incorrupt.

Venerable Solanus Casey was especially noted for his humility and confidence in God's providence. He was a doorkeeper for many years, which put him in touch with many prayer-requesting visitors. He worked miracles during his lifetime and enjoyed playing baseball. He said, "Do not pray for easy lives; pray to be stronger people. Do not pray for tasks equal to your powers; pray for powers equal to your tasks."

Saint John Paul II studied secretly for the priesthood during Nazi Germany's occupation of Poland. He was the first Polish pope and had the third-longest papacy in Church history, spanning from 1978 to 2005. Saint John Paul II enjoyed hiking, soccer, and ice hockey. He said: "Every Christian is called to become a strong athlete of Christ, that is, a faithful and courageous witness to his Gospel. But to succeed in this, he must persevere in prayer, be trained in virtue and follow the divine Master in everything."

///

SPORTS PRAYERS FOR INDIVIDUALS

Eternal Father, in the name of your Only Begotten Son, Jesus Christ, I ask for the grace to be a man of integrity. Grant that I see creation for what it truly is, respecting and serving others through the proper use of material goods, directing all my worship to You alone. Grant that I never put material results above purity of intention and humble acceptance of Divine Providence, so that I may anticipate in this life the everlasting joy You have prepared for your faithful servants in Heaven.

Holy Spirit, the Eternal Love between the Father and the Son, grant me the grace to accept proper guidance from coaches, engage in productive work with teammates, and enjoy every opportunity to deny my own sinful inclinations. Show me that true joy is only possible through self-sacrifice for higher goods, and that new opportunities to gain your powerful wisdom are presented to me every day, if I only look for them. Holy Spirit, remain in me as the life of my soul.

Jesus, my Redeemer and Lord, grant that I may successfully navigate the battlefield of life and share in the victory over sin and death You have won for us. Help me to remember that sin is weak and shameful, while virtue is strong and praiseworthy. Help me to see and use sports to prepare myself for the greater battles of life, always remembering that the greatest team I will compete with in this life is the Catholic Church, to which I've been united in Baptism. Grant that I may preserve baptismal grace and one day share in the blessedness of the Most Holy Trinity.

///

TEAM PRAYER

Eternal Father, help us to see that all things here below come to an end, and that only eternity lasts forever. Grant that we let go of things we cannot control, and spend our time on the things we can control. Grant that, through cooperation with your grace, we become the men you intend us to be. We ask this through Christ, Our Lord. Amen.

///

PRAYER OF ST. JOHN PAUL II IN A HOMILY FOR THE "JUBILEE OF SPORTS PEOPLE" IN OCTOBER 2000

O Christ, we fix our gaze on you, who offer every person the fullness of life. Lord, you heal and strengthen those who, trusting in you, accept your will. .

And those, like the athlete, who are at the peak of their strength recognize that *without you, O Christ, they are inwardly like the blind man*, incapable, that is, of seeing the full truth, of understanding the deep meaning of life, especially when faced with the darkness of evil and death.

Even the greatest champion finds himself defenseless before the fundamental questions of life and needs your light to overcome the demanding challenges that a human being is called to face.

Lord Jesus Christ, help these athletes to be your friends and witnesses to your love. Help them to put the same effort into personal asceticism that they do into sports; help them to achieve a harmonious and cohesive unity of body and soul.

May they be sound models to imitate for all who admire them. Help them always to be athletes of the spirit, to win your inestimable prize: an imperishable crown that lasts forever. Amen!

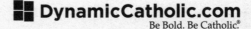

NOTES

NOTES

NOTES

NOTES